LEO SPITZER ON LANGUAGE AND LITERATURE

A Descriptive Bibliography

E. Kristina Baer
Daisy E. Shenholm

THE MODERN LANGUAGE ASSOCIATION
NEW YORK, NY

Library of Congress Cataloging-in-Publication Data

Baer, E. Kristina, 1947-
Leo Spitzer on language and literature: a descriptive bibliography / E. Kristina Baer, Daisy E. Shenholm.
p. cm.
Includes indexes.
ISBN 0-87352-195-1
1. Spitzer, Leo, 1887-1960 – Bibliography. 2. Philology – Bibliography. I. Shenholm, Daisy E., 1924- II. Title.
Z8831.18.B34 1991
[P85.S65]
016.41 – dc20 91-9845

Published by The Modern Language Association of America
10 Astor Place, New York, New York 10003-6981

Contents

PREFACE

This descriptive bibliography of Leo Spitzer's scholarship, including posthumous collections, makes available for the first time a comprehensive overview of his publications. Although many of his literary essays have been anthologized, his work in etymology and lexicology, and in grammar, morphology, and syntax, remains largely unknown and unevaluated.

Within the bibliography, books and monographs are listed chronologically and include tables of contents. Bracketed numerals following individual chapters refer to the journals in which the pieces first appeared and/or were translated from as well as to other collections in which they appear. Book reviews are listed alphabetically by author.

Articles are organized topically by discipline: "Etymology and Lexicology," "Grammar, Morphology, and Syntax," "Semantics," "Literary Criticism and Theory," "Stylistics," and "Miscellany." "Etymology and Lexicology," "Grammar, Morphology, and Syntax," and "Literary Criticism and Theory" are subdivided by language. Within each category, articles are listed chronologically and alphabetically by journal of publication. Summaries are supplied for each article entry. Bracketed numerals following individual journal articles refer to the books in which they also appear. Whenever possible, we give simple definitions in English in the following format: OProv. *(per)digastendos* (= 'with malicious intention').

Here is an example of how to use this cross-referencing system. A researcher locates Spitzer's study of Fr. *chef d'oeuvre*, item 231 under "Etymology and Lexicology, French." The study originally appeared in *GRM* (*Germanisch-Romanische Monatsschrift*), volume 6, in 1914. If this volume of *GRM* is unavailable, the researcher has an alternative source: as indicated at the end of the summary provided for item 231, the article also appears in 6. The researcher then can turn to item 6, *Aufsätze zur romanischen Syntax und Stilistik* (Halle: Niemeyer, 1918; Tübingen: Niemeyer, 1967), and locate the article by the cross-reference [231]. To facilitate cross-referencing of articles that address similar topics, person, subject, and word indexes are provided, which reference items by entry number.

The list of journal abbreviations includes only those journals in which Spitzer's work appeared. When, as occasionally happens, a journal is cited in the title of an article by another scholar, that journal is not abbreviated unless Spitzer published in the same journal. The list of language abbreviations used in the bibliography follows.

We wish to acknowledge the financial assistance provided by the Regents of the University of California and by the Research Council of Rutgers, the State University of New Jersey, for portions of our work. We would also like to express our gratitude to the library staffs throughout the country without whose diligent help the gathering of the material encompassed in the bibliography would have been impossible. Many individuals assisted in the bibliography's compilation and production. We wish to thank especially Edward J. Buckbee, J. Alan Moore, David A. Pharies, and Carolyn Stein, who read and summarized approximately three hundred articles, and Yakov Malkiel and René Wellek, who reviewed and commented on portions of the bibliography in its early stages.

Leo Spitzer did not always provide complete bibliographic information on works to which he referred in his articles, nor did he always give the first name of scholars whom he cited. We have supplied this information wherever possible. Given the scope of his scholarship and productivity over the course of his publishing career, which began in 1910 with his doctoral dissertation and continued without interruption for the next fifty years, it is possible that we have overlooked items in the Spitzer oeuvre. We hope that fellow *Romanisten* who discover such material will bring it to our attention.

Leo Spitzer on Philology: An Introduction

In an interview published in 1952, Leo Spitzer called himself a humanist, whom he described as a window opening onto a panoramic view of other civilizations. To anyone familiar with Spitzer's voluminous oeuvre, this description will seem woefully inadequate. To be sure, Spitzer here articulates his commitment to understand linguistic phenomena in comparative terms and to serve in some sense as the transmitter of this approach to others. However, Spitzer was anything but a passive, transparent conduit between the vast cultural landscape he surveyed and his colleagues, students, and readers. Any one of his publications shows that his performance of the humanist's task does not accord with the metaphorical description he supplied his interviewer.

Not a single article Spitzer published takes a dispassionate, passive, or objective view of its subject, for he was a polemicist who assumed that his readers were well versed in his areas of expertise, and he had no patience with those who were not. In his introduction to *Les études de style* [44],[1] Jean Starobinski likens Spitzer's contentious approach to that of a lover whose ardor is kindled by the presence of a rival.[2] That Spitzer considered his life's work to be a courtship of the truth through the related processes of discovery and refinement helps to account for his habit of publishing his ideas in essays and notes, most of which take as their point of departure observations or conclusions published by others.[3]

For him, scholarship carried over into the public domain a debate that originated when he read something that caught his attention. The result is that his publications usually begin as a refinement of someone else's ideas that is couched in refutations displaying his erudition and acerbic wit in a spirited defense of philology.

To Spitzer, scholarship *was* debate, an active encounter between a scholar and an object of study on one side and an audience on the other.

This view is succinctly stated in the appendix to *Romanische Stil- und Literaturstudien* [22]: if a work is to survive, it must be the image of the battle waged by its creator, transmitting to readers the fervor of the struggle. In view of Spitzer's combative style, it is not surprising that some scholars whom he challenged considered themselves victims rather than colleagues engaged in the same pursuit. Indeed, his parti pris left it clear that only the philologist cast in Spitzer's mold could aspire to serve philology as he conceived it (Hytier).

Above all, Leo Spitzer was a reader. His humanism was defined by and through the linguistic phenomena and texts he scrutinized. Given his intellectual predisposition and formal training, it is natural that what began early in life as a reading habit – underscoring unusual passages – later developed into an interest in describing irregularities and idiosyncrasies and determining their relation to a linguistic or literary whole.

Leo Spitzer was born in Vienna on 7 February 1887, the eldest son of a wealthy Jewish merchant. He graduated at the top of his class from Vienna's Franz-Joseph-Gymnasium and studied at the University of Vienna with the great Swiss Romance philologist Wilhelm Meyer-Lübke and with Elise Richter. After receiving his doctorate in 1910 – his dissertation on grotesque word formations in Rabelais was published by Max Niemeyer that year [1] – he spent the better part of the next several years doing postdoctoral work in France with Antoine Thomas and Jules Gilliéron.

Invited by Meyer-Lübke in 1913 to accept a nontenured position as *Privatdozent* at the University of Vienna, Spitzer seemed destined for an academic career in his mentor's shadow. However, in 1914 he was drafted into the Austrian army and spent World War I working in the Austrian censor's office. On the basis of this experience, he later wrote a study of circumlocutions for hunger in the letters of Italian prisoners of war [16].

After the war he went to the University of Bonn, where from 1922 to 1925 he was associate professor of Romance philology. Although he had inherited a large fortune from his father, postwar inflation depleted it. Reflecting later on his diminished circumstances during these years, Spitzer wryly commented, "It had looked as though I were cut out to be a noble parasite. It turned out I was just a worker. This was the better thing" (Spitzer 21).

In 1926 he secured a full professorship at Marburg. He enjoyed the town and relished the youth of the university's students and faculty members. His recollections of this period evoke the utopian, free-spirited learning environment described by Renaissance writers like Rabelais: "There was drinking and carousing and noise. Every Saturday afternoon we would all get together and go dancing at a café, high on the mountain overlooking the town. And amid the simple gaiety, serious study thrived" (Spitzer 21).

After five years at Marburg, Spitzer moved on to a full professorship at the University of Cologne, where he became editor of the journal *Kölner Romanistische Arbeiten*. At forty-three, well-known in Europe and abroad, he was at the threshold of a distinguished career. He had established a name for himself as an innovative, challenging scholar, and talented students throughout Europe came to study with him. Then, in 1933, political conditions in Germany changed the direction of his career. Notified by telegram from the minister of public education that he was to "take a 'leave of absence,' " Spitzer left the country with his wife and son.

In retrospect, it appears Spitzer was dismissed by the Nazi regime for two reasons: his Jewish background and two liberal pamphlets he wrote in 1918 [5, 9]. He was offered a post at the University of Manchester but decided to accept a position at the University of Istanbul, where he was charged with organizing classes in four languages for three thousand students. With a view overlooking the Sea of Marmara, the setting was magnificent if dilapidated, but there were no books. Asking the dean the reason for this appalling lack of resources, he was informed, "We don't bother with books. They burn" (Spitzer 26).

In 1934 Spitzer was invited to join the faculty at Johns Hopkins University, where he would be virtually free of teaching and administrative responsibilities and could pursue his research interests full-time. Since he still had a three-year contract to fulfill in Istanbul, Johns Hopkins held the position open for him. In 1936 he came to the United States, one of the émigré scholars whose arrival in this country during the thirties and forties was to have tremendous impact on teaching and research in the humanities.[4]

At Johns Hopkins, where he remained until he retired in 1956, Spitzer found an ambience conducive to his work. When he arrived, the study of the history of ideas was taking shape under the guidance of Arthur Lovejoy, with whom Spitzer would engage in spirited discussions on the nature and value of the discipline (Coser 265). Once established at Johns Hopkins, Spitzer did not suffer the same hardships as other émigrés, whose English was poor and whose expectations and intellectual needs could not be met in their new milieus (Coser 3–15; Fleming and Bailyn 3–10).

The thirties and forties were an exciting time in the development of literary theory, critical practice, and new approaches to the study of linguistics. In Chicago the New Critics were promulgating theories of critical method and practice. Behavioral linguists increasingly challenged the traditional positivist views of language development. Spitzer was in his element: he vigorously opposed many of the ideas put forth by the New Critics as reductive and denounced the behaviorists for replacing one set of mechanistic views of language with another.

Spitzer felt called on to defend his positions and challenge those individuals he considered wrongheaded or inadequately trained for the task he held sacred.[5] Accused in turn of "mentalist" or "impressionistic" scholarship, of "conservatism" or "absolutism," even, eventually, "destructive" criticism, Leo Spitzer generally held true to the course he had set for himself at the outset of his career.

In the United States Spitzer found an arena in which to display his formidable knowledge and experience, his taste for lively debate, his impatience with sloppy thinking, and a sense of urgency in matters as diverse as the style of American advertising and the Middle English lyric. With the zeal of a true proselytizer he set about defining issues and expounding matters of practice, building steadily on the foundation he had laid in the twenties.

Spitzer's introduction to *Linguistics and Literary History* [29] offers a cogent summary of his training, the direction he subsequently pursued, and the development of his method.[6] Early in his career he renounced the positivist philology espoused by Meyer-Lübke in favor of the antimechanistic approach inaugurated by the Grimm brothers and refined by Hugo Schuchardt, whom he revered. In his book on Schuchardt [17], published in 1922, Spitzer placed himself in the tradition of those who, while not denying that laws govern certain aspects of language development, seek first to understand how the individual speaker affects language change (Starobinski 8).

Intrigued by the irregular and unstable elements in language, Spitzer isolated and described neologisms and deformations that disclosed the speaker's full powers. An advocate of exploring word roots from within the language under study, rather than seeking outside influences to explain origins, he was one of the first European scholars to champion the speaking community's role in linguistic innovation over the arbitrary rules then in vogue. For Spitzer, as for Charles Bally, the question of how a given variation occurred was less important and, consequently, less interesting than why it occurred.

As his debate with Ernst Gamillscheg and others shows, Spitzer considered philology an intuitive process, not a matter of logical differentiation [534, 975]. In general, Gamillscheg's rejection of etymologies based on onomatopoeia led to analyses that were inadequate to explain language's vitality, because he was more concerned with identifying sources than with tracing development [539, 542]. Modeled on Karl Vossler's approach, Spitzer's premise is that language is expression and that grammar arbitrarily codifies rather than reveals the dynamic processes of linguistic change and development. To Spitzer, linguistic creativity derives from individual use of language, as revealed, for example, in neologisms [967]. (His study of his wife's language with their son is a brilliant example of this postulate in action [19].)

The guiding precepts of Spitzer's approach to etymology are outlined in "Aus der Werkstatt der Etymologien" (1925) [968]. Etymologies must be found by accident rather than through "intentional investigation"; stylistic information about a given word or word family must be considered along with phonetic and semantic information; documentation is to be preferred to reconstruction. Above all, the etymologist must have broad-based training in a variety of disciplines and be fully knowledgeable about the present state of the language being studied.

In 1927, Spitzer developed these ideas when he discussed the postwar fate of the study of Romance languages and cultures at German universities. The task of the university instructor of Romance languages, he averred, was to revitalize interest in the field in order to counteract postwar political tensions in western Europe [972]. Because modern philologists' training, broadly construed, encompassed cultural and intellectual history, it was incumbent on them to rise above the fragmentarism characteristic of positivist thinking. The implications of this view were not solely pedagogical: they were deeply rooted in Spitzer's approach to literary analysis.

In part through an early interest in semantics and syntax, Spitzer turned in the late teens and early twenties to an analysis of literary texts in which he blended aesthetic and linguistic approaches in the study of literary style. In 1923, in "Pseudo-objective Motivierung (Eine stilistisch-literaturpsychologische Studie)" [952], he introduced an idea that, subject to minor modifications, remained a cornerstone of his work in literary analysis. In this study of Charles-Louis Philippe's novel *Bubu de Montparnasse*, he presented a method of interpreting literature by relating an author's distinctive linguistic characteristics to his psychological makeup. Spitzer based his literary interpretation on the work itself, not the author's biography. A further refinement of this idea appeared in 1928. "Vigny's 'Le cor' " [759] emphasizes that clarification of style must remain within the work: a priori aesthetic views, as well as biographical, geographical, and philological criticism regarding the influence of other texts, inhibit rather than foster an understanding of the text at hand.

At first, Spitzer's work in this area was strongly influenced by Freud and by Wilhelm von Humboldt, who believed that a literary work is the expression of the psychological activity that conceived and formed it.[7] In his efforts to trace a writer's "psychological etymon" through stylistic deviations from normal linguistic usage, however, Spitzer revealed the limits of his knowledge of Freud's neurosis theories. In the twenties he abandoned this psychological approach, because he realized that the analysis of style is an analysis of the writer's participation in language as an institution. The work itself is the meeting ground for an individual style and the language the writer knows and manipulates.

For this reason, Spitzer as a literary critic was profoundly sensitive to the relation between authors and their time. Spitzer was quick to castigate scholars of medieval literature who applied contemporary standards of creativity or originality to early writers. His essays on Dante [839, 840, 841, 858], on Marie de France [762, 785], on the Archpriest of Hita [902], and on the general notion of the poetic "I" in the Middle Ages [732] are key statements. As Starobinski states, "Pour Spitzer, l'histoire est partout implicite, sous-jacente, environnante: la forme d'une oeuvre est toujours obtenue à partir d'un matériau daté, et toute oeuvre forte peut être dite *marquante* parce qu'elle qualifie son moment historique autant qu'elle est qualifiée par lui" (12).

Spitzer's acute awareness of a work's historicity led him to renounce efforts to trace an author's psychology through style. Instead, he argued for mapping the artistic coherence of the work itself. Although this approach links him with the New Critics, Spitzer distanced himself from them because he believed they divorced stylistics from literary history. For Spitzer, it was an error to hang the analysis of a literary text on a single element, such as imagery. Structure, conception, and even psychology must also be considered.

The method Spitzer used to elaborate the reading of a text and to understand it stylistically was similar to the method he used to plot the relations among the words in a given word family, for he never disavowed the connection between his linguistic training and his literary criticism. The basic operations of induction and deduction, regardless of the material scrutinized, compose what he called "the philological circle" [29, p. 1]. As he knew, there was nothing new about the method: it originated in what Wilhelm Dilthey and Friedrich Schleiermacher described as the *Zirkel zum Verstehen* in their theories of hermeneutics. What Spitzer advocated was an approach to literary analysis based on careful observation of detail, analysis of the relation between the detail and its context. Only this approach permitted one to reach an understanding of the literary work as more than a heterogeneous linguistic phenomenon.

Spitzer's critics took issue with the method primarily because of the way he described how it worked. It was disingenuous of him to argue that, beginning tabula rasa, he had arrived at a particular interpretation through a rigorous step-by-step process. In fact, Spitzer himself recognized that even the first moment in the analytical process—what he called the "click"—is conditioned by previous experiences: to read is to have read [29, p. 20].

Fundamentally, in an era of reaction against historical positivism, many concurred with Spitzer that the introduction of material extrinsic to the literary work led inevitably to a distortion of its integrity as an aesthetic fact. Still, while most seemed to agree that Spitzer's definition of literary aesthetics is not mere aestheticism or pure formalism, Spitzer was faulted for his absolutism. Not even his prodigious knowledge or his use of grammatical, stylistic, and historical categories, which often produced exceptional insights into how a literary text works, silenced his critics. Here Spitzer was his own worst enemy, for by emphasizing and debating his method, he often obscured the more important practical and theoretical implications of his analyses.

In a study of émigré scholars, Lewis Coser observes that Spitzer was a "stormy petrel" among scholars and that he spent much of his energy in "protracted feuds, partisan tracts, and vitriolic book reviews." However, while Spitzer's attacks on fellow scholars were occasionally destructive, he may have helped raise standards of scholarship by making younger scholars, fearful of his attacks, much more careful about what they wrote (Coser 266–67). In any case, more careful or not, younger scholars did not shy from debate with this formidable interlocutor any more than their seniors did.

In 1957 in an eloquent defense of their fellow Hispanist Stephen Gilman, J. Richard Andrews and Joseph H. Silverman took issue with Spitzer's review of Gilman's book *The Art of "La Celestina"* [941].[8] Andrews and Silverman did not challenge Spitzer's method but pointed out how Spitzer himself had deviated from his own principles in order "destructively" to criticize Gilman's approach to the Spanish classic. In their view, Spitzer's entire argument was based on arbitrary and absolutist assumptions and critical criteria he had elsewhere repudiated. For example, Spitzer took Gilman to task for describing intuition as the springboard to critical insight. As Andrews and Silverman show, Spitzer himself championed intuition in another context—his introduction to *Linguistics and Literary History*—and made it quite clear that an inner "click" led him to the crucial understanding of a literary text.

Still, for all the apparent inconsistency in the Gilman review, a key passage cited by Andrews and Silverman suggests what drove Spitzer's argument:

> If I must choose between any old-fashioned, but first-rate positivist, whose aesthetic creed may be unsophisticated and crude, but who knows the exact meaning of his technical terminology, is able to handle textual, historical and linguistic questions and to focus his undivided attention on a particular problem at the time, and a contemporary ambitious creator of new bold aperçus and new terminology behind which vagueness of thought, hazy associations and verbalism are hidden, I definitely prefer today the former. [29, pp. 23–24]

Andrews and Silverman concluded that Spitzer was a neopositivist, that he considered literary texts museum artifacts or laboratory experiments, and that he was more interested in continuity than in change. With additional reference to Spitzer's ongoing battle with Américo Castro [715], whose work *España en su historia* Spitzer had decried, Andrews and Silverman maintained that Spitzer's real target was not Gilman, but his great teacher, Castro. That Spitzer might have chosen to assail Castro in this manner is possible, but he had other reasons to take on Gilman. Spitzer considered Gilman's interpretation invalid because it was based on tenuous or unfounded assertions.

Spitzer's dominant criticism of Gilman's study centered on fuzzy thinking and terminological ambiguity, which could lead to critical abuses he had spent a lifetime combating. Spitzer could not countenance a method that masked ill-informed analysis, which often characterized young American scholars' work because of inadequate training and the inordinate administrative and teaching demands placed on their time and energies [998]. But Spitzer's critique also raised broader questions concerning the nature of scholarly discourse, in which he took a profound interest. (It is worth noting that when, in 1928, Spitzer himself was roundly chastised by Gamillscheg for his critique of the latter's *Französisches Etymologisches Wörterbuch* [534] – Gamillscheg claimed that Spitzer's etymologies were based on unsubstantiated flashes of inspiration and that he used nonexistent words – Spitzer expressed his hope for greater tolerance of dissent in scholarly circles [975].)

When Jean Hytier reviewed *Essays in Historical Semantics* [28] in 1950, he responded favorably to Spitzer's having created a bridge – stylistics – between linguistics and literary history (Hytier 42). This connection was a singularly important contribution that had grown out of a modern humanist's commitment to antimaterialism, antimechanism, and antipositivism. Calling Spitzer a theologian of literary aesthetics – on account of his stance as an apologist for the internal beauty of the work of art – Hytier balked nevertheless at the aprioristic way in which Spitzer applied the circular method he championed.

He cited as one example Spitzer's definition of the baroque in a discussion of *Phèdre* [22, 44, 48, 758]. According to Hytier, the definition works only because Spitzer rejects anything that doesn't fit. In addition, Hytier disparaged Spitzer's postulate – that the work of art constitutes a unity so complete, so perfect, that its internal organizing principles are reflected equally in all its parts – as being too absolute to offer guidance to a deeper understanding of the text. As Hytier put it, "Dans ce cas, la méthode de M. Spitzer serait moins une méthode de découverte qu'une méthode d'exposition" (54). Although hardly unsympathetic to Spitzer's work, Hytier damned him with faint praise.

These charges of absolutism, conservatism, and arbitrariness are not groundless. No one who is passionately engaged in the quest for truth can easily escape the one-sidedness that results from a deeply held belief in the essential rightness of one's position. While the vigor of Spitzer's conviction at times flaws his argument, it gives even the briefest of his notes an astonishing vitality. Starobinski sheds light on the problems in Spitzer's expository method and emphasizes its positive aspects:

> [Pour Spitzer] le savoir philologique est un composé, où entrent en rapport dialectique la reconnaissance de la matérialité du texte, et *la qualité toujours singulière et particulière*. Dans tous les textes où il précise ses vues théoriques, nous le voyons insister non sur la description objective de la structure, mais sur les aspects subjectifs de la recherche. . . . *Sa méthodologie est la description d'un cheminement de l'esprit*: elle n'est pas une recette, un mode d'emploi, un procédé, mais une réflexion portant sur les étapes progressives où se modifie, de proche en proche, la relation du lecteur au texte, à mesure qu'il en saisit mieux le sens global (29; my emphasis).

By calling attention to Spitzer as a reader, Starobinski focuses on a singularly important element in Spitzer's work and on his impact as a scholar and thinker, as a "poet of ideas" (15). For Spitzer, a forerunner of the structuralists, is a phenomenologist of reading and therefore a forerunner of reception theorists who, like Hans Robert Jauss, have acknowledged their debt to his work. Ever attentive to the text's dynamic, Spitzer is incontrovertibly aware of the reader's relation to it. This awareness is applied evenly to great and minor works: of his several essays on the way *erlebte Rede* is used by different writers, "Zeitgebung im Französischen Gerichtssaalbericht" [961] comments on the way the blending of simple past and pluperfect tenses and the use of indirect narrative emphasize the reader's role as participant instead of as witness, in contemporary newspaper reports as well as in Old Spanish romances.

That Spitzer applied his skills and intelligence to such disparate phenomena—and indeed noted the resemblances between or among them—tells us something about him as an intellect. It is not that he didn't value or appreciate the difference between, say, American advertising slogans and a sonnet by Milton. Nor was he indiscriminate; to make that assumption is to misunderstand the way he approached his work. Spitzer viewed all linguistic phenomena as susceptible to scrutiny and analysis. While he was often intolerant of other scholars, he was not an intellectual snob, content to barricade himself within the walls of his specialized training. Fundamentally, to Spitzer language was a living thing. All its forms, however idiosyncratic or peculiar, were worthy of the philologist's attention. His motto sums up this belief: "No linguistics without philology; no philology without linguistics!" [992].

Spitzer's prodigious oeuvre, mostly articles and notes, testifies to the scope of his effort. Some of the pieces he himself collected in book form; some have been assembled since his death at Forte dei Marmi on 16 September 1960. Most, however, remain scattered among the more than one hundred journals to which he contributed. This preference for the "micrological" has led one recent commentator to suggest that, as an intellectual, Spitzer was too restless, too impatient to produce the synthetic work one associates with eminent scholars (Malkiel).[9] (Of the same generation, Erich Auerbach, with whom Spitzer is frequently compared, published his influential *Mimesis*, some of it written at the University of Istanbul, where he replaced Spitzer.)

Spitzer's habit of firing off notes, comments, and correspondence makes it difficult to arrive at an overall assessment of his work, especially in the areas of etymology and lexicology and of grammar, morphology, and syntax. Still, there are key studies that summarize, reiterate, or refine major points, and all Spitzer's work is underpinned by a remarkable consistency of approach. This uniformity makes it possible for a reader to recognize themes and developments and to profit from the comparisons branching out from them.

Spitzer's study of the polygenesis of *Stimmung* [708, 710] epitomizes the way in which he could and did reach out beyond the narrow confines of the micrological. In this contribution to historical semantics, he shows his preoccupation with continuity over time of a concept rooted in classical antiquity. He is also attentive to the interplay between continuity and discontinuity and the dynamic relation between conservatism and innovation. Fascinated by the impulses that fuel the tensions implied in the processes he describes, he carried on this study in several subsequent articles.

In most of Spitzer's literary studies, a comprehensive blend of semantics, grammar and syntax, and historical structuralism provides the bridge between linguistics and literary criticism. His interest in the survival of certain concepts or topoi leads him to explore their permutations, sometimes with unexpected results. For example, after his study of *Stimmung* appeared, he turned to the concept of world harmony that survives in Walt Whitman's "Out of the Cradle Endlessly Rocking" [737]. Linking Whitman to Dante through both poets' conviction "that the Here and the Hereafter collaborate toward [their] poetry," he makes a distinction that clearly characterizes Whitman's new treatment of the theme:

> . . . in contrast to Dante who knew of an eternal order in this world as in the Beyond, Whitman finds himself faced with an earthly reality whose increasing complexity made correspondingly more difficult his achievement of poetic mastery. . . . Out of the hydra-like anarchy he has created unity; and, as we see, he has gained not only an emotional but an intellectual triumph; he represents himself as "taking all things, but swiftly leaping beyond them" like a master theologian or a medieval glossator. . . . (237–38)

Although Spitzer examines the continuity of particular concepts such as these and moves easily through intricate series of sources and influences, he was firmly opposed to the atomism that results when critics unreflectively apply extraneous material to the literary text.

In "Two Dante Notes" [840] and "Understanding Milton" [741] he protests the use of biographical information for its own sake in the analysis of a literary text. The explicator must stringently evaluate the personal information introduced in the text in order not to explain away the literary by reference to the empirical. When a poet introduces reality, it is only to convince the reader of the significance of the scene being portrayed.

This theme in Spitzer's theoretical pronouncements, always expressed in terms of his dominant concern for the boundaries between art and reality, complements his rejection of any approach that fragments the text. Although he more than occasionally drew on an array of sources, he remained opposed to reducing a text to an unrelated series of sources and influences, or to the intellectual framework it embodies, or to the status of a historical document. Biographical information, sources, ideas, or historical context are admissible only to the extent that they do not interfere with the text's status as an aesthetic entity. The inductive-deductive process that characterizes the to-and-fro movement of the critical pendulum must be rigorously controlled by the critic's acknowledgment of the text's aesthetic autonomy.

Absolutist in that he was a vocal proponent of the literary text's autonomy, conservative in that he considered continuity and innovation interdependent, Spitzer also recognized that his method could not be reduced to a program. Having described the importance of past experiences with "the philological circle" that conditioned his reading of a new and unfamiliar text, he noted, "For every poem the critic needs a separate inspiration, a separate light from above. . . . Indeed, a Protean mutability is required of the critic, for the device which has proved successful for one work of art cannot be applied mechanically to another . . . " [29, p. 28].

Today, we do not read Spitzer for his methodology or his theory. What accounts for the durability of his work in semantics and literary criticism is that Spitzer takes the text at face value. Because Spitzer's reading seeks above all to understand the text as a given, rather than force it to obey an interpretation imposed on it from outside, his readings are productive.

As a guide through texts as various as *Inferno* and *La modification*, Spitzer stands second to none. Jean Hytier noted that Spitzer's method is less a method of discovery than a method of exposition. Spitzer would have agreed. Far from being flawed for this reason, the method is strengthened. Too often methodology interposes itself between reader and text so that the text becomes merely a proving ground for theoretical postulates.

Spitzer's legacy is this: by always seeking to understand the text on its own terms, he challenges his readers to engage with him in that most difficult of tasks—to comprehend how the fundamental arbitrariness of language has been shaped into meaningful utterance.

E. Kristina Baer

NOTES

1 The numbers in square brackets refer to works listed in the bibliography.

2 "Comme tant d'amoureux qu'anime la présence d'un concurrent, Spitzer semblait souhaiter que sa conquête du sens des textes litigieux coïncidât avec la déconfiture du rival. Au demeurant, rectifier un malentendu, réfuter un contre-sens, contredire un collègue, c'était pour lui repartir d'un point périphérique et se replacer dans la position externe d'où pouvait être lancée l'offensive victorieuse en direction du centre" (Starobinski 14).

3 In his appraisal of Spitzer, René Wellek laments Spitzer's reluctance to produce "a single unified book" and attributes it to German academic methods, that is, detailed commentary on passages chosen for particular exercises.

4 See Coser for an account of this period. *Comparative Literature* appeared in 1949, and Spitzer contributed articles to five of its first six issues. Yale had no program in comparative literature until Wellek arrived in 1946, and no full-fledged department until 1959. Harvard decided to resuscitate its comparative literature program in 1945 under the leadership of

Harry Levin. The Linguistic Society of America had been founded in 1925, and Leonard Bloomfield had published his influential book *Language* in 1933.

[5] In his personal recollection of Spitzer and Auerbach, Harry Levin remembers Spitzer in 1950 as "the greatest living virtuoso of the explication de texte."

[6] See Wellek, 313-15, for a thoughtful summary of milestones in the development of Spitzer's thinking and method.

[7] Freud's ideas were widely discussed in the Viennese circles Spitzer frequented as a young man. See David Bellos ix-xxi for comments on Spitzer's imperfect grasp of Freudian theories.

[8] See Gilman, "Rejoinder," for a response to Spitzer's review.

[9] While Spitzer may have been a master of the linguistic note, many of his contemporaries, especially those whom he engaged in debate, published their work in the same form. In certain areas, such as etymology and lexicography, notes and articles are the rule rather than the exception.

WORKS CITED

Andrews, J. Richard, and Joseph H. Silverman. "On 'Destructive Criticism': A Rejoinder to Mr. Leo Spitzer." *Modern Language Forum* 42 (1957): 3-24.

Bellos, David, ed. *Essays on Seventeenth-Century French Literature.* By Leo Spitzer. Cambridge: Cambridge UP, 1981.

Bloomfield, Leonard. *Language.* New York: Holt, 1933.

Castro, Américo. *España en su historia: cristianos, moros, y judíos.* Buenos Aires: Losada, 1948.

Coser, Lewis A. *Refugee Scholars in America: Their Impact and Their Experiences.* New Haven: Yale UP, 1986.

Fleming, Donald, and Bernard Bailyn, eds. *The Intellectual Migration.* Cambridge: Belknap, 1969.

Gilman, Stephen. *The Art of "La Celestina."* Madison: U of Wisconsin P, 1956.

——. "A Rejoinder to Leo Spitzer." *Hispanic Review* 25 (1957): 112-21.

Hytier, Jean. "La méthode de M. Leo Spitzer." *Romanic Review* 41 (1950): 42-59.

Levin, Harry. "Two *Romanisten* in America: Spitzer and Auerbach." Fleming and Bailyn 463-84.

Malkiel, Yakov. "Leo Spitzer (1887-1960): The Most Controversial Romance Philologist of His Generation." Lecture. University of Kentucky, 1985.

Spitzer, Leo. Interview. *Johns Hopkins Review* Apr. 1952: 19-26.

Starobinski, Jean. Introduction. *Les études de style.* By Leo Spitzer. Trans. Éliane Kaufholz, Alain Coulon, and Michel Foucault. Paris: Gallimard, 1970.

Wellek, René. "Leo Spitzer (1887-1960)." *Comparative Literature* 12 (1960): 310-334.

ABBREVIATIONS

Journals (in Acronym Order)

AGI	*Archivio Glottologico Italiano*
Agonia	
AJP	*American Journal of Philology*
Anales del Instituto de Lingüística (U.N. de Cuyo)	
ANS	*Archiv für das Studium der Neueren Sprachen*
ArL	*Archivum Linguisticum*
A Rom	*Archivum Romanicum*
AS	*American Speech: A Quarterly of Linguistic Usage*
Asomante	
Belfagor	
BFL	*Boletim de Filologia, Lisboa*
BHi	*Bulletin Hispanique*
BICC	*Boletín del Instituto Caro y Cuervo*
BIIH	*Boletín del Instituto de Investigaciones Históricas*
BInst	*Bulletin Linguistique, Bucarest*
BSLP	*Bulletin de la Société de Linguistique de Paris*
Bulletin	*Bulletin of the History of Medicine*
Cahiers	*Cahiers Sextil Puscariu*
CL	*Comparative Literature*
CN	*Cultura Neolatina*
Conv	*Convivium*
Critique: Revue Générale des Publications Françaises et Etrangères	
La Cultura Moderna	
Dacoromania	
ELH	*A Journal of English Literary History*
Euph	*Euphorion*
Expl	*The Explicator*
Fil	*Filología*
FM	*Le Français Moderne: Revue de Linguistique Française*
FR	*The French Review*
GGA	*Göttingen gelehrte Anzeigen*
GR	*The Germanic Review*
GRM	*Germanisch-Romanische Monatsschrift*

GSLI — *Giornale Storico della Letteratura Italiana*
l'Herne
HR — *Hispanic Review*
IF — *Indogermanische Forschungen*
Investigaciones Lingüísticas, Mexico
Ital — *Italica*
JbP — *Jahrbuch für Philologie*
JEGP — *Journal of English and German Philology*
JHI — *Journal of the History of Ideas*
Johns Hopkins Review
Les Langues Néo-Latines
Lg — *Language*
LI — *Lettere Italiane*
Literaturblatt für Germanische und Romanische Philologie
LN — *Lingua Nostra*
MDU — *Monatshefte*
Mitteilungen des Rumänischen Instituts an der Universität Wien
MLN — *Modern Language Notes*
MLQ — *Modern Language Quarterly*
MLR — *Modern Language Review*
MP — *Modern Philology*
Neue Jahrbücher für Wissenschaft und Jugendbildung, Leipzig
NM — *Neuphilologische Mitteilungen*
NMo — *Neuphilologische Monatsschrift*
NRFH — *Nueva Revista de Filología Hispánica*
NS — *Die Neueren Sprachen*
Palatina
Philosophy and Phenomenological Research
PMLA — *Publications of the Modern Language Association*
PQ — *Philological Quarterly*
Psychiatry
QIA — *Quaderni Ibero-Americani*
Renaissance
Revue Celtique
Revue de Dialectologie Romane
Revue des Etudes Indoeuropéennes
Revue d'Histoire de la Philosophie
Revue Internationale des Etudes Balkaniques
Revue Internationale des Etudes Basques
RF — *Romanische Forschungen*
RFE — *Revista de Filología Española*
RFH — *Revista de Filología Hispánica*
RHM — *Revista Hispánica Moderna*
RJb — *Romanistisches Jahrbuch*
RLiR — *Revue de Linguistique Romane*
Rom — *Romania: Revue Trimestrielle Consacrée à l'Etude des Langues et Littératures Romanes*
RP — *Revista de Portugal. Seria A. Lingua Portuguesa*
RPF — *Revista Portuguesa de Filologia*

RPh	*Romance Philology*
RR	*Romanic Review*
SFI	*Studi di Filologia Italiana*
SFr	*Studi Francesi*
SMed	*Studi Medievali*
SoR	*Southern Review*
SP	*Studies in Philology*
Speculum	
Lo Spettatore Italiano	
StRen	*Studies in the Renaissance*
Studia Neophilologica	
Traditio	
Travaux du Séminaire de Philologie Romane (Istanbul)	
Trivium	
Ulisse	
VKR	*Volkstum und Kultur der Romanen*
VRo	*Vox Romanica*
Word	
WS	*Wörter und Sachen*
WW	*Wirkendes Wort*
ZDP	*Zeitschrift für Deutsche Philologie*
ZFS	*Zeitschrift für Französische Sprache*
ZRP	*Zeitschrift für Romanische Philologie*
ZVS	*Zeitschrift für Vergleichende Sprachforschung*

References

EWF	*Etymologisches Wörterbuch der französischen Sprache*
EWRS	*Etymologisches Wörterbuch der romanischen Sprachen*
FEW	*Französisches Etymologisches Wörterbuch*
Lex a. d. Kat.	*Lexikalisches aus dem Katalanischen und den übrigen iberoromanischen Sprachen*
REW	*Romanisches Etymologisches Wörterbuch*

Languages

AFr.	Anglo-French
ALat.	Anglo-Latin
Alav.	Alavés
Alb.	Albanian
Amer.	American
AN	Anglo-Norman
Anc.Prov.	Ancien Provençal
Andal.	Andalusian
Anj.	Anjevin
Apul.	Apulian
Ar.	Arabic
Arag.	Aragonese
Aran.	Aranés
AS	Anglo-Saxon
Ast.	Asturian

Blais.	Blaisois
Bonorva.	Bonorvese
Bret.	Breton
Bulg.	Bulgarian
Calabr.	Calabrese
CanFr.	Canadian French
Castil.	Castilian
Catal.	Catalan
Celt.	Celtic
Comelico.	Comelicese
Cors.	Corsican
Eccl.Lat.	Ecclesiastical Latin
Egypt.	Egyptian
Emil.	Emilian
Eng.	English
Flor.	Florentine
Fr.	French
Frank.	Frankish
Gael.	Gaelic
Gall.	Galician, Gallego
Gall. Port.	Galician-Portuguese, Gallego-Portugués
Ger.	German
Gk.	Greek
GrecoLat.	Greco-Latin
Heb.	Hebrew
Ht.-Maine	Haut Maine
Hung.	Hungarian
IE	Indo-European
Ir.	Irish
Istr.	Istrian
It.	Italian
JudeoSp.	Judeo-Spanish
Lat.	Latin
LLat.	Late Latin
Log.	Logudorese
Lomb.	Lombard
Lucca.	Lucanian, Lucchese
Mall.	Mallorcan
MEng.	Middle English
MexSp.	Mexican Spanish
MFr.	Middle French
MHG	Middle High German
MLat.	Medieval Latin
Montañ.	Montanés
MSp.	Modern Spanish
Murc.	Murcian
Neap.	Neapolitan
New Gk.	New Greek
NHG	New High German
NProv.	New Provençal
OCatal.	Old Catalan
OEng.	Old English
OFr.	Old French
OHG	Old High German
OIr.	Old Irish
OIt.	Old Italian
ON	Old Norman
ONorse	Old Norse
OPort.	Old Portuguese
OProv.	Old Provençal
ORom.	Old Romanian
OSp.	Old Spanish
OVenet.	Old Venetian
Pic.	Picard
Pied.	Piedmontese
Pistoj., Pist.	Pistoiese
Port.	Portuguese
Prov.	Provençal
Rom.	Romanian
Russ.	Russian
Sal.	Salamancan
Santand.	Santander
Sax.	Saxon
SFr.	Southern French
SGer.	Southern German
Sicil.	Sicilian
SIt.	Southern Italian
Skt.	Sanskrit
Slav.	Slavic
Sp.	Spanish
Swed.	Swedish
Tessin.	Tessinois

Trevig.	Trevigiano
Turk.	Turkish
Tusc.	Tuscan
Valen.	Valencian
Venet.	Venetian
Veron.	Veronese
VLat.	Vulgar Latin
Wall.	Walloon
Yid.	Yiddish

Books and Monographs

1. *Die Wortbildung als stilistisches Mittel exemplifiziert an Rabelais, nebst einem Anhang über die Wortbildung bei Balzac in seinen "Contes drôlatiques."* Beiheft zur *ZRP* 19. Halle: Niemeyer, 1910.

2. *Die Namengebung bei neuen Kulturpflanzen im Französischen.* Heidelberg: Winter, 1912 [226].

3. *Syntaktische Notizen zum Katalanischen.* Köthen: Schulze, 1914.

4. *Die Bezeichnungen der "Klette" im Galloromanischen.* With Ernst Gamillscheg. Halle: Niemeyer, 1915.

5. *Betrachtungen eines Linguisten über Houston Stewart Chamberlains Kriegsaufsätze und die Sprachbewertung im allgemeinen.* Leipzig: n.p., 1918.

6. *Aufsätze zur romanischen Syntax und Stilistik.* Halle: Niemeyer, 1918; Darmstadt: Niemeyer, 1967.
   (1) Zur Syntax des italienischen Possessivpronomens [622]. (2) Frz. *Sa conversation . . . ne sentait point son curé de village*—ptg. *seu burro.* (3) Frz. *chef d'oeuvre* [231]. (4) Frz. *payer comptant* und Verwandtes [232]. (5) Frz. *vous avez beau parler.* (6) Über ital. *così* [361]. (7) Über frz. ital. *là* [563]. (8) Über span. *que* [668]. (9) Ital. *pazienza* [621]. (10) *Facere* mit dem Infinitiv zur Umschreibung des Verbum finitum [570]. (11) Über syntaktische Einordnung des Individuellen unter die Allgemeinheit. (12) Über das Futurum *cantare habeo.* (13) Über den Imperativ im Romanischen [636, 637]. (14) Persona pro re [638]. (15) Span. cat. *y* 'und.' (16) Über "Rahmenstellung" im Romanischen. (17) Rom. *Noctem et diem.* (18) Die syntaktischen Errungenschaften der Symbolisten [also in 34]. (19) Ein Ersatzwort für "Syntax." (20) Nachträge und Verbesserungen.

7. *Motiv und Wort, Studien zur Literatur- und Sprachpsychologie.* With Hans Sperber. Leipzig: Reisland, 1918.
   (1) Hans Sperber. Motiv und Wort bei Gustav Meyrink. (2) Leo Spitzer. Die groteske Gestaltungs- und Sprachkunst Christian Morgensterns.

8. *Über einige Wörter der Liebessprache. Vier Aufsätze.* Leipzig: Reisland, 1918.

9. *Fremdwörterhatz und Fremdvölkerhass. Eine Streitschrift gegen die Sprachreinigung.* Wien: Manzsche, 1918.

10. *Katalanische Etymologien* (excerpted from *Jahrbuch der hamburgischen wissenschaftlichen Anstalten* 6 [1917]). Hamburg: Meissner, 1918.

11. *Studien zu Henri Barbusse.* Bonn: Cohen, 1920.

12. *Über Ausbildung von Gegensinn in der Wortbildung.* Genève: Olschki, 1921.

13. *Beiträge zur romanischen Wortbildungslehre.* With Ernst Gamillscheg. Biblioteca dell'Archivum Romanicum Series 2.2. Genève: Olschki, 1921.

14. *Italienische Kriegsgefangenenbriefe.* Bonn: Hanstein, 1921.

15. *Lexikalisches aus dem Katalanischen und den übrigen iberoromanischen Sprachen.* Biblioteca dell'Archivum Romanicum Series 2.1. Genève: Olschki, 1921.

16. *Die Umschreibungen des Begriffes "Hunger" im Italienischen.* Beiheft zur *ZRP* 68. Halle: Niemeyer, 1921.

17. *Hugo Schuchardt-Brevier: Ein Vademecum der allgemeinen Sprachwissenschaft.* Halle: Niemeyer, 1922; Tübingen: Niemeyer, 1976 [976].

18. *Italienische Umgangssprache.* Bonn: Schroeder, 1922.

19. *Puxi: Eine kleine Studie zur Sprache einer Mutter.* München: Hueber, 1927 [350].

20. *Stilstudien.* München: Hueber, 1928, 1961.
Vol. 1: (1) Attributive Anreihung von Substantiven im Französischen [572]. (2) Asyndetische Vergleiche im Italienischen und Rumänischen. (3) Providentielle Finalbestimmungen. (4) Über Personenvertauschung in der Ammensprache [624, 625]. (5) *Par exemple—peut-être—déjà* [577]. (6) "Il ne faut pas que tu meures" [578]. (7) Zur pronominalen Verwendung von *des* im Frz. [575]. (8) Warum frz. *énormément* und warum romanisch *-mente*? [255]. (9) Zwillingsformeln: Singen und Sagen—Schorlemorle [640, 641]. (10) Paronomasie im Spanischen. (11) Grammatische Rückdatierung im Spanischen [674]. (12) *Dieu possible*—die Grammatikalisierung der nomina sacra [623]. (13) Spreizstellung bei präpositionalen Ausdrücken im Französischen [579]. (14) Das synthetische und das symbolische Neutralpronomen im Französischen. (15) Romanisch **facit* 'er sagt'—Zur Bewertung des Schöpferischen in der Sprache [694]. (16) *Fait-accompli*—Darstellung im Spanischen [677].
Vol. 2: (1) Sprachwissenschaft und Wortkunst. (2) Ehrenrettung von Malherbes "Consolation à Monsieur du Périer" [757; also in 36]. (3) Zur Kunstgestalt einer spanischen Romanze [890]. (4) "Umkehrbare Lyrik." (5) Über Zeitliche Perspektive in der neueren französischen Lyrik (Anredelyrik und evokatives Präsens) [951]. (6) Sprachmischung als Stilmittel und als Ausdruck der Klangphantasie [950]. (7) "Inszenierende" Adverbialbestimmungen in der neueren französischen Literatur [948]. (8) Pseudo-objektive Motivierung bei Charles-Louis Philippe [952; also in 49]. (9) Der Unanimismus Jules Romains' im Spiegel seiner Sprache (Eine Vorstudie zur Sprache des französischen Expressionismus) [754; also in 34]. (10) Zu Charles Péguy's Stil [760; also in 22, 34]. (11) Zum Stil Marcel Proust's [also in 34, 44]. (12) Wortkunst und Sprachwissenschaft [967; also in 31, 32].

21. *Meisterwerke der romanischen Sprachwissenschaft.* 2 vols. München: Hueber, 1929–30.

22. *Romanische Stil- und Literaturstudien.* Marburg: Elwert, 1931.
Vol. 1: (1) Zur sprachlichen Interpretation von Wortkunstwerken [761, 955; also in 23, 31, 32]. (2) Marie de France–Dichterin von Problem-Märchen [762]. (3) Zu einer Stelle bei Eustache Deschamps. (4) Zur Auffassung Rabelais' [816]. (5) Die klassische Dämpfung in Racine's Stil [758; also in 44, 48].
Vol. 2: (1) Saint-Simons Porträt Ludwigs XIV [trans. in 817; also in 48]. (2) Zur Kunst Quevedos in seinem *Buscón* [in 37, 45]. (3) Zu Góngoras "Soledades" [893; also in 49]. (4) Das Gefüge einer cervantinischen Novelle [898]. (5) Über die Eigennamen bei Gracián [trans. from 894]. (6) Pedro Calderón de la Barca [896]. (7) Einige Voltaire-Interpretationen [in 44]. (8) Vigny's "Le cor" [759]. (9) Zu Péguy's Stil [760; also in 20, 34]. (10) Zum Problem des französischen Argot: Schluss-Aphorismen [585].

23. *Introducción a la estilística romance.* With Karl Vossler and Helmut Hatzfeld. Buenos Aires: Imp. de la U de Buenos Aires, 1932.
(1) Karl Vossler: Formas gramaticales y psicológicas de lenguaje. (2) Leo Spitzer: La interpretación lingüística de las obras literarias [trans. from 761, 955; also in 22, 31, 32]. (3) Helmut Hatzfeld: La investigación estilística en las literaturas románicas.

24. *Die Literarisierung des Lebens in Lopes "Dorotea."* Bonn: Röhrscheid, 1932; New York: Russell, 1968.

25. *Quelques remarques sur J. Coromines "El parlar de Cardos i Vall Ferrera."* Barcelona: Macia, 1937.

26. *L'amour lointain de Jaufré Rudel et le sens de la poésie des troubadours.* University of North Carolina Studies in the Romance Languages and Literature 5. Chapel Hill: U of North Carolina P, 1944 [883; also in 35, 44].

27. *La enumeración caótica en la poesía moderna.* Trans. Raimundo Lida. Colección de Estudios Estilísticos 1. Facultad de Filosofía y Letras de la Universidad de Buenos Aires, Instituto de Filología. Buenos Aires: Coni, 1945 [in 33].

28. *Essays in Historical Semantics.* New York: Russell, 1948.
(1) *Muttersprache* und *Muttererziehung* [356]. (2) Er hat einen Sparren (Span.). (3) *Schadenfreude* [355]. (4) *Race* [153; also in 31, 32]. (5) *Gentiles* [711]. (6) *Milieu* and *Ambiance* [704].

29. *Linguistics and Literary History: Essays in Stylistics.* Princeton: Princeton UP, 1948; New York: Russell, 1962.
(1) Linguistics and Literary History [in 31, 33, 43, 49]. (2) Linguistic Perspectivism in *Don Quijote* [in 33, 37, 43, 49]. (3) The "Récit de Théramène" [in 31, 48]. (4) The Style of Diderot [in 43]. (5) Interpretation of an Ode by Paul Claudel [784; also in 34, 49].

30. *A Method of Interpreting Literature.* Smith College Lectures. Northampton: Smith, 1949; New York: Russell, 1967.
(1) Three Poems on Ecstasy (John Donne, St. John of the Cross, Richard Wagner) [in 37, 38, 41]. (2) Explication de Texte Applied to Voltaire [in 31, 41]. (3) American Advertising Explained as Popular Art [in 38, 41, 49].

31. *Critica stilistica e storia del linguaggio.* Ed. and introd. Alfredo Schiaffini. Bari: Laterza, 1954, 1975.
Part 1: La critica stilistica. (1) Stilistica e linguistica [967; also in 20, 32]. (2) L'interpretazione linguistica delle opera letterarie [761, 955; also in 22, 23, 32]. (3) Linguistica e storia letteraria [trans. from 29; also in 32, 33, 43, 49]. (4) L'arte della "transizione" in La Fontaine [trans. from 774; also in 32, 35, 44, 48]. (5) Il "Récit de Théramène" [trans. from 29; also in 32, 48]. (6) *L'explication de texte* applicata a Voltaire [trans. from 30; also in 32, 41].
Part 2: Storia del linguaggio. (1) Semantica storica. (2) Storia della parola "razza" [trans. from 153; also in 28, 32].

32. *Critica stilistica e semantica storica.* Ed. and introd. Alfredo Schiaffini. Bari: Laterza, 1955, 1964 [same contents as 31].

33. *Lingüística e historia literaria.* Biblioteca Románica Hispánica 2; Estudios y Ensayos 19. Madrid: Gredos, 1955, 1961, 1968.
(1) Lingüística e historia literaria [trans. from 29; also in 31, 43, 49]. (2) La lírica mozárabe y las teorías de Theodor Frings [trans. from 931]. (3) En torno al arte del Arcipreste de Hita [trans. from 902]. (4) Perspectivismo lingüístico en el *Quijote* [trans. from 29; also in 37, 43, 49]. (5) El conceptismo interior de Pedro Salinas [921; also in 37]. (6) La enumeración caótica en la poesía moderna [in 27].

34. *Marcel Proust e altri saggi di letteratura francese.* Ed. and introd. Pietro Citati. Torino: Einaudi, 1959.
(1) Le innovazioni sintattiche del simbolismo francese [in 6]. (2) Lo stile di Charles Péguy [trans from 760; also in 20, 22]. (3) L'interpretazione di un'ode di Paul Claudel [trans. from 784; also in 29, 49]. (4) L'unanimismo di Jules Romains [trans. from 754; also in 20]. (5) Sullo stile di Proust [trans. from 20; also in 44]. *Appendice 1.* Lo stile di Proust e quello di Albrecht Schaeffer. *Appendice 2.* Saint-Simon e Proust. *Appendice 3.* L'etimologia di un "cri de Paris" [724; also in 35, 44]. (6) Schemi di pensiero nello stile di Albert Thibaudet [trans. from 797, 798; also in 35].

35. *Romanische Literaturstudien, 1936–1956.* Tübingen: Niemeyer, 1959; Paris: SABRI, 1960.
Part 1: Französische Literatur. (1) The Prologue to the *Lais* of Marie de France and Medieval Poetics [785]. (2) La lettre sur la baguette du coudrier dans le *Lai du Chievrefeuil* [796]. (3) Un hapax ne peut être expliqué par la linguistique seule: *Gormont et Isembard* [790]. (4) Des guillemets qui changent le climat poétique (note au fragment d'Alexandre d'Albéric) [788].

(5) *Aucassin et Nicolette*, v. 2 [795, 801]. (6) Die Branche VIII des *Roman de Renart* [779]. (7) Le style "circulaire" [730]. (8) Note on the Poetic and Empirical "I" in Medieval Authors [732]. (9) Etude ahistorique d'un texte: "Ballade des dames du temps jadis" [782]. (10) The Poetic Treatment of a Platonic-Christian Theme [Du Bellay's Sonnet of the Idea] [734]. (11) Die Kunst des Übergangs bei La Fontaine [774; also in 31, 44, 48]. (12) Les *Lettres portugaises* [805; also in 43, 48]. (13) *La vie de Marianne* [806; also in 43, 44, 49]. (14) Zu Victor Hugo's "Le rouet d'Omphale" [770, 771; also in 36]. (15) Baudelaire's "Spleen" [802; also in 36]. (16) Patterns of Thought in the Style of Albert Thibaudet [797, 798; also in 34]. (17) Le style chez Ch.-F. Ramuz: Le raccourci mystique [787]. (18) La genèse d'une poésie de Paul Valéry [789]. (19) L'étymologie d'un "cri de Paris" [chez Proust] [707; also in 34, 44].
Part 2: Provenzalische Literatur. (1) L'amour lointain de Jaufré Rudel [883; also in 26, 44]. (2) *Parelh paria* chez Marcabrun [886].
Part 3: Italienische Literatur. (1) The Text and Artistic Value of the "Ritmo cassinese" [851]. (2) "Il cantico di frate sole" [856, 860, 865; also in 47]. (3) Il detto del "Gatto lupesco" [862]. (4) A proposito del "Mare amoroso" [861, 866]. (5) L'episodio di Travale [849]. (6) "For de la bella cayba" (una questione estetica) [870, 871]. (7) Speech and Language in *Inferno* XIII [839; also in 47, 49]. (8) Farcical Elements in *Inferno*, XXI-XXIII [841; also in 47, 49]. (9) The Addresses to the Reader in the *Commedia* [858; also in 47, 49]. (10) *Crai, poscrai, posquacquera* [990, 995]. (11) Zum Aufbau von Petrarcas *Trionfi* [843; also in 47]. (12) L'originalità della narrazione de *I Malavoglia* di Verga [859; also in 47].
Part 4: Spanisch-Portugiesische Literatur. (1) Sobre el carácter histórico del *Cantar de mio Cid* [925; also in 39]. (2) "Razón de amor" [930; also in 39]. (3) "Eya velar" [929; also in 39]. (4) El romance de *Abenámar* [923; also in 39]. (5) A Folkloristic Pre-stage of the Romance *Conde Arnaldos* [938; also in 39]. (6) Fray Luis de León, *Profecía del Tajo* [933]. (7) "No me mueve, mi Dios" [935; also in 39]. (8) A Central Theme in Lope's *Fuenteovejuna* [939; also in 49]. (9) Lope de Vega's "Al triunfo de Judit" [937]. (10) El barroco español [922; also in 37, 49]. (11) Die "Cantiga da garvaya" [926, 936]. (12) Fleur et rose.
Part 5: Rumänische Literatur. *Mioriţa* [733].
Part 6: Mittel- und Neulateinische Literatur. (1) The Epic Style of the Pilgrim Aetheria [237, 844]. (2) Zu Pontans Latinität [847]. (3) The Problem of Latin Renaissance Poetry [735].

36. *Interpretationen zur Geschichte der französischen Lyrik*. Ed. Helga Jauss-Meyer and Peter Schunck. Heidelberg: Selbstverlag des Romanischen Seminars der U Heidelberg, 1961.
(1) Ronsard: *Le second livre des amours*, seconde partie. (2) Ronsard: *Sonnets pour Hélène*, livre II, XLIII. (3) Clément Marot: "Eglogue au roy, soubs les noms de Pan et Robin" (1539) [807]. (4) François de Malherbe: "Consolation à Monsieur du Périer gentilhomme d'Aix en Provence, sur la mort de sa fille" [757; also in 20]. (5) Jean de La Fontaine: "Le meunier, son fils, et l'âne. A.M.D.M." (6) Jean de La Fontaine: "Les deux pigeons" [811].

(7) André Chénier: "La jeune captive." (8) Alfred de Musset: "La nuit de mai." (9) Victor Hugo: "Le rouet d'Omphale" [770, 771; also in 35]. (10) Victor Hugo, *Légende des siècles*: "Booz endormi." (11) Victor Hugo, *Les rayons et les ombres*: "Tristesse d'Olympio." (12) Baudelaire, *Les fleurs du mal*: LXXVII, "Spleen" [802; also in 35]. (13) Mallarmé: Autre éventail de Mademoiselle Mallarmé.

37. *Cinque saggi di Ispanistica*. Ed. Giovanni Maria Bertini. Torino: Giappichelli, 1962.
(1) San Giovanni della Croce: "El cántico espiritual" [trans. and derived from 30; also in 38, 41]. (2) Prospettivismo nel *Don Quijote* [trans. from 29; also in 33, 43, 49]. (3) Il barocco spagnolo [trans. from 922; also in 35, 49]. (4) L'arte di Quevedo nel *Buscón* [trans. from 22; also in 45]. (5) Il concettismo interiore di Pedro Salinas [trans. from 921; also in 33].

38. *Essays on English and American Literature*. Ed. and introd. Anna Granville-Hatcher. Foreword Henri Peyre. Princeton: Princeton UP, 1962.
(1) On Yeats's Poem "Leda and the Swan" [745]. (2) Explication de Texte Applied to Walt Whitman's Poem "Out of the Cradle Endlessly Rocking" [737]. (3) "Tears, Idle Tears" Again [743]. (4) A Reinterpretation of "The Fall of the House of Usher" [742]. (5) The "Ode on a Grecian Urn," or Content vs. Metagrammar [746]. (6) Marvell's "Nymph Complaining for the Death of Her Faun" [748]. (7) Understanding Milton [741]. (8) Herrick's "Delight in Disorder" [749]. (9) Three Poems on Ecstasy: John Donne, St. John of the Cross, Richard Wagner [in 30, 37, 41]. (10) Spenser, "Shepheardes Calendar, March" (Lines 61–114), and the Variorum Edition [738]. (11) Explication de Texte Applied to Three Great Middle English Poems [739, 740]. Appendix: American Advertising Explained as Popular Art [in 30, 41, 49].

39. *Sobre antigua poesía española*. Buenos Aires: U Nacional, 1962.
(1) Sobre el carácter histórico del *Cantar de mio Cid* [925; also in 35]. (2) Sobre la cantica "Eya velar" [929; also in 35]. (3) "Razón de amor" [930; also in 35]. (4) El romance de Abenámar [923; also in 35]. (5) La unidad artística del *Auto da Sibila Cassandra* de Gil Vicente [trans. from 942]. (6) Período previo folklórico del *Romance del Conde Arnaldos* [938; also in 35]. (7) "No me mueve, mi dios" [935; also in 35].

40. *Classical and Christian Ideas of World Harmony: Prologomena to an Interpretation of the Word "Stimmung."* Ed. Anna Granville-Hatcher. Pref. René Wellek. Baltimore: Johns Hopkins UP, 1963 [708, 710, 722].

41. *Eine Methode Literatur zu interpretieren*. Trans. Gerd Wagner. München: Hauser, 1966 [trans. from 30].
(1) Drei Gedichte der Ekstase (John Donne, Saint John of the Cross, Richard Wagner) [30, 31, 38]. (2) *Explication de Texte* angewandt auf Voltaire [30, 31]. (3) Amerikanische Werbung – verstanden als populäre Kunst [30, 38, 49].

42. *L'armonia del mondo: Storia semantica di un'idea*. Trans. V. Poggi. Bologna: Mulino, 1967 [722].

43. *Texterklärungen: Aufsätze zur europaïschen Literatur.* Trans. Gerd Kenninger et al. München: Hauser, 1969.
(1) Sprachwissenschaft und Literaturwissenschaft [trans. from 29; also in 31, 33, 49]. (2) Die Werke Rabelais' [trans. from 803]. (3) Sprachlicher Perspektivismus im *Don Quijote* [trans. from 29; also in 33, 37, 49]. (4) Die *Lettres portugaises* [trans. from 805; also in 35, 48]. (5) Über *Das Leben der Marianne* [trans. from 806; also in 35, 44, 49]. (6) Der Stil Diderots [trans. from 29]. (7) Matthias Claudius' *Abendlied* [831]. (8) Zu einer Landschaft Eichendorffs [830].

44. *Les études de style.* Trans. Eliane Kaufholz, Alain Coulon, and Michel Foucault. Introd. Jean Starobinski. Paris: Gallimard, 1970.
(1) Art du langage et linguistique. (2) L'amour lointain de Jaufré Rudel et le sens de la poésie des troubadours [883; also in 26, 35]. (3) Rabelais et les "rabelaisants" [812]. (4) L'art de la transition chez La Fontaine [trans. from 774; also in 31, 35, 48]. (5) L'effet de sourdine dans le style classique: Racine [trans. from 758; also in 22, 48]. (6) Quelques interprétations de Voltaire [in 22]. (7) A propos de *La vie de Marianne* (lettre à M. Georges Poulet) [806; also in 35, 43, 49]. (8) Le style de Marcel Proust [trans. from 20; also in 34]. (9) L'étymologie d'un "cri de Paris" [707, 724; also in 34, 35]. (10) Quelques aspects de la technique des romans de Michel Butor [813, 814].

45. *L'art de Quevedo dans le "Buscón."* Trans. B. and C. D. R. Dauer. Paris: Ediciones Hispano-Americanas, 1972 [trans. from 22; in 37].

46. *Lettere di prigionieri di guerra italiani 1915–1918.* Trans. Renato Solmi. Introd. Lorenzo Rienzi. Linguistic notes Laura Vanelli. Torino: Boringhieri, 1976.

47. *Studi italiani.* Ed. Claudio Carpati. Letteratura e Cultura dell' Italia Unita 4. Milano: Vita e Pensiero, 1976.
(1) Nuove considerazioni sul "Cantico di frate sole" [856, 860, 865; also in 35]. (2) La bellezza artistica dell'antichissima elegia giudeo-italiana [869]. (3) Osservazioni sulla *Vita nuova* di Dante [trans. from 836]. (4) Il canto XIII dell'*Inferno* [trans. from 839; also in 35, 49]. (5) Un episodio autobiografico nel canto XIX dell'*Inferno* [trans. from 840]. (6) Gli elementi farseschi nei canti XXI-XXIII dell'*Inferno* [trans. from 841; also in 35, 49]. (7) La "tipologia ideale" nel *De vulgari eloquentia* di Dante [trans. from 857]. (8) Gli appelli al lettore nella *Commedia* [trans. from 858; also in 35, 49]. (9) La struttura dei *Trionfi* del Petrarca [trans. from 843; also in 35]. (10) L'*Aspasia* di Leopardi [872]. (11) L'originalità della narrazione nei *Malavoglia* [859; also in 35].

48. *Essays on Seventeenth-Century French Literature.* Trans., ed., and introd. David Bellos. Cambridge: Cambridge UP, 1981.
(1). Racine's Classical *piano* [trans. from 758; in 22, 44]. (2) Saint-Simon's Portrait of Louis XIV [trans. from 817; also in 22]. (3) Corneille's *Polyeucte* and the *Vie de Saint Alexis* [trans. from 763]. (4) The Art of Transition in La Fontaine [trans. from 774; also in 31, 35, 44]. (5) The "Récit de Théramène" in Racine's *Phèdre* [in 29, 31]. (6) The *Lettres portugaises* [trans. from 805; also in 35, 43].

49. *Leo Spitzer: Representative Essays.* Ed. Alban Forcione, Herbert Lindenberger, and Madeline Sutherland. Foreword John Freccero. Stanford: Stanford UP, 1988.

(1) Linguistics and Literary History (1948) [in 29, 31, 33, 43]. (2) Pseudo-objective Motivation in Charles-Louis Philippe (1923) [trans. from 952; in 20]. (3) Two Essays on Góngora's *Soledades* (On Góngora's *Soledades* [1930] [trans. from 893; also in 22]; Selections from Góngora's First *Soledad*: Critical and Explanatory Notes on Dámaso Alonso's New Edition [1940]) [trans. from 915, 919, 920]. (4) The Spanish Baroque (1944) [trans. from 922; also in 35, 37]. (5) Three Essays on Dante's *Commedia* (Speech and Language in *Inferno* XIII [1942] [839; also in 35, 47]; The Farcical Elements in *Inferno* XXI–XXIII [1944] [841; also in 35, 47]; The Addresses to the Reader in the *Commedia* [1955] [858; also in 35, 47]). (6) *Geistesgeschichte* vs. History of Ideas as Applied to Hitlerism (1944) [991]. (7) Linguistic Perspectivism in *Don Quijote* (1948) [in 29, 33, 37, 43]. (8) Interpretation of an Ode by Paul Claudel (1948) [784; also in 29, 34]. (9) American Advertising Explained as Popular Art (1949) [in 30, 38, 41]. (10) Apropos of *La vie de Marianne* (Letter to Georges Poulet) (1953) [trans. from 806; also in 35, 43, 44]. (11) A Central Theme and Its Structural Equivalent in Lope's *Fuenteovejuna* (1955) [939; also in 35]. (12) Development of a Method (1960) [trans. from 1004].

Book Reviews

50. *Silloge linguistica dedicata alla memoria di Graziado Isaia Ascoli nel primo centenario della nascita* (Torino: Chiantore, 1929). *IF* 50 (1932): 147–53.

51. Bally, Charles, *Linguistique générale et linguistique française* (Paris: Leroux, 1932). *IF* 53 (1935): 207–12.

52. Bazin, Simonin, *"Voilà taxi!"* (Paris: Gallimard, 1935). *VRo* 3 (1938): 182–91.

53. Behrens, D., *Giessener Beiträge zur romanischen Philologie* (Giessen: Selbstverlag des Romanischen Seminars, 1921). *ANS* 143 (1922): 155–57.

54. Bertoni, G., *Lingua e cultura (studi linguistici)* (Firenze: Olschki, 1939). *MLN* 54 (1939): 548–50.

55. Bottiglioni, G., *Atlante linguistico-etnografico italiano della Corsica* (Pisa: STID, 1935). *MLN* 52 (1937): 270–75.

56. ——, *Les raisons et les principaux caractères de l'"Atlante linguistico-etnografico italiano della Corsica"* (Pisa: STID, 1936). *MLN* 52 (1937): 270–75.

57. Brémond, Henri, *Racine et Valéry: Notes sur l'initiation poétique* (Paris: Grasset, 1930). *ZFS* 58 (1934): 240–50.

58. Brown, L. P., *Some Romance Words of Arabic or Germanic Origin*, USC Romance Philology Series 1 (Los Angeles: U of Southern California P, 1938). *MLN* 54 (1939): 627.

59. Brzywacz, Margot, *"Eifersucht" in den romanischen Sprachen* (Pöppinhaus: Bochum-Langendreer, 1937). *Rom* 64 (1938): 256–61.

60. Castro, Américo, *Glosarios latino-españoles de la edad media* (Madrid: *Revista de filología española*, Anejo 22, 1936). *MLN* 53 (1938): 122–46.

61. Corominės, Juan, *Diccionario crítico-etimológico de la lengua castellana* 1 [A–C] (Bern: Francke, 1954). *MLN* 71 (1956): 271–73.

62. ——, *Diccionario crítico-etimológico de la lengua castellana* 2 [Ch–K] (Bern: Francke, 1954). *MLN* 71 (1956): 373–86.

63. ——, *Diccionario crítico-etimológico de la lengua castellana* 3 [L–Re] (Bern: Francke, 1954). *MLN* 72 (1957): 579–91.

64. ——, *Diccionario crítico-etimológico de la lengua castellana* 4 [Ri–Z; Indices] (Bern: Francke, 1954). *MLN* 74 (1959): 127–49.

65. Curtius, Ernst Robert, *Europäische Literatur und lateinisches Mittelalter* (Bern: Francke, 1948). *AJP* 70 (1949): 425-31.

66. Damm, Otto, *Der deutsch-französische Jargon in der schönen französischen Literatur* (Berlin: Ebering, 1911). *ZFS* 41 (1913): 82-88.

67. Damourette, J., and E. Pichon, *Des mots à la pensée: Essai de grammaire de la langue française* 1-2 (Paris: d'Artrey, 1930). *ZRP* 52 (1932): 628-33.

68. ——, *Morphologie du verbe: Essai de grammaire de la langue française* 3 (Paris: d'Artrey, 1933). *ZRP* 53 (1933): 612-20.

69. ——, *Des mots à la pensée: Essai de grammaire de la langue française 1911-1936: Auxiliaires, temps, modes, voix* 5 (Paris: d'Artrey, 1936). *RR* 30 (1939): 436-42.

70. Etienne, S., *Défense de la philologie*, Bibliothèque de la Faculté de Philosophie et Lettres de l'Université de Liège, fasc. 4 (Paris: Droz, 1933). *NM* 37 (1936): 312-14.

71. Ettmayer, Karl von, *Vademecum für Studierende der romanischen Philologie* (Heidelberg: Winter, 1919). *NM* 21 (1920): 135-40.

72. Falgui, E., and A. Prati, *Diccionario de Marina medievale e moderno* (Roma: Reale Accademia d'Italia, 1937). *MLN* 54 (1939): 157.

73. Franz, Artur, *Zur galloromanischen Syntax*, Supplementheft 10 der *ZFS* (Jena-Leipzig: Gronau, 1920). *ANS* 142 (1921): 151-58.

74. Gamillscheg, Ernst, *Studien zur Vorgeschichte einer romanischen Tempuslehre* (Wien: Nachtr. d.l. Aufl., 1913; Tübingen: Tübinger Beitr. 2 Linguistik, 1920). *ANS* 131 (1913-14): 466.

75. Gerig, Walther, *Die Terminologie der Hanf- und Flachskultur in den frankoprovenzalischen Mundarten mit Ausblicken auf die umgebenden Sprachgebiete*, Beiheft zu *WS* (Heidelberg: Winter, 1913). *ZRP* 38 (1917): 368-71.

76. Gillet, Joseph E., *"Propalladia" and Other Works of Bartolomé de Torres Naharro* 3 (Menasha: Banta, 1943-61). *HR* 21 (1963): 62-75.

77. Gilliéron, Jules, *L'aire clavellus d'après* l'Atlas linguistique de la France (Bern: Beerstecher, 1912). *ZFS* 40 (1912-13): 139-49.

78. Gilliéron, Jules, and Mario Roques, *Etudes de géographie linguistique* (Paris: Champion, 1912). *ZFS* 42 (1914): 25.

79. Giol, Pere Barnils, *Die Mundart von Alacant* (Barcelona: Palau de la Disputació, 1913). *ZRP* 40 (1919-20): 239-42.

80. Glaser, Kurt, *Zum Bedeutungswandel im Französischen* (Ergänzende Skizzen zu Nyrop, *Grammaire historique de la langue française* 4 [Copenhagen: Bojesen, n.d.]), Sonderabdruck aus *NS* 29-30. *ZRP* 43 (1923): 252-54.

81. Glässer, Edgar, *Denkform und Gemeinschaft bei Jules Romains*, Romanische Studien 46 (Berlin: Ebering, 1938). *MLN* 54 (1939): 223-25.

82. Göhri, Karl, *Die Ausdrücke für Blitz und Donner im Galloromanischen, eine onomasiologische Studie*, Sonderabdruck aus der *Revue de dialectologie romane* (Hamburg: n.p., 1912). *ZFS* 42 (1914): 166-69.

83. Green, H. J., *"Anseÿs de Mes" according to Ms N [Bibl. de l'Arsenal 3143]* (Paris: Belles Lettres, 1939). *MLN* 55 (1940): 624–26.

84. Grégoire, Antoine, *Le style des chroniqueurs financiers* (Genève: n.p., 1939). *FM* 9 (1941): 67–72.

85. Gregorio, Giacomo de, *Contributi al lessico etimologico romanzo con particolare considerazione al dialetto e ai sub dialetti siciliani [Studi glottologici italiani VII]* (Torino: Chiantore, 1920). *ZRP* 44 (1924): 376–80.

86. ——, *Studi glottologici italiani* 8 (1925). *ZRP* 50 (1930): 252–56.

87. Griera, A., *Atlas lingüístic de Catalunya* (Barcelona: Inst. d'Estudis Catalans). *ZRP* 45 (1925): 614–23.

88. Haas, J., *Grundlagen der französischen Syntax* (Halle: Meyer, 1912). *ANS* 130 (1913): 451–54.

89. Hachtmann, Otto, *Die Vorherrschaft substantivischer Konstruktionen im modernen französischen Prosastil, eine stilistische Studie* (Berlin: Ebering, 1912). *ZFS* 42 (1914): 157–65.

90. Hanzen, W., W. Muschg, and E. Staiger, eds., *Weltliteratur: Festgabe für Fritz Strich zum siebzigsten Geburtstag* (Bern: Francke, 1952). *MLN* 69 (1954): 460–63.

91. Hatzfeld, Helmut, *Führer durch die literarischen Meisterwerke der Romanen, II. Spanische Literatur* (München: Hueber, 1923). *ZRP* 44 (1924): 373–76.

92. *Mélanges de linguistique romane offerts à M. Jean Haust* (Liège: n.p., 1939; Genève: Slatkine, 1972). *MLN* 55 (1940): 401–02.

93. Holbrook, Richard Th., *Etude sur Pathelin*, Elliott Monographs 5 (Paris: Champion, 1917). *ZRP* 44 (1924): 368–73.

94. Jaberg, K., *Aspects géographiques du langage* (Paris: Droz, 1936). *MLN* 52 (1937): 227–28.

95. Jeanroy, Alfred, and J.-J. Salverda de Grave, *Uc de Saint-Circ: Poésies* (Toulouse: Privat, 1913). *ZFS* 41 (1913): 10–17.

96. Jennings, Augustus Campbell, *A Linguistic Study of the "Cartulario de San Vicente de Oviedo"* (New York: Vanni, 1940). *RFH* 2 (1940): 391–96.

97. Juilland, A., ed., *Cahiers Sextil Puscariu (linguistique-philologie-littérature roumaines)* 1, fasc. 1 and 2 (Roma: Valle Hermoso, 1952). *Word* 9 (1953): 300–07.

98. Juillière, Pierre de la, *Les images dans Rabelais*, Beiheft zur *ZRP* (Halle: Niemeyer, 1912). *ZFS* 42 (1914): 66–67.

99. Kalepky, Theodor, *Neuaufbau der Grammatik* (Leipzig: Teubner, 1928). *ZRP* 55 (1935): 705.

100. Kayser, Wolfgang, *Das Groteske, seine Gestaltung in Malerei und Dichtung* (Oldenburg: Stalling, 1957). *GGA* 212 (1958): 95-110.

101. Kellermann, W., *Aufbaustil und Weltbild Chrestiens von Troyes im Percevalroman, ZRP* Beiheft 88 (Halle: Niemeyer, n.d.). *MLN* 55 (1940): 222–26.

102. Keniston, H., *The Syntax of Castilian Prose: The Sixteenth Century* (Chicago: U of Chicago P, 1937). *Lg* 14 (1938): 218-30.

103. Koukal, Gustav, *Etymologische Streifzüge [Beiträge zur französischen Wortgeschichte]* (Wien: n.p., 1911). *ANS* 128 (1912): 263-64.

104. Lecoy, Félix, *Recherches sur le* Libro de buen amor *de Juan Ruiz, archiprêtre de Hita* (Paris: Droz, 1938). *RFE* 1 (1939): 266-74.

105. Le Gentil, Pierre, *Le virelai et le villancico (le problème des origines arabes)* (Paris: Belles Lettres, 1954). *HR* 23 (1955): 312-14.

106. *Homenaje a la memoria de Dr. Rodolfo Lenz,* Anales de la Facultad de Filosofía y Educación, Sección de Filología, 2.1 (Santiago de Chile: U de Chile, 1938). *MLN* 35 (1940): 156-57.

107. Lerch, Eugen, *Prädikative Partizipia für Verbalsubstantive im Französischen,* Beiheft zur *ZRP* (Halle: Niemeyer, 1912). *ANS* 131 (1913-14): 225.

108. ——, *Das invariable Participium praesentis des Französischen (une femme aimant la vertu),* Sonderabdruck aus den *RF* 33 (1913-15): 369-488. *ZRP* 39 (1917-19): 372-76.

109. Levi, Attilio, *Le palatali piemontesi* (Torino: Bocca, 1918). *ANS* 141 (1921): 262-64.

110. Löfstedt, Einar, *Syntactica Studien und Beiträge zur historischen Syntax des Lateins* (Lund: Gleerup, 1933). *VRo* 2 (1937): 197-208.

111. ——, *Vermischte Studien zur lateinischen Sprachkunde und Syntax* (Lund: Gleerup, 1936). *VRo* (1939): 129-35.

112. Lombard, Alf, *L'infinitif de narration dans les langues romanes, étude de syntaxe historique* (Uppsala: Almqvist, 1936). *VRo* 3 (1938): 172-81.

113. Lommatzsch, Erhard, *Gautier de Coincy als Satiriker* (Halle: Niemeyer, 1913). *ZFS* 41 (1913): 184-86.

114. Lucero, T. M., and A. Dornheim, eds., *Homenaje a Fritz Krüger* (Mendoza: U de Cuyo, 1952). *Lg* 30 (1954): 295-98.

115. Malkiel, Yakov, *Das substantivierte Adjektiv im Französischen* (Berlin: Jastrow, 1938). *MLN* 54 (1939): 148-50.

116. ——, *Development of the Latin Suffixes -antia and -entia in Romance Languages, with Special Regard to Ibero-Romance,* University of California Publications in Linguistics 1.44 (Berkeley: U of California P, 1944). *AJP* 67 (1946): 380-82.

117. Meyer-Lübke, Wilhelm, *Historische Grammatik der französischen Sprache, 2 Teil: Wortbildungslehre* (Heidelberg: Winter, 1921). *A Rom* 7 (1923): 194-210.

118. Meyer-Riefstahl, Rudolf, and Marcel Flandin, *Villatte: Parisismen* (Berlin-Schöneberg: Langenscheidt, 1912). *ZFS* 40 (1912-13): 34-37.

119. Migliorini, B., and G. Devoto, eds., *Lingua nostra* 1 (Firenze: Sansoni, 1939). *MLN* 55 (1940): 469-71.

120. Moreiro, Julio, *Estudios da lingua portuguesa* 2 (Lisboa: Teixeira, 1913). *Literaturblatt für germanische und romanische Philologie* 2.3 (1914): 65–79.

121. Nicholson, G.-G., *Recherches philologiques romanes* (Paris: Champion, 1921). *ZRP* 42 (1922): 741–42.

122. ——, *Un nouveau principe d'étymologie romane* (Paris: Droz, 1936). *MLN* 52 (1937): 605–07.

123. Nitze, W. A., ed., *Le haut livre du Graal: Perlesvaus* 3, Commentary and Notes (Chicago: U of Chicago P, 1938). *MLN* 53 (1938): 604–08.

124. Notholt, Edwin, *Das Adverb, der präpositionale Ausdruck und der ganze Satz als Prädikat in Verbindung mit dem Verb in der Entwicklung der französischen Sprache* (Diss. Göttingen, 1913). *ZFS* 43 (1915): 62–63.

125. Pei, Mario, *The Italian Language* (New York: Columbia UP, 1941). *MLN* 57 (1942): 148–54.

126. Pflaum, Hiram, *Die religiöse Disputation in der europäischen Dichtung des Mittelalters: I. Der allegorische Streit zwischen Synagoge und Kirche* (Genève: Olschki, 1935). *Speculum* 13 (1938): 356–60.

127. Place, E. B., ed., *"L'histoire de Gille de Chyn" by Gautier de Tournay*, Northwestern University Studies in the Humanities 7 (Evanston: Northwestern UP, 1941). *MLN* 58 (1943): 132–41.

128. Riffaterre, Michael, *Le style de Pléiades de Gobineau, essai d'application d'une méthode stylistique* (New York: Columbia UP, 1957). *MLN* 63 (1958): 68–74.

129. Rogger, K., *Vom Wesen des Lautwandels*, Leipziger Romanistische Studien 1.6 (Leipzig: Selbstverlag des Romanischen Seminars, 1934). *MLN* 50 (1935): 341.

130. Rohlfs, Gerhard, *Ager, area, atrium* (Borna-Leipzig: Noske, 1920). *ANS* 142 (1921): 154–55.

131. ——, *Historische Grammatik der italienischen Sprache und ihrer Mundarten* 2: Formenlehre und Syntax, 1. Teil. (Bern: Francke, 1949). *Word* 8 (1952): 276–79.

132. Sainéan, Constantin, *Lettres de L. Sainéan, le grand philologue* (Bucuresti: n.p., 1936). *FM* 5 (1937): 185–86.

133. Saint-Amour, Comte de Caix de, *Belgicismes* (Anvers: J. van Hille-de Backer, 1911). *ZFS* 40 (1912–13): 149–53.

134. Sayce, R. A., *Style in French Prose: A Method of Analysis* (Oxford: Oxford UP, 1953). *Critique* 98 (1955): 595–609.

135. Schmidt, W. Fritz, *Die spanischen Elemente im französischen Wortschatz*, Beiheft 54 zur *ZRP* (Halle: Niemeyer, 1914). *ZFS* 44 (1917): 215–21.

136. Schoch, Josef, *Perfectum historicum und Perfectum praesens im Französischen von seinen Anfängen bis 1700* (Halle: Niemeyer, 1912). *ZRP* 37 (1913): 372–75.

137. Schrader, L., *Panurge und Hermes, zum Ursprung eines Characters bei Rabelais* (Bonn: Romanisches Seminar der U Bonn, 1958). *CL* 12 (1960): 263–65.

138. Schramm, Franz, *Sprachliches zur Lex Salica: Eine vulgärlateinisch-romanische Studie* (Marburg: Ebel, 1911). *ANS* 28 (1912): 252.

139. Schultz, I., *Bildhaftigkeit im französischen Argot*, Giessener Beiträge zur Romanischen Philologie 27. (Giessen: Im Selbstverlag des Romanischen Seminars, 1936). *MLN* 53 (1938): 74-75.

140. Seidler, H., *Allgemeine Stilistik* (Göttingen: Vandenhoeck, 1953). *CL* 8 (1956): 146-49.

141. Stern, Samual Miklos, *Les chansons mozarabes* 1 (Palermo: Manfredi, 1953). *HR* 23 (1955): 303-05.

142. Strohmeyer, Fritz, *Der Stil der französischen Sprache* (Berlin: Weidmann, 1910). *ZRP* 36 (1912): 110-16.

143. Sturtevant, E. H., *An Introduction to Linguistic Science* (New Haven: Yale UP, 1947). *AJP* 71 (1950): 90-99.

144. Ullman, S., *Style in the French Novel* (Cambridge: Cambridge UP, 1957). *CL* 10 (1958): 368-71.

145. Vossler, Karl, *Frankreichs Kultur im Spiegel seiner Sprachentwicklung: Geschichte der frz. Schriftsprache von den Anfängen bis zur klassischen Neuzeit* (Heidelberg: Winter, 1913). *ZFS* 42 (1914): 139-50.

146. Wagner, Max Leopold, *Das ländliche Leben Sardiniens im Spiegel der Sprache*, Beiheft zu *WS* (Heidelberg: Winter, 1921). *ZRP* 43 (1923): 486-88.

147. Wartburg, Walter von, *Französisches etymologisches Wörterbuch* (Bonn: Klopp, 1929). *NS* 33 (1925): 49-53; *NS* 35 (1927): 356-60; *NS* 36 (1928): 109-13, 601-04; *NS* 37 (1929): 653-54; *NS* 39 (1931): 34-36, 597-99; *NS* 40 (1932): 161-62; *NS* 41 (1933): 25-27.

148. ——, *Französisches etymologisches Wörterbuch: eine Darstellung des galloromanischen Sprachschatzes* 3 (D-F) (Leipzig: Teubner, 1934). *MLN* 51 (1936): 39-43.

149. ——, *Die Entstehung der romanischen Völker* (Halle: Saale, 1939). *MLN* 54 (1939): 547-48.

150. Wegmann, Franz, *Syntaktische Eigentümlichkeiten der Sprache des Pierre Loti* (Schweinfurt: Programm d. k. Humanistischen Gymn., 1913-14). *ZFS* 44 (1917): 222-23.

151. Williams, E. B., *From Latin to Portuguese, Historical Phonology and Morphology of the Portuguese Language* (Philadelphia: U of Pennsylvania P, 1938). *MLN* 54 (1939): 376-78.

152. Wind, B. H., *Les mots italiens introduits en français au XVIè siècle* (Amsterdam: Deventer, 1926). *ZRP* 55 (1935): 705.

Etymology and Lexicology

Linguistic Symbols

*	Reconstructed, not attested
<	Derives from
>	Produced the derivative
=	Is the same as; means
X	Blended with

American, Anglo-French, and English

153. *"Ratio > race."* *AJP* 62 (1941): 129–43.
With reference to Aristotle, Augustine, and Thomas Aquinas, Spitzer clarifies the semantic development *ratio* > *razza* > *race* and discusses its contemporary political connotations in France, Germany, and Italy, emphasizing, in particular, ideological deformation [in 28, 31, 32].

154. "*Curmudgeon* 'Miser.'" *JEGP* 41 (1942): 150–51.
Curmudgeon is related to OFr. *chamorge* (= 'glandered [horse]').

155. "Eng. *Dismal* < OF **dism-al.*" *MLN* 57 (1942): 602–13.
Previous derivations of *dismal* are rejected in favor of OFr. *disme* (= Lat. *decima* [sc. *pars*]) + the suffix *-al*, a variant of *-el* = Lat. *-alis*. A **dies decimales* > OFr. *(di) dism-al* (or a *decimale* [*tempus*] > *dis* (*jours*) *dismals* involving the idea of a 'tithe of time') must have included the idea of a 'time of self-mortification.'

156. "*Pageant*: Lat. *pagina*." *AJP* 64 (1943): 327–30.
ALat. *pagina* (= 'apparatus, machinery, something well-constructed and prepared for a purpose'), the root of Eng. *pageant*, is among the descendants of the *pangere-compages*, *impago* family.

157. "*Conundrum–Quandary.*" *JEGP* 42 (1943): 405–09.
Eng. *conundrum* stems from a foreign source adapted in different ways, perhaps Fr. *calembour* < **calembourdon* (**calembredon*). The *qu-* spelling is probably

pseudoetymological. The original pronunciation of *quandary* = 'quandáry,' in common use from circa 1580, supposes a form in *-ariu*; secondary dialectal forms help set up a continuous chain from *conundrum, quonundrum, quorundum,* to *quandáry,* from **calembredaine.*

158. "Anglo-French Etymologies." *AS* 19 (1944): 16–24.
By way of illustrating the need for progress in the study of AFr. word families, this article is a discussion of *bludgeon, cabrie* (= 'antelope'), *épergne, flimsy, scoundrel,* and *sculduddery* (Amer. *skulduggery*), all of which have Fr. roots.

159. "*(Gri)malkin.*" *JEGP* 43 (1944): 94–97.
Grimalkin = *grimal-kin* and not *grey-malkin*. The Fr. proper name, *Grimaud, Grimouard* (= 'devil, evil spirit, heretic'), shows that Macbeth's *grimalkin* (= 'name of a fiend') stays well within the French tradition.

160. "Anglo-French Etymologies." *MLN* 59 (1944): 223–50.
Earlier sources and more probable antecedents are given for the following: *cantankerous, culprit, dally, flaunt, foist, gravy, jaunt, rum, trance-prance,* and *trudge.*

161. "*Nincompoop.*" *MLN* 59 (1944): 565–66.
Fr. *hypocondre* + *-omp* probably gave **i(m)pocomp,* which underwent metathesis, **i(m)compoop,* later acquiring the *-n* of the Fr. or Eng. indefinite article to become *nincompoop.*

162. "Anglo-French Etymologies." *SP* 42 (1944): 521–43.
The etyma for *harlot, lampoon, lapel, loiter, per(s)nickety, squander, (s)queazy,* and *turmoil* are explained, and previous theories are rejected in favor of Fr. dialectal word families or analogues.

163. "*Highball.*" *AS* 20 (1945): 72–73.
Notes a parallel semantic development in Fr. slang terms denoting various types of intoxicating beverages that, like the Amer. word, hearken back to railroad terms.

164. "*Cahoots.*" *AS* 20 (1945): 154–55.
The word's slightly pejorative sense in its modern usage may be a vestigial trait reflecting its origins: Fr. *cahot* (= 'the jumpe, hop or jogge of a coach, etc., in a rugged or uneven way' [Cotgrave]; fig., 'difficulté, obstacle': "C'est une affaire et qui aura bien des cahots" [Littré]). Thus, "he is in cahoots with me" was originally equivalent to "he is in the same boat with me."

165. "Three Etymological Notes." *JEGP* 44 (1945): 94–97.
Fr. borrowings or roots are found for *gun, car(ri)w(h)itchet,* and *gallivant.*

166. "Anglo-Latin *buzones.*" *MLN* 60 (1945): 285–86.
Meaning 'county knights on whose nod (*nutus*) depends the action of others in the county court,' *buzones* is explained as a latinization of popular OFr. *bu(i)son* (= 'buzzard') < Lat. *buteo.*

167. "Anglo-French Etymologies (Second Series, cf. *MLN* 59, 223–50)." *MLN* 60 (1945): 503–21.
Balderdash, caterwaul, curlicue, dudgeon, pilliwinks, prowl, tantrum(s), doldrum(s), and *vagary.*

168. "Anglo-French Etymologies." *PQ* 24 (1945): 20–32.
Fr. origins for *askance-asquint, frill, peevish, saunter, squirm, toy.*

169. "Patterns of Thought and of Etymology (I) *Nausea* > OFr. (> Eng.) *Noise*." *Word* 1 (1945): 260–76.

Numerous examples show the semantic development of classical Lat. *nausea* (= 'seasickness, vomiting, disgust, boredom') > OFr., OProv. *noise* (= 'quarrel, strife, discord, noise'). A more careful examination of medieval thought patterns – textually accessible in this case – is required to understand semantic development.

170. "Mots anglo-français." *FM* 14 (1946): 87–99.

The dearth of studies dealing with AFr. etyma is attributed to the hyper-specialization of Anglicists and Gallicists. Neglect of Fr. etyma is due to oversight, disdain for the hapax, positivistic timidity, dismissal of semantic resources, misclassification of homonyms, and chronological conservatism.

171. "Three Etymologies." *PQ* 25 (1946): 273–77.

(1) Proposes as the origin of Eng. *to interlope* the Lat. *interlopare* (= 'to interpolate') in the form **to interpole*. (2) Suggests a Fr. dialectal origin for *to jam*, Wall. *djamer* (= 'to couple, to yoke together'). (3) The OFr. word family *reborser* (= 'to brush the hair the wrong way, to stem the tide, to act in opposition to something or somebody, to retrace one's steps') is at the origin of *rubbish* perhaps as **rebrous* in a meaning close to that of *mâquis*.

172. "Patterns of Thought and of Etymology (II).". *Word* 2 (1946): 142–54.

A consideration of the etymology and semantic development of *curse* traces the word to a use of the classical Lat. verb *incurrere* (= 'running into ills of any kind').

173. "*Scalawag*." *AS* 22 (1947): 188–91.

A Fr. origin lies at the root of this Americanism in the modern Eng. word family that also includes *scavenger*. *Scalawag* may reflect **(e)scalvage* postulated by Fr. *esclavage* and OFr. *escaul(e)vage*.

174. "*Ragamuffin*, *Ragman*, *Rigamarole* and *Rogue*." *MLN* 42 (1947): 85–93.

Traces Eng. *rageman* (= 'devil') to the Old Testament king Rehoboam, whose name, through secondary developments contributed by folk etymology, eventually came to mean 'rag-gatherer, -dealer.'

175. "*Shenan(n)igan*." *AS* 23 (1948): 210–13.

The Amer. slang term is related to Ger. – or Rotwelsch – *schinägeln* (= 'to live in debauchery') (cited by Hermann von Fischer, *Schwäbisches Wörterbuch*, Tübingen: Lauppe, 1920, v. 844).

176. "*Basket*." *MLN* 63 (1948): 58–59.

Traced to an ON or Pic. form **baskot* parallel to Ht.-Maine *bachot* (= 'reed hut').

177. "*Racket* and *Logorrea*." *Word* 4 (1948): 127–28.

(1) For *racket* (= 'scandalous affair [of fraud]'), Spitzer postulates a semantic development similar to that of colloquial *pétard* (= 'rocket' > 'noise'); *racket* (= 'a disturbance, loud noise') is connected with *rocket* (= 'an apparatus consisting of a cylindrical case of paper containing an inflammable composition by the ignition of which it may be projected to a height or distance'). (2) *Logorrea* (= 'excessive talkativeness') is a learned coinage based on the model of *diarrhea*.

178. "*Noise* and *Curse*." *Word* 4 (1948): 128–30.

The semantic development *nausea* > *noise* (= 'disgust, vomiting > illness, grief > [loud lament of] mourning') is paralleled in Port. *nojo* (< Lat. *inodiare*), which developed the same meanings. Cites additional examples of the tendency to attribute human attitudes to God.

179. *"Cavort."* *JEGP* 48 (1949): 132–37.

The word family Fr. *chahuter, chahut* (= '[to raise] an uproar, scandal') is the etymon for *cavort*.

180. *"Casket, Cask."* *MLN* 64 (1949): 44–46.

Probably derives from Prov. **casquet* (= 'shell or skull'); the simple form in both Eng. and Fr. may be a back-formation from the *-et* form considered as a diminutive.

181. *"Kanke(r)dort* 'a state of suspense, a difficult position.'" *MLN* 64 (1949): 502–04.

This term is related to the word family represented by *quandary* and *conundrum* (which go back to Fr. **calembredaine* 'nonsense talk'); it may be the oldest attestation of Fr. *calembour(d)* in Eng.

182. "The *Schmoo.*" *AS* 25 (1950): 69–70.

The origin of this Amer. term appears to be Heb. *shemu-a* (= 'what one hears, gossip'), from which the Yid. *schmu* (= 'profit') developed. Al Capp is credited with having freed the term from its ironic connotation and with having used its onomatopoeic value to symbolize his "genuine American pantheism."

183. "Two Etymologies: 1. *Gibberish,* 2. *Goon.*" *AS* 25 (1950): 152–53.

(1) **En-guibrage* (= 'messy, cumbersome array of heterogenous objects [as found at the county fair of Guibray]') underlies Anj. *enguibrage* and is at the origin of Eng. *gibb(e)ridge* (the original form of *gibberish*), which was secondarily associated with names of languages ending in *-ish.* (2) *Goon* derives from Lyonnais and Mâconnais *gone* (= 'gamin'), a back-formation of the verb *se go(u)ner* (= 'to dress badly or ridiculously, to be dirty or ridiculous').

184. *"Pun."* *JEGP* 49 (1950): 352–54.

Like *conundrum* and *carwitchet, pun* is of Fr. origin. Eng. *punnet* and *pundigrion* (circa 1676) < **poignette* < *poindre* (= 'to sting'), and **poindrillon* or **poindirillon* (also, possibly, **pointrillon,* **pointilleron*) < Fr. *pointe* (= fig., 'pun').

185. "A Chaucerian Hapax Legomenon: *Upon the viritoot.*" *Lg* 26 (1950): 389–93.

The etymon of *viritoot* is OFr. *vire-vou(s)te* < *vire! voute!* < Lat. **volvitare.* Analogies illustrate the processes of dissimilation and assimilation in its development.

186. "On the Etymology of *Pet.*" *Lg* 26 (1950): 533–38.

All meanings of the Eng. noun are derived from Lat. *peditum* through semantic developments of Fr. *pet.*

187. *"Funny Bone."* *AS* 26 (1951): 306–07.

Dismisses the etymology, which suggests a play on *humerus,* and cites a parallel colloquial expression, *das damische Aderle* (Carinthia, Austria) 'the crazy, giddy vein,' used in reference to the funny bone.

188. *"Hurlewayn."* *NM* 52 (1951): 13–14.

The term *hurlewayn's kynne* is not etymologically identical to OFr. *mesnie Hellequin.* Rather it is a reflection of the *milites Herlewini,* the 12th-c. Lat. prototype of OFr. *mesnie Hellequin.*

189. *"Trousers* < OF **treüs.*" *PQ* 30 (1951): 437–41.

Isidore of Seville's *tubrucus, -i,* a word that came into VLat. as early as the 5th or 6th c., is probably reflected in Gallo-Romance, for example, OProv. *trabucs* or *trebucs* and OFr. *trebus.*

190. "Two Anglo-French Etymologies." *Word* 7 (1951): 211–21.

(1) *Pimpernel, pimp, whimbrel.* This Eng. word family is traced first to **pipinella,* a hypocoristic word from nursery language. Spitzer suggests deleting **pimpernella* from *REW* and replacing it with **pipinnus,* which, as his examples, parallels, and study of semantic developments show, has a much broader hypocoristic-onomatopoeic meaning. (2) *Tarry.* Adduces evidence from MEng. and OFr. translations of identical passages from Psalms to demonstrate that MEng. *tary* is derived from OFr. *entarier* (both are used to render Lat. *irritare*).

191. *"Snallygaster."* *AS* 27 (1952): 237–38.

Related to *schnelle Geister* (= 'fast-flying ghosts'), *snallygaster* is eventually linked to the "seven whistlers" of folklore, a popular derivation of the Wild Host.

192. *"Burglar."* *JEGP* 51 (1952): 95–96.

Postulates **buricare* (a variant of **furicare* < Lat. *fur* [= 'thief']) meaning 'to rummage' as the origin of AN *burguier* (= 'to rummage, to pillage') and *burguëor* < ALat. *burgator* (= 'burglar'). MLat. and Eng. *-l-* forms (*burglatoria, burglator, burgulare, burglar*) may go back to OFr. **burgu-el-er* or **burg-ailler.*

193. *"Confusion Shmooshun."* *JEGP* 51 (1952): 226–33.

The ironic repetition of a word or word-ending prefixed by *shm-* reflects the speech habits of Jews of the Bronx, New York. This type of jocose word formation is traced ultimately to a Turk. or Yid. origin.

194. *"Slang."* *MLN* 67 (1952): 99–103.

Supports Partridge's etymology and hypothesis concerning the word's semantic development (*Society for Pure English* 55 [1940]) and includes parallels and a definition of the social foundation of the term: (1) OFr. *eslinguer,* literally, 'to throw stones with a sling' meaning 'to speak'; (2) examples showing that the word belonged originally to the milieu of itinerant peddlers (or showmen). *Slang* is a phonetic variant of *sling.*

195. *"Salpeter."* *MLN* 67 (1952): 358–59.

Discusses Philipp Forchheimer's article, "The Etymology of *salpeter*" (*MLN* 67 [1952]: 103) and refutes his reasoning that *salpeter* < *sal nitrum* through dissimilation *n* > *b, p.* Instead, Spitzer claims, all forms (Ger. *Salpeter,* Fr. *salpêtre,* Eng. *saltpeter*) go back to Lat. *salpetrae,* Gk. *alas petras.*

196. *"To Pelt* < Dialectal Fr. *empeuter."* *RR* 43 (1952): 205–07.

Like *skulduggery* and *conundrum, to pelt* may be traced to OFr. words of popular origin. Saintonge *empeuter,* like Prov. *empeltar,* is a representative of **impeltare.* Its transfer to English soil is due to the fact that Saintonge belonged for some time to the English crown.

197. "A Further Note on *Snollygaster."* *AS* 29 (1954): 85.

A brief discussion of *snallygaster* and *snollyg(h)oster,* confirming the hypothesis in the Baltimore *Evening Sun* (3 Sept. 1952) that both words derive from "Teutonic *schnelle Geister*" in a unilinear development: "the Wild Host" > "bird(s) of prey that terrorize(s) man" > "ostentatious, vociferous politico."

198. *"Stubborn."* *MLN* 69 (1954): 550–51.

Relates *stubborn* to the Fr. dialectal word family *estibourner* and concludes that the Eng. word probably represents a postverbal adjective *estibourne* (= 'strong, resistant as a palisade').

199. "The Etymology of the Term *Syphilis*." *Bulletin* 29 (1955): 269–73.
Spitzer rejects previous explanations. Girolamo Fracastoro changed an already existing *erysipelas* into *syphilis*, eliminating its first two syllables.

200. "Karl Heisig, *Gentiles* (*NS*, 1954, 503–5)." *RF* 66 (1955): 446–47.
Heisig's theory is that the word was used by French troops in America in the 18th c. to mean 'non-Jewish' and that later it was commonly used by American Jews. But Spitzer traces the word back to biblical Lat. *gentiles* and biblical Gk. *ta ethne* and ultimately to Old Testament Heb. *goyim*. The use of the word *gentiles* by American Christians in speaking of themselves is traced to the Old Testament mentality of the Calvinist colonists.

Catalan and Provençal

201. "Etymologisches aus dem Katalanischen." *NM* 15 (1913): 157–79.
Additions to Meyer-Lübke's *Romanisches Etymologisches Wörterbuch* are supported by S. Vogel's Catalan-German dictionary.

202. "Katl. *tramitar* 'weitergeben,' *tràmit* 'Instanz,' span. *trámite* 'Instanzenweg.'" *ANS* 136 (1917): 162–63.
The semantic development of this word family parallels the development of Fr. *canal* (= 'paths of influence') in the 18th c.

203. "Zu REW Nr. 9544a: *Winald*." *ANS* 136 (1917): 163–64.
Concerns the common terms for fox, including *volp*, *renart*, *guinarda*, and *guinen*. In the south of France, *reinal* > *winald*. Spitzer speculates on the use of the expression "le grand guignol" meaning 'le grand usurier' in reference to Jews.

204. "Katalanische Etymologien." *ZRP* 40 (1919–20): 215–26.
(1) OCatal. *asit* < OCatal. *asít*. (2) Catal. *atohell*, *tuducalare*. (3) OCatal. *axalo* < Fr. Châlons. (4) Catal. *axonar* (= 'to pick olives, to cut branches') < **axó* not **aixó*. (5) *Fer s'ebré* < *abrer* < *arbor*. (6) Catal. *hach* is the result of adding *ka* to *ha* in order to distinguish the name of the letter *h* from the name of the letter *a*. (7) Catal. *perbocar* (= 'to vomit') < *provocare*, but Mall. *perbocar* (= 'steel cutting edge') and Aran. *perbocar* (= 'to plaster a wall') < *per* + *boca*. (8) NProv. *sencèr* (= 'intact'), Catal. *sencer* (= 'upright, entire') = Lat. *sincerus*. (9) It. *via* (= 'time') = Lat. *via* (= 'way'). (10) Catal. *xollar* (= 'to shave one's head') = **eix-sullar*, except that **sullar* is replaced by **fullar* (= Valen., 'to abort').

205. "Kat. *aixecar* 'heben.'" *NM* 21 (1920): 21–22.
O. J. Tallgren errs in tracing this verb (= 'to lift') to *exsiccare*. Spitzer suggests OProv. *eslaiser* (= 'to hurl oneself, to hurry').

206. "Kat. *nissaga* 'Rasse,' 'Geschlecht.'" *NM* 21 (1920): 78–79.
The noun *nissaga* (= 'race, species') derives from *nidus* with an additional *-s*, not, as Tallgren contends, from *neptiaca* and *nid-ici-aca*.

207. "Kat. *tortosa*, *bémis* m. 'imbécil, idiota.'" *NM* 21 (1920): 79–80.
Bémis relates to *Bohème* (= Languedoc, 'cajoler, flunkey'). Frédéric Mistral notes that *bòumian* or *Bohemian* originated in Rousillon and Catalonia.

208. "Katalanisch . . . *y tot*." *NM* 22 (1921): 50–53.

In defense of his treatment of Catal. *y tot* (*Revue de Dialectologie Romane* 6 [1915]: 119ff.), Spitzer focuses on the use of Sp. *y todo* (= 'also, even, even though, although') and shows semantic parallels in dialectal It. *e tot*, It. *e tutto*, and Fr. *et tout*. Also discusses *así y todo*, *así y con todo*, *con todo y con eso*, and *después y todo*.

209. "Zu Brüchs Bemerkungen *Bibl. arch. rom.* II/3, 26ff." *A Rom* 6 (1922): 494–504.

Spitzer defends his Catal. etymologies against Josef Brüch's criticisms.

210. "Cat. *anyorar* 'echar de menos, desear con viveza.'" *RFE* 10 (1923): 311–13.

Defense of the etymology *anyorar* (= 'to miss, long for') < Catal. *entranyorar* (= 'idem'), by regression < *interanea* (= 'entrails'), cf. *Lex. a. d. Kat.* 14–15.

211. "Prov. *coderc* 'pacage communal.'" *A Rom* 11 (1927): 396–97.

For mainly semantic reasons, Spitzer prefers the postverbal etymon, Lat. *condirigere* (= 'to use and enjoy [particularly of land]') > Prov. *coderc* (= 'common pasture land') to the etymon proposed by J. Jud (*Rom* 52 [1926]: 331), Cymric *cytir* (= 'communal') > Gall. **coteric*. Furthermore, a postverbal derivation with a guttural sound in final position is more plausible than the addition of the suffix *-icu*, which is attested only in country names (e.g., Armorica).

212. "Cat. ¡*ray*!" *RFE* 15 (1928): 284–89.

Spitzer defends his etymology *ray*, an affective postposed adverb < *radius* (*Lex a. d. Kat.* 110), against M. de Montolíu's suggestion that it is an interjection indicating indifference or disgust.

213. "Anc. prov. *estalbiar*, *-viar*, cat. *estalviar*, 'épargner, garder.'" *Revue Internationale des Etudes Basques* 20 (1929): 428–29.

Estalbiar is related to **es-taub-iar* (= 'to render wise or prudent'). The Ger. etymon *-taub* > *dauf* (= 'deaf') would have passed into Prov.

214. "Katal. *arna* 'Bienenstock.'" *ZRP* 49 (1929): 86–87.

Catal. *arna* (= 'beehive') < *urna* (= 'urn') phonetically influenced by *arca* (= 'box, coffin') or by the feminine definite article (*l'urna* < *l'arna*).

215. "Kat. *baluerna* 'Ungetüm.'" *NM* 32 (1931): 247–48.

Catal. *baluerna* (= 'large crowd') < Lat. *bedua* (= 'wild animal').

216. "Nprov. *gueissá* 'taller, drageonner.'" *ZFS* 56 (1932): 254.

Sp. *guájete por guájete* (= 'tit for tat') should be distinguished from Prov. *gueissá*, since Sp. ¡*guaj*! is an interjection.

217. "Kat. *malaguanyat*, *malagonyat*." *NM* 35 (1934): 41.

According to Vogel, *malaguanyat* = 'referring to the deceased'; *malagonyat* = 'cried over, blessed.' According to Spitzer, both terms mean 'to won.'

218. "Katal. *andróminas*, *endróminas* 'Habseligkeiten,' 'im Wege stehende Gegenstände,' 'lästige Bitten,' kat., sp., ptg. *andromina* 'Schwindel,' 'Lügen.'" *ZRP* 55 (1935): 171–72.

In Catal. these words derived from **endemoni(a)r*, **endomeni(a)r*. The influence of *drach* (= 'devil') explains the *-dro-* segment.

219. "Catalan *migrar-se* 'to be bored.'" *Lg* 13 (1937): 146–48.

Catal. *migrar-se* (= 'to be bored') and Prov. *migra* (= 'be nervous') are probably reductions of a **mingrar* < *minuare* (= 'to diminish') influenced phonetically by *magre* (= 'thin, weak').

220. "Aprov. *baderna* chez le moine de Montaudon." *A Rom* 22 (1938): 377–78.
Baderna in this lai is 'an old sot,' otherwise *galerna*. Modern Fr. *baderne*, a marine term, was strangely out of use for centuries.

221. "Prov., catal. *avol* 'mauvais, vil.'" *Rom* 65 (1939): 537–39.
Reversing his opinion (*ZFS* 45 [1919]: 370), Spitzer proposes Prov., Catal. *avol* (= 'bad, vile') < Gk. *aboylos* (= 'imprudent, ill-advised').

222. "Cat. *melangia*, anc. cat. *merarchia*." *A Rom* 24 (1940): 99–100.
Spitzer does not agree that *melangia* < *merarchia* < *melancolia*; it is unlikely that the medical term *merarchia* for *menorragia* (= 'woman's ailment') entered the common language. Instead, a Gk. term used by Plutarch, *maraygia* > *maralgia* > *merargia* (= 'loss of sight'), is the source.

223. "Etymologies catalanes et provençales." *Miscellania fabra: Recull de treballs de lingüística catalana i romànica, dedicats a Pompeu Fabra pels seus amics i deixebles amb motiu del 75 aniversari de la seva naixença.* Buenos Aires: Coni, 1943. 264–79.
Includes the following: (1) Catal. *quelcom*, Prov. *calacom*, *que(z)com*; (2) Un sens métaphorique du catalan *ram*; (3) OProv. *(per)digastendos* (= 'with malicious intention'); (4) Catal. *melangia*; (5) Catal. *alda*, *olda* (= 'old').

224. "Catalonian *ensenestrer, ensinistrar* 'enseñar, adestrar, preparar, ejercitar.'" *HR* 12 (1944): 177.
The title verb is added to attestations of OFr. *(a)senestrar.*

225. "Remarques additionnelles aux 'Contributions à la lexicographie provençale' de M. Kurt Lewent (*Rom* 71, 289–329)." *Rom* 72 (1951): 227–30.
Concost < *congustus*, like Catal. *congost* (= 'mountain pass'), Sp. *congosto* (= 'idem'), Port. *congosta, cangosta*; *deviza* = *a devis'a* (= 'Il a comme intention . . . ,' not 'à perfection'); *deyops* in the phrase "qu'etz plans deyops e rama" is read as *d'y(s)ops*; *encreza* in "passar al portestreig de gran encressa" = 'profound darkness,' however, Spitzer reads this metaphorically as 'harshness, stress'; *perdensa* in "amena lo joc en perdença" = '(the designated player) upsets the game.'

French

226. "Die Namengebung bei neuen Kulturpflanzen im Französischen." *WS* 4 (1912): 122–65.
This wide-ranging study of European vegetable nomenclature, including corn, buckwheat, and potatoes, traces each term to the New World and the development of food terminology there [2].

227. "Dialekt-Französisch *échaler* 'Nüsse Herunterschlagen.'" *WS* 4 (1912): 165.
Eskilot derives from *(es)cal(y)* or *(als)scal(r)*, not, as Meyer-Lübke suggests, from *eskeroun*.

228. "Zu 'carnaval' im Französischen." *WS* 3 (1912): 193–95.
Examines the relationship among *carnavas*, *carnaval*, and *carême* and the evolution from *mardi gras* and *Don Carnal* to *Donna Cuarisma*.

229. "Afrz. *haut tondu* = anmassend?" *ZFS* 40 (1912–13): 127–29.

In response to Schulz-Gora's explication (*ZRP* 36 [1912]: 84) of this OFr. locution, Spitzer clarifies two neglected points: the choice of *haut* and not *bas tondu* and the frequent placement of *si* before the expression. In the first case, the expression mocks the size of a monk's tonsure, and, in the second, it contains a conscious comic ambiguity that *si* reinforces.

230. "Die Namengebung bei neuen Kulturpflanzen im Französischen (Nachtrag)." *WS* 5 (1913): 124–28.

(1) Fr. *terrine* (= 'soup tureen' > 'potato') is an example of folk etymology at work. (2) As Spitzer explained (*WS* 4 [1912]: 122 ff.), SFr. *blé de Barbarie* (= 'corn') is a modification of *blé de Turquie*. The Pied. form *barbayá* (= 'a mixture of corn, rye, and other grains; also, chocolate, coffee, milk drink mixture') derives from the SFr.

231. "Frz. *chef d'oeuvre*." *GRM* 6 (1914): 117–19.

A discussion of the earliest attestations of this term meaning 'masterpiece,' not 'master craftsman' (Etienne Boileau, *Le Libre des mestiers*), and a look at similar constructions, for example, *prud'homme* [in 6].

232. "Frz. *payer comptant* und Verwandtes." *ZRP* 38 (1914–17): 358–65.

A review of many similar phrases and uses, referring chiefly to Littré: "Dieu a payé comptant." *Comptant* < *computante* [in 6].

233. "Frz. *couper* = **colaphare* oder **cuppare*?" *ZFS* 43 (1915): 270–79.

Although Fr. *couper* < Lat. *cuppare*, Meyer-Lübke is wrong to assert that Fr. *couper* (= 'to cut') is unrelated to OFr. *colper* (= 'to hit,' cf. Pic. *couper, colper*). Meyer-Lübke is correct to separate OFr. *coup* (= 'cuckold') from Lat. *cuculus* (= 'cuckoo'). T. Atkinson Jenkins (*MP* 10 [1913]: 3) shows that Fr. *cocu* (= 'cuckold') < Lat. *cuculus*; Spitzer lists supporting evidence: Prov. *cogul*, Catal. *cugul*, Sp. *cuclillo*. A discussion follows concerning the use of *cuckoo* to refer to the husband of an unfaithful wife.

234. "Frz. *boire d'autant*." *GRM* 7 (1915–19): 279–80.

The phrase is associated with 16th-c. *pleigier d'autant*. Examples are drawn from works by Rabelais and Voltaire.

235. "Frz. *printemps*, ital. *primavera*." *ANS* 135 (1916): 417–20.

Primum tempus > *printemps*, and *primum ver* > *primavera*.

236. "Altfranz. *daser* 'rêver, être en proie à l'illusion, au vertige,' *daserie* 'rêverie, illusion, erreur, folie, vertige,' *dasion* 'vertige.'" *ANS* 136 (1917): 165.

Fr. *daser* is the root of Ger. *doesig* and *daase* and Eng. *to daze*.

237. "Franz. *console* 'Kragstein'; franz. *ouche*." *ZFS* 44 (1917): 246–55.

(1) *Console*. Einar Löfstedt (*Philologischer Kommentar zur "Peregrinatio Aetheria,"* Uppsala: Almquist, 1911) cites Fr. *console* (= 'corbel stone') = 'architectural support' < 'support in general' < 'consolation' < Lat. *consolari* (= 'to support') as an example of the semantic development of the concrete to the abstract. But Spitzer says that there can be no direct relationship between Fr. *console* and Lat. *consolari* since Fr. *consoler*, the root of *console*, first appears in the 15th c. At most there is a parallel between the development of Lat. *consolatio* and Fr. *console*. (2) *Ouche*. Fr. *ouche* (= Prov. *olca*) bears no semantic relation to Lat. *aula* (= 'courtyard'), contrary to Adolphe L. Terracher (*Studier i modern språkvetenskåp* 4 [n.d.]: 257). Johannes Hoops (*Paul und Braune's Beiträge zur Geschichte der deutschen Sprache und*

Literatur 37 [n.d.]: 313) rightly points out that OEng. *occa* = Prov. *olca* and not Lat. *occa* (= 'harrow'); but he is wrong to relate Prov. *olca* to a Celt. root.

238. "Franz. *gravir*." *ZRP* 38 (1917): 111–15.

Fr. *gravir* (= 'climb with effort, using the hands') cannot derive from Lat. *gradus* (= 'step, stair, degree'), as suggested by Friedrich Diez (*EWRS* 603) and Meyer-Lübke (*REW* 3831), because (a) the *-d-* > *-v-* phonological development is undocumented, (b) the original meaning of *gravir* seems to have been 'creep, crawl,' and (c) the intervocalic *-p-* of the variant *graper* is unexplained. There are three more likely etyma, all of which depart from the semantic notions of 'creeping' and 'grasping,' that could have developed into 'climb.' These are (1) Ger. **grab* (= 'grasp,' cf. Eng. *grab*, Ger. *grapsen* 'snatch'), (2) Ger. *krappa* (= 'hook'), and (3) Celt. **crab*, the reconstructed etymon of Celt. words meaning 'hand,' 'grasp,' and 'scraper.'

239. "Franz. *charivari*." *ZRP* 39 (1917–19): 370–71.

The origins of this word are uncertain; it first appeared in the 14th c. Mount Calvary is the proposed root: *calvarium* > SFr. *calvari* > northern Fr. *calivari* > *chalivali* > *charivari*. All derive from Gk. *karevaria*.

240. "Zu Frz. *omelette* 'Eierkuchen.'" *ANS* 138 (1919): 110–11.

Lamella > *alumelle* > *amelette* as shown in Littré. Spitzer describes a similar transfer of several words for *mushroom*, including Port. *cagumelo*, Austr. *kuckemucke*, and Fr. *coucoumelle*.

241. "Frz. *habiller*, prov. *avol*—frz. *billet*." *ZFS* 45 (1919): 366–74.

Contrary to *REW*, Spitzer claims that Fr. *habiller* (= orig., 'to get ready to arm') does not derive from Fr. *habit*, since the apparent relationship is merely a chance convergence of phonetic development. The meaning of *habiller* was influenced by *habit*, so that it eventually developed the meaning 'to dress' and many specialized meanings in fashion and cooking.

242. "Frz. *marmouset*, *marmot*; Frz. *échelle* 'Landungsplatz.'" *ZRP* 40 (1919–20): 103–08.

(1) *Marmouset*, *marmot*. Fr. *Marmouset* (= 'grimace, insignificant youth') < OFr. *marmouset* (= 'ape, grotesque figure'). The later influence of Fr. *marmot* (= 'child'), OFr. *merme* (= *minimus*) accounts for the 'ape' > 'child' development as a term of affectionate abuse, similar to Eng. *monkey*. *Marmouset* cannot < *merme*. As pointed out by Leo Wiener (*RF* 35 [1914–16]: 954) *marmouset* < *mormos-*. (2) *Echelle*. In Mediterranean ports, Fr. *mettre l'échelle*, It. *l'escala* = 'to put your boat ashore (on the shells).' Levantine and Gk. words conformed. The term, from the word for 'ladder,' or possibly from *scaffold*, came to mean 'the platform from which justice is dispensed.'

243. "Französische Etymologien." *ZRP* 40 (1919–20): 695–706.

(1) Frz. *bernard-l'hermite*. This term for 'hermit crab' is associated with Saint Bernard and other hermits who, like the crab who hides, withdrew from the world. (2) *Brouiller* (= 'to confuse') and *grouiller* (= 'to team with'). *Brouiller* < Ger. *brodeln*, *grouiller* < Ger. *grodeln*. (3) *Cagnard*, *cagneux*. Gamillscheg is in error: *cagnard* derives not from *calina* but from *canus*. (4) *Caillebote*. This word is not composed of OFr. *caye* (= 'column') and *boter* (= 'to lay out'). It probably derives from one of two homonyms, *caillebotter* (= 'to soften') or *caillebotte* (= 'cheese curds'). (5) *Exaucer une prière* 'to hear a prayer.' The linguistic development, *exaudire* < *exaudi*, does not completely explain this expression; there is also a biblical influence, OFr. *exhalcier*. (6) *Pauvre hère* (= 'poor devil'). *Hère* has no connection with Ger. *Herr*.

244. "Nochmals frz. *bémi*." *NM* 21 (1920): 134.

Fr. *bé-a-ba* (= 'nonplussed') can be compared to Fr. "ne seit pas aré, bémi." In this expression, the terms *aré* and *bémi*, which signify the musical scale, have been abbreviated to *bémi*.

245. "Französische Etymologien, einige verblasste Tier- und Pflanzenmetaphern." *ZRP* 41 (1921–22): 161–75.

(1) *Fringuer, fringant, frinson,* and *fringuetlo* are all associated with the motions of birds. *Coquet, coqueter* and *piper* > *pimpant* are further examples. (2) *Pékin* (= 'dunderhead') derives from Prov. *pé(c)* (= 'ignorant'). (3) *Enchifrené* (= 'to have a cold') < *chifoine* < *sifoine* is related to the flower *symphonia* (= 'hellebore'). (4) Spitzer proposes derivations for three debate terms: *baffouer, courtier, trimer.*

246. "Frz. *bègue* 'stotternd.'" *ZRP* 41 (1921–22): 351–54.

Agrees with Brüch, who traces Fr. *béguine* to *bégart* and to Netherlandish tribes called *Beguinen* and *Begharden*. These terms are related to Flemish *beggen* (= 'to pray').

247. "Zur Wortgeschichte. Frz. Etymologien." *ZRP* 42 (1922): 192–207.

Etymologies for these words: *arlouys; bernique; blafard; cagibi; cent double = centuplum; daron; gamin; goujat, gouge; Gros-jean; plamus(s)e; purer, purée; purin; sémillant; sindrèse.*

248. "Französische Etymologien." *ZRP* 42 (1922): 337–43.

(1) Lazare Sainéan is mistaken in his claim that Blais. *calibourde* (= 'stilt') and *caliboudon* derive from the game *chat enfourché*. (2) Contrary to Gamillscheg, Spitzer believes Fr. *carcaise* (= 'melting oven used in glass manufacturing') < Prov. *carqueso* (= Fr. *carquois*), not from It. *calcaria*. (3) Fr. slang *faffes* (= 'papers, banknotes') as Fr. *faffiot* was a 17th-c. card game chip and stems from an onomatopoeic origin. (4) Discussion of L. Sainéan's derivations of Fr. *gosse* and *goître*. (5) Diezen misleads Romance philologists with his warning that OFr. *page* (= 'page, boy attendant') is not to be confused with *pagensis*.

249. "Afrz. dialektfrz. *corneille* (Zwerchfell)." *ZRP* 42 (1922): 606–07.

In response to Antoine Thomas (*Rom* 46 [1920]: 481ff.), who first argues that *corneille* (= 'diaphragm') comes from *cornu* (= 'horned') and then maintains that it derives from *cornillière*, Spitzer shows that it is actually related to *corneille* (= 'crow').

250. "Französische Etymologien." *ZRP* 43 (1923): 321–51.

(1) Gaston Paris is probably mistaken in deriving Fr. *antenois* from Rom. *annotinus*. (2) *REW* 8526 rightly rejects Diezen's suggestion that OFr. *antainer* derives from MHG *tagadinc* but offers no solution in its stead. (3) Gamillscheg is mistaken to say that the suffix *-able* in Fr. *cartable* derives from *-abilis*; rather it derives from *-abulum*. (4) A. Horning and Marchot agree with Spitzer in rejecting *darutt* as the source of *chasse au daru*. (5) A variety of possible etymologies for the Fr. diminutive *riquiqui* are considered.

251. "Französische Etymologien." *ZRP* 43 (1923): 587–600.

(1) OFr. *castiche* < Ger. *kasten*, not from Lat. *castellum* as Gamillscheg believes. (2) Lat. **caluginare* > OFr. *cluignier* (= 'to blink'). Spitzer explains the change from *cal-* to *cl-* with reference to *claudere* > OProv. *clause*, **clusus* > OProv. *clus*. (3) According to Gamillscheg, *despareiller* = 'to deprive of' as well as 'to make unequal'; Spitzer disagrees because of the tension between the first meaning and the mean-

ing of *pareil* (= 'equal'). (4) While Fr. *falot* < Ar. *falâti*, Austr. *falott* does not. (5) A reaffirmation that Fr. *piaffer* stems from onomatopoeic sources is found in Lazare Sainéan's recent work. (6) Contrary to *REW* 8406, Spitzer argues that Fr. *sonde* (= 'sounding lead') cannot < Lat. *subundare*. Rather, as Walter Skeat shows (*Etymological Dictionary of the English Language*, Oxford: Clarendon Press, 1882, s.v. *sound* 4), the etymon is Ger. *sund-* attested in Gael. and Ir. (7) A discussion of the exuberant semantic distribution of the Fr. *zig-zag* family of words, including *zeste de noix*, explained in terms of evocative phonetics and the charm of word repetition.

252. "Nochmals Frz. *biffe*, Schweizerfrz. *jaffer*." *NM* 25 (1924): 7–14.
Further support for the onomatopoeic derivation of OFr. *biffe*.

253. "Französische Etymologien." *ZRP* 44 (1924): 188–200.
(1) *Bigot*. A term of abuse in the 15th c. related to *bique* (= 'goat'). (2) *Crécelle* (= 'Good Friday rattle'). *Crécelle* and *crécerelle*, meaning a religious instrument and a type of bird, are one and the same word, both based onomatopoeically on *krek*. (3) *Faubert* (= 'ship's broom'). The word originally means 'slow or dull,' from OFr. *foubert* (= 'simple-minded'). (4) *Guenipe* (= 'wench'). The *gue-* in *guenipe* is probably related to *guenon*, a 16th-c. word for a long-tailed ape. *Guenon* in turn is related to a series of words derived from *guene*, *gane* (= 'wetness, swamp') from Lat. *aquana*. *Guenipe* therefore means 'dirty or immoral woman.' (5) *Pantoufle* (= 'slipper'). Probably related to Prov. *pantouqueto* (= 'woman or daughter of the country') and a host of other words beginning with *pant-*, which have to do with rustic or rural things. (6) *Regrattier*. Related to *regratter* (= 'to scrape together') means 'to peddle.' (7) Fr. *Roussin*, OFr. *roncin*, OProv. *ronci*, Sp. *rocín* (= 'packhorse, small horse, jade or used-up horse'). There are no viable hypotheses for the variety of meanings that these words, all from the same family, possess. They also seem related to colloquial Fr. *rousser* (= 'to pass wind'). (8) *Tromper* and its synonyms again. Dante's *Inferno* 21.137–39 provides more evidence that *tromper* and *trompe* signified mocking someone by farting.

254. "Altfrz. *luire* 'bespringen (von Widdern).'" *ZRP* 44 (1924): 725–27.
If OFr. *luire* (= 'to mount, of rams') comes from *luctari* it must be very old, in which case it would probably be more widespread than it is. It is more likely related to OFr. *luiser*, Prov. *lusi* (= 'to make light, to lighten'). The similarity between the movement of lightning and the rapid movements made by animals in heat is documented.

255. "Zur Wortgeschichte." *ZRP* 45 (1925): 281–89.
(1) Why Fr. *énormément* and why Romance *-mente*? The ending *-ément* for adverbs in Fr. probably stems from the creation of adverbs from participles (*aveuglé*—*aveuglément*). These participial adverbs are popular because they are considered more elegant and more active since the force of the verb lingers in the participle. Both *-ément* and *-mente* are modifications of the traditional Latin use of adjectives in the accusative as adverbs (e.g., Lat. *magnum clamare*). (2) *Serpe-Dieu*. This 16th-c. curse is derived from *sacredieu* (cf. *saperdi*, *saprebleu*), not from OFr. *par la cervelle Dieu*. (3) *Marcher*. *Marhan* (= 'to walk') is clearly the etymon. *Marcus* (= 'hammer') does not work, since it is both unsupported and illogical. More likely, a connection exists between *marcher* and Fr. *marche* (= 'border, borderland') and Ger. *marka* (= 'sign, border') [in 20].

256. "Zur Wortgeschichte: Zur französischen Wortgeschichte." *ZRP* 45 (1925): 584–92.

(1) Romance *gönnen*–German feeling? The only Romance synonyms for Ger. *gönnen* (= 'to allow, to grant, not to begrudge') occur on the periphery of the Romance world. Some linguists argue that Romance speakers, coming in contact with Ger. *gönnen*, created a semantic equivalent from Lat. *cupere*. It is much more likely that these words developed from Lat. on their own; in general, one linguistic family does not influence another. (2) Fr. *houblon* 'hops.' Ever since *houp* meaning 'beer' was documented, there has been a tendency to see Fr. *houblon* as related to Ger. *Hopfen*. The *-b-* in the Fr. words makes it much more likely that it is related to OFr. *hober* (= 'to move'), just as the Ger. word is descended from an OHG word having to do with movement. (3) Why Fr. *le quart* 'the fourth' but *le quatrième* 'the fourth item'? *Le quart* is one of the original ordinals. In current usage, they rarely appear in a series like "one third, one fourth, one fifth," so no common ending exists. *Le quatrième*, however, is one of a later group of ordinals, which often appear in a series. (4) Fr. *vétilles* 'trifles.' The word is related to *vectis* (= 'male member') and *vetiy* (= 'little brush for pastries') as well as to *veiller* (= 'to trifle, to quibble'). (5) Fr. *virer* 'to turn around.' *Virer*, like Ger. *Wirrwarr* (= 'muddle'), is onomatopoeic. Although onomatopoeia can be overused as an explanation for word origins, to deny that it ever occurs is to deny the creative, chaotic element of language.

257. "Nochmals afrz. *haut tondu*." *ZFS* 48 (1926): 379–81.

In this addition to his earlier remarks (*ZFS* 40 [1912–13]: 127ff.), Spitzer concludes that *haut tondu* means 'shorn on top' and specifies a particularly elegant type of tonsure, an ironic contradiction of the symbolic meaning of a haircutting, that is, the loss of power and the humility of worldly denial.

258. "Altfrz. *enrede* 'gewalttätig, heftig.'" *A Rom* 11 (1927): 393–94.

According to Meyer-Lübke (*REW* 4452), OFr. *enrede* < OFr. *irrepere* (= 'to sneak into') < **inrepidus* (= 'violent'). But how does 'to sneak into' derive from 'violent'? In the interest of not forcing matters, one can relate *enrede* to *raid* (= 'stiff, rigid'). *Enroider* (= 'to become rigid') > *enrede*, where *rede* = 'impetuous.'

259. "Frz. *heur*." *ZFS* 49 (1927): 319–23.

A refutation of Gilliéron's thesis concerning *heur* (*Pathologie et Thérapeutique Verbales* 3 [1921]: 12ff.), which holds that in contemporary parlance the word refers only to people. Adducing scholarly evidence and testimony from two native French speakers, Spitzer shows how this archaism functions to associate the speaker with an aristocratic milieu or to distance the speaker from a situation.

260. "Altfrz. *acesmer*, aprov. *(a)sesmar, (a)sermar* 'herrichten.'" *A Rom* 12 (1928): 322–24.

FEW is wrong in asserting that OIt. *accismare* (= 'to prepare') > *acesmer*. Since *ad-* is clear, one can see *schisma* in the term. As a possibility, *adschismare* could mean 'to prepare for battle, to make ready,' hence OFr. *acesmer* = 'to form up for battle.' The semantic transition of *acesmer* is typical of a medieval tendency to generalize, that is, 'to prepare for battle' > 'to prepare.' The construction **ad-schism-are* suggests 'church fractionalization' > 'struggle.' Since Port. *scismar* = 'to ponder' and the schismatic was seen as an abstruse dreamer, perhaps *acesmer* originally meant 'to think' > 'to prepare.'

261. "Frz. *voler* (zur Frage der Homonymenvermeidung)." *ZFS* 51 (1928): 460–69.

Beginning with an anecdote about an airplane tour of Rotterdam harbor, Spitzer examines why in Fr. the verb *voler* (= 'to fly') is restricted to the pilot, while in Ger. *fliegen* can also apply to the passengers. With respect to *voler*, the difference has to do with the "dangerous homonym" *voler* (= 'to steal') through its former reference to hunters who robbed people instead of catching birds.

262. "Zu *Zeitschrift* 51, 456." *ZFS* 52 (1929): 128.
Kalepky's explanation of "ce sont les lapins qui ont été étonnés" is essentially the same as Spitzer's in *ZRP* 36 (1912): 115, inter alia.

263. "*Aller chercher quelqu'un, prendre*, 'abholen.'" *ZFS* 52 (1929): 311–14.
Disagrees with L. Jordan (*ZFS* 51 [1928]: 469) on two points: *prendre* and *chercher* do not now have the same meaning nor do they differ only in stylistic usage; *prendre* was preferred in the previous generation since *chercher* was considered somewhat vulgar.

264. "Frz. *type*." *ZRP* 49 (1929): 709–12.
The semantic development from generic to individual in Fr. *type* 'fellow' < *type* 'type' must have originated in the practice among females of referring to a man as their 'type.' *Son type* would have gradually become synonymous with *son homme*.

265. "Frz. *donjon* 'befestiger Turm.'" *ZFS* 53 (1930): 289–90.
Defends the derivation of Fr. *donjon* from Ger. *Dung* < Prov. *domnhg* < Lat. *dominus, -io*.

266. "Frz. *piot* und *gibier*." *ZRP* 50 (1930): 736–37.
Spitzer defends his etymologies of *piot* (= 'wine') < *pie* (= 'magpie') and *gibier* (= 'wild game') < *gib-* (= 'roam').

267. "*L'avant-guerre* 'Vorkriegszeit.'" *ZFS* 54 (1931): 326–36.
This response to K. Lewent (*NS* 37 [1929]: 207) traces a development of the phrases *avant-guerre* and *après-guerre*. Before World War I the term *prewar* had an abstract sense denoting a period that preceded any war. After the war the term was established as a substantive to date events in their historical period. The formation of substantives signals a sense of history, of accomplished change.

268. "Aprov. *saludar de lonh*—altfrz. *fils de bast, bastart*." *ZRP* 51 (1931): 291–96.
(1) The phrase *saludar de lonh* refers to a courtier's act of greeting a lady according to protocol, but from such a distance or with such minimal effort that no further conversation is likely to take place. This social act of courtesy is used to keep someone at a distance. (2) OFr. *bastart* 'bastard' derives from *fils de bast* (< *bastum*) 'saddle boy.' Both the mule-saddle and the bastard son make one uncomfortable.

269. "Frz. *lapereau* 'junges Kaninchen,' ptg. *laponço, láparo*." *ZRP* 51 (1931): 705–06.
Port. *laponço, láparo* (= 'young rabbit') < *lapa* (= 'overhanging rock, burrow') < *lapp-* (= 'blow, slap'), which is possibly onomatopoeic.

270. "Altfranz. *ta char* = Neufranz. *ta viande*?" *NS* 40 (1932): 483–86.
These locutions are not related: *char* has a religious connotation, 'the body of Christ,' whereas *viande* always means 'animal flesh.'

271. "Frz. *poussif* 'herzschlächtig' (von Pferden)." *ZFS* 56 (1932): 68.
A note to Gamillscheg (*ANS* 50 [1926]: 256ff.).

272. "Notizen zu *bayadère*." *VKR* 6 (1933): 169.
Bayadère < Port. *balhadeiras* (1630) and a work by Bernardin de Saint-Pierre using *bayadères*.

273. "*Le business*." *ZFS* 57 (1933): 364.
A. Barth (*ZFS* 57 [1933]: 118) is wrong about the origin of this loan word's gender. Barth blames the English and the Americans who speak French badly and say "le business." Spitzer equates *le business* with *le travail*. The article relates the loan word to its Fr. semantic equivalent.

274. "*Autarchie*." *FM* 2 (1934): 19–32.
Fr. *autarchie* (= 'autarchy') can be pronounced [otarki] or [otarši]. The former pronunciation is original, reflecting that of the etymon, Ger. *Autarkie* (< Gk. *autarkhia*); the latter is due to analogical leveling with *monarchie*, *oligarchie*, and so on.

275. "La vie du mot *nazi* en France." *FM* 2 (1934): 263–69.
The Ger. noun *Nazi*, an abbreviation of *National-Sozialist*, was formed on the model of *Sozi* < *Sozialist*. Both retain strong ironic overtones. In Fr. the word *nazi* [nadzi] or [nazi] has lost these overtones and has become the standard technical term, used as both noun and adjective. This is due to the absence of the *sozi* model, the grammatical unacceptability of *national-socialiste*, and the fact that nationalism and socialism strike the French as an unusual ideological combination.

276. "A. fr. *en aine(s)*, *en l'ain*." *RLiR* 10 (1934): 166–67.
Ain = Ger. *eigen* (= 'the same'). The *-s* of *en aines* is the adverbial *-s* of its synonym *mesmes*. *En l'aine* = *à mesme* (= 'on the spot').

277. "Frz. *chanceler* 'schwanken.'" *ZFS* 58 (1934): 65–66.
Contrary to Meyer-Lübke (*REW* New Edition) and Brüch (*ZFS* 50 [1927]: 304; 57 [1933]: 447), Spitzer corroborates Diez's derivation of Fr. *chanceler* (= 'to stagger') from OFr. *chanceler* (= 'to screen, cross out, ramble through'), ultimately from Lat. *cancelli* (= 'railing').

278. "Frz. *vanneau* 'Kiebitz.'" *ZFS* 58 (1934): 316–17.
A discussion of the etymology of *vanneau* in relation to its homonyms.

279. "Fr. *tâter*." *A Rom* 9 (1935): 436.
REW accepts an onomatopoeic **tust* (= 'to knock, to push, to feel') for SFr. *tutejar* (= 'to feel') and rejects an onomatopoeic **tast* for Fr. *tâter*, *tastar* (= 'to feel'). This is because Meyer-Lübke adds the meaning 'to taste' to *tâter* in support of his etymology *tangere* + *gustare*. But this meaning can also be derived from 'to strike a tentative blow.' Spitzer notes the existence of OProv. *tist*, which would suggest the trio **tist*- **tast*- **tust*- (cf. Fr. *pif paf puf*, *bim bam bum*, etc.).

280. "Le *business*." *FM* 3 (1935): 53.
The masculine gender of Fr. *business* (= 'complicated affair') < Eng. *business* may be attributed to the model of *la machine* (= 'machine'), *le machin* (= 'complicated machine'), *la chose* (= 'complicated thing'). The word's status as a borrowing accounts for the nuance of complexity.

281. "*Galfâtre*." *FM* 3 (1935): 54.
Fr. *galfâtre* (= 'good-for-nothing person,' orig., 'boy who works at an inn') < *calefactor*, cf. Ger. *Kalfakter* (= 'student in charge of heating').

282. "J. Orr, '*Autre*, *outre* et *foutre*,' *Revue des Langues Romanes* 9 (1933): 59–85." *FM* 3 (1935): 180–87.
General critique with corrections.

283. *"Abasoudir, basir,* etc." *NM* 36 (1935): 289–90.
Fr. *basir* < Ger. *abasoudir* (= 'to lose composure').

284. "A. fr. *enjouter*." *Rom* 61 (1935): 481–82.
OFr. *enjouter* (= 'coax, charm, intoxicate') < OFr. *jote* (= 'beet, one of a variety of vegetables put in soup'). The latter meaning suggests 'mix up, render confused.'

285. *"Faire patelavare."* *Rom* 61 (1935): 482–83.
OFr. *faire patelavare*, which seems to mean 'care little for, turn up one's nose at,' is a Fr.-Lat. hybrid; Fr. *patte* (= vulg., 'hand') + Lat. *lavare* 'wash' < familiar expression "se laver les mains d'une chose."

286. "Frz. *révérence parler* 'mit Verlaub (zu sagen).'" *ZFS* 59 (1935): 91–93.
Spitzer questions the derivation of this locution and its use as a form of feigned respect in society. He stresses one of the main informing principles of his study of etymology: Seek out the etymology first within the language under study. Once this field has been fully explored, then it is acceptable to investigate the possibility of a foreign source.

287. "J. Orr, *'Autre, outre* et *foutre,' Revue des Langues Romanes* 9 (1933), 59–85." *FM* 4 (1936): 92–93.
Orr responded (*FM* 3 [1935]: 287) to Spitzer's original critique of his article. This is Spitzer's reply to Orr.

288. *"Frontalier."* *FM* 4 (1936): 329–32.
Fr. *frontalier* (= 'frontier regions, person living on the frontier') presents a case of suffixal dissimilation, since the more natural derivation should have been **frontièrier*, which is inadmissible for reasons of euphony. The suffix *-al* may have been chosen by analogy with *hospitalier, journalier*, and so on.

289. *"Nasi* (argot français) 'syphilis,' 'syphilitique.'" *MLN* 51 (1936): 35–36.
Fr. argot *nazi* (= 'syphilis, syphilitic') is not derived from *lazi* (= 'mal de Saint-Lazare') – Saint-Lazare being a Parisian prison for women – as Lazare Sainéan (*Le langage parisien du XIXè siècle*, Paris: Boccard, 1920, 93) and others suppose, but from Prov. *naser* (= 'to detest') < *nas* (= 'nose').

290. *"Arlouyn* bei Villon; frz. *fredaine*; frz. *pilori* 'Pranger.'" *ZRP* 56 (1936): 70–79.
(1) In *ZRP* 42 (1922): 192, Spitzer proposed that Villon's *arlouyn* (= 'pimp') was a derivative of the *arlot* (= 'rogue') family. It is instead a variant of *hardouin* (= 'matchmaker, go-between'), whose etymon is the Ger. personal name *Hardwin*. The change *d* > *l* occurred by analogy with *arlot*. (2) Fr. *fredaine* (= 'worthless thing') is probably an expressive derivative of *fredon* (= 'trill'), created when the latter was chosen as a headword of a refrain on the model of *dondon-dondaine, ribon-ribaine*, and so on, and resulting in *fredon-fredaine*. (3) Fr. *pilori* (= 'pillory, machine of punishment which turns while holding the victim's extremities immobile') is from the onomatopoeic root **pirl-*, **birl-* (= 'drag, whirl,' cf. *REW* 6522b).

291. "Frz. *danse, danser*." *ZRP* 56 (1936): 643–44.
Fr. *danse* < Lat. **dantia* < *dare* (= 'hit, make a movement'), cf. Sp. *dar una vuelta* (= 'take a walk'), Bigorre *non saber oun da* (= 'not know where to go').

292. "O. Bloch, 'Notes étymologiques et lexicales,' *RLiR* 11 (1935), 313–42." *FM* 5 (1937): 188–90.
Comments on individual etymologies.

293. "Afrz. *chief* 'Hauptstadt, Vorort.'" *ZRP* 57 (1937): 564–77.

Brüch (*ZRP* 55 [1935]: 452) is mistaken to claim that OFr. *chief* meant 'capital city' only in Picardy, where Germanic influence was strongest (cf. *Haupstadt*). The evidence seems to indicate that this was the case because such a great percentage of 13th-c. French literature is written in Pic. In fact, the use of 'head' for 'capital city' is a biblical-literary commonplace: examples abound in Lat. and medieval It., Prov., and Sp.

294. "*Tēmoin.*" *A Rom* 22 (1938): 372–75.

Tēmoin is traced from Lat. *testimonium* and the use of the verb *testis* through the 10th-c. *Glosas Emilianensis* to modern Fr. and Sp. The same word can signify either the actor or the action.

295. "Afrz. *luire* 'das weibliche Schaf bespringen,' 'brebis luisoire (en chaleur).'" *A Rom* 22 (1938): 379–80.

Several examples of current usage for this term meaning 'sexual pleasure' are related to OFr. *luire* in its meaning 'an animal in heat.'

296. "Un Français 'cent pour cent.'" *FM* 6 (1938): 49–51.

The phrase "100 percent American," originally used to differentiate "real" Americans from "hyphenated" Americans (e.g., "Italo-Americans"), was born in reactionary commercial contexts and eventually acquired pejorative nuances. The equivalent French borrowing, however, "un Français cent pour cent," continues to be used among true patriots.

297. "A. Kuhn, 'Das französische Neuwort,' *GRM* 25 (1937), 296–313." *FM* 6 (1938): 91–92.

Kuhn's study of Nazi terminology in France is incomplete.

298. "*Sacral.*" *FM* 6 (1938): 127–30.

The word *sacrale* (= 'affirming the sacred') is an apparent French theological neologism. Although it could easily have been formed directly from Lat., it was actually first used in Eng. and Ger. as an anthropological term referring to sacred rites and as a medical term referring to the bones of the lower part of the body. The theological meaning is only apparently original.

299. "Fr. *chef-d'oeuvre.*" *Lg* 14 (1938): 287–88.

Fr. *chef-d'oeuvre* (= 'masterpiece') originally meant 'piece of work,' not 'leader of work' as *FEW* (s.v. *caput*) claims.

300. "*Davi(d) fausse-clê.*" *Rom* 64 (1938): 101–02.

Fr. criminal argot *David fausse-clê* (= 'skeleton key') is a sacrilegious reference to Isaiah 22:22 in which the house of David is referred to as the key to heaven.

301. "*Gâteau.*" *Rom* 64 (1938): 395–98.

Fr. *gâteau* (= 'cake') is a derivative of *gâter* (= 'to spoil'), having originally denoted a certain type of pastry made with dry crumbs (cf. *gratin*) remaining from the preparation of other breads.

302. "Old French *esterminals.*" *Speculum* 13 (1938): 461–62.

OFr. *esterminals* (*Roland* v. 1662) is a gross Latinism (< **exterminalis* < *exterminus* [= 'beyond a boundary']) used as an adjective meaning 'exotic, outlandish,' modifying the noun *topazes* (= 'topazes') in the previous verse.

303. "Fr. *console* = ital. **consola?*" *A Rom* 23 (1939): 92–93.

Fr. *consoler* derives from *soulas* = *solacium* (= 'to help'), not from It. *consola*, which comes from *solum* > *suola* (= 'to establish').

304. "Néologismes, *aérodynamique*." *FM* 7 (1939): 15–19.

Concerning words that do not evolve: Amer. *streamline* was immediately adapted to other contexts besides the automotive industry; Fr. *aérodynamique* was restricted to aviation.

305. "*Total*." *FM* 7 (1939): 20–25.

In Fr., Sp., and Catal. the word *total* followed by a colon is often used in the quasi-mathematical sense of 'in summary' or 'in consequence,' the colon acting as the equivalent of the equal sign (=). This usage is considered vulgar in France but not on the Iberian peninsula.

306. "*Photogénique*." *FM* 7 (1939): 125–32.

In 1829 the Englishman W. H. Fox Talbot coined the term *photogenic* (= 'photographic, produced by light'). Ten days later the word *photography*, a blend of *photogenic* and Fr. *héliographie*, was proposed and immediately won wide acceptance. By the early 1900s the term *photogenic* (Fr. *photogénique*) had made a comeback—this time, however, with the meanings 'capable of producing certain chemical effects through light,' 'having physical characteristics that are well captured by photography.' The new meaning is etymologically incorrect ('producer of' is rendered by *-genetic*, Fr. *-genêtique*).

307. "Eugen Lerch, '*Quitter*,' *ZRP* 58 (1938)." *FM* 7 (1939): 187–88.

The semantic development of Fr. *quitter* is not yet fully understood.

308. "*Dénudément*." *FM* 7 (1939): 225–28.

For stylistic reasons the neologism *dénudément* (= 'nakedly') is today preferred to *nu(e)ment* 'idem' in literary contexts. The former, owing to its resemblance to a present participle, suggests activity and will, thus satisfying the author's need for emphasis.

309. "*Zèbre*." *MLN* 54 (1939): 78.

Addition to a previous article on *zèbre* and cognates (*RFE* 15 [1928]: 375–76).

310. "Additions à l'article de M. Tilander sur le fr. *mot* (*Rom* 64, 347ff.)." *Rom* 65 (1939): 223–25.

(1) Lat. *muttus*, etymon of *mot*, was created out of the sound and movement of the syllable *mu-*. (2) The phrase *ne sonner mot* 'ne dire mot' emphasizes affectively the passivity of someone. (3) *Ne tinter mot* is a reinforcement of *ne sonner mot*. (4) *Mot* 'word' is an ulterior semantic development; the original meaning was 'gestural manifestation.' (5) *Mot* denotes a minimal sound vis-à-vis *parole* and an independence of thought vis-à-vis *terme*. (6) *Mot*! 'silence!' represents a reversion to the original meaning.

311. "Encore une fois *gâteau*." *Rom* 65 (1939): 374–75.

Lines 304–05 from Chrétien's *Perceval* support the theory that *gâteau* < *gâter*, as proposed in *Rom* 64 (1938): 395–98.

312. "*Tantaliser*." *FM* 8 (1940): 115–17.

Fr. *tantaliser* (= 'tantalize') was introduced into Fr. in the 18th c. by Mirabeau, who borrowed it from Eng. (first attestation, 1597).

313. "*Beffroi*." *FM* 8 (1940): 320–22.

Fr. *beffroi* (= 'belfry, alarm bell, movable tower') < **bis-fridare*.

314. "A. fr. *eschar(e)votee* 'écorchée.'" *MLN* 55 (1940): 447–49.

OFr. *escharevotee* (= 'skinned') and the related words *charevoste* (= 'cadaver') and *charevate* (= 'piece of flesh') are attributed by Jud (*Studies in French Language and Medieval Literature Presented to Professor Mildred Katherine Pope*, Manchester: Manchester UP, 1939, 225–41) to *carne reposita* (= 'buried flesh'). This etymology is doubtful because the phrase was not current in Lat. and thus could not have crystallized into the single Romance word. Moreover, it fails to explain *charevate*. The etymon *scarabaeus* (= 'scarab') > OFr. *esc(h)arbote* 'idem' is preferable because the tracks of this insect could have suggested 'scrawling,' whence the notions 'scratch,' 'flail,' and 'skin' could have been derived.

315. "*Trouver*." *Rom* 66 (1940–41): 1–11.

The history of Fr. *trouver* (= 'find') is as follows: Gk. *tropos* (= 'musical mode, style') > Lat. *tropus* (= 'musical harmony') > *contropare* (= 'harmonize,' later 'agree, compare') > Fr. *controuver* (= 'find a solution [accord] together') > Fr. *trouver* (= 'find [alone],' later 'compose a song').

316. "Zwei französische Neologismen." *Corona: Studies in Celebration of the Eightieth Birthday of Samuel Singer*. Ed. A. Schirokauer and W. Paulsen. Chapel Hill: Duke UP, 1941. 100–16.

Fr. *paramilitaire* (= 'a German organization which, without being military, gives its members military training') appeared during the drafting of the Treaty of Versailles. Later it was adopted by left-wing French groups that used similar tactics. The prefix *para-* to express a camouflage (civilians as members of the military) refers also to something considered pathologically unhealthy by the French (cf. Fr. *paraptyphoïde*). The neologism contains a critical judgment. Similarly *mouscoutaire* (= 'spiritual disciple of Moscow teaching') expresses a French view, judgment, and criticism of a Russian entity.

317. "Anc. fr. *Açopart* 'Ethiopien.'" *MLN* 57 (1942): 252–59, 486.

A response to E. C. Armstrong's summary of the present state of knowledge of this name (*MP* 38 [1940–41]: 243ff.). *Açopart* is a Fr. word: *Açopart* (*achopart*) = *acoper* + *-ard* < *achopper* (= 'stumble, knock against, bump'). That Crusaders associated this term with Ethiopians has perhaps to do with the Ethiopian custom of beginning battle in a flexed knee position.

318. "Fr. *mitant* 'the middle,' 'the half.'" *MLN* 57 (1942): 356–58.

Criticizing former attitudes in Romance etymology that favored phonetics and construction over morphology and semantics, Spitzer rejects the bold construction **medietante* for the simple *medium tantum* as the root of *mitant*.

319. "Three French Etymologies." *Lg* 19 (1943): 156–61.

(1) OFr. *mais* (= 'mauvais') is not a doublet of *mauvais* (< *malifatius*) via a bilabial *w*. It has a Frank. or Saxon etymon from the word family represented by Swed. *mas* (= 'slow, lazy') > **mazi* (= 'putrefaction') > OFr. *mais* (= 'wicked'). (2) Fr. *ribon-ribaine* 'coûte que coûte, bon gré mal gré.' The French phrase is not a modification of Prov. *arribe sou qu'arribe* (= 'come what may, willy-nilly'). *Ribon-ribaine* and its variants from OFr. *riber* < OHG *hrîba* (= 'whore'), signifying originally 'to give oneself up to pleasure,' must have followed the verb's development of a more general meaning and established the suggestion of two types of blows given as part of a series, cf. *de coutin, de coutan*. (3) Fr. *semelle* 'sole.' **Sem-* < Lat. *semis* (= 'half'). In view of *semiplotia* = *dimidiatae soleae*, Spitzer admits a **sem-ella* in proto-Fr. meaning 'half-shoes' or 'reinforcement of a sole by a half-sole.'

320. "A. fr. *esmarve*." *MLN* 58 (1943): 519–21.

Esmarve meaning 'dead, frozen' > 'terrified, surprised' is a postverbal adjective from OFr. **esmarver* or **esmarvir*.

321. "Comment." *MLQ* 4 (1943): 389.

Spitzer challenges Y. Malkiel's explanation of *subtilis* > OFr. *soutif*. Proposes *subtilis* > *soutieus* (cf. *vilis* > *vieus*), fem. (analogical) *soutive*, masc. *soutif* (a regressive form, cf. *Judaeus*, *juieus*, fem. *juive* on whose basis *juif* was formed). Sp. *solitariu* 'bachelor' and Port. **solitosu* are derivations of **solvitus*.

322. "Français populaire *moche*." *RR* 34 (1943): 150–53.

Mouche (= 'ugly, vile') is coupled with *toc* (= 'poor imitation') in the ironic sense of 'très, beaucoup, grandement.' *Mouche* 'vile,' originally used by gangsters and attested as a common slang term in 1849 along with *toc*, passed into theater slang (*mouche* [= 'mauvais']). The form *moche*, attested in 1900, may be a dialectal variant.

323. "Fr. *travail*." *RR* 34 (1943): 374–79.

Travailler is derived from MLat. *tripalium* (= 'instrument of torture') as proposed by P. Meyer (*Rom* 17 [1888]: 421), not from **trapaliare* < **trapalium* < **trapu* < IE **tere-pe* as proposed by L. Gray (*RR* 33 [1942]: 163). Examples of the most ancient meaning of Fr. *torture*, *tourment* are given to support the argument against recourse to nonexistent words when precise textual evidence is available.

324. "The Name of the Holy Grail." *AJP* 65 (1944): 354–63.

OFr. *graäl* originates in **cratalis*, *-e* < Lat. *cratis*, *-es* (= 'something woven, plaited, interlaced'). Eventually this word signified bowls of wood and of tin and, later, bowls of silver and other precious metals. It is in the latter sense that it appears in Chrétien and Helimandus.

325. "Deux notes argotiques." *FR* 18 (1944): 17–23.

(1) *Larbin* (= 'laquais, valet de grande maison'), meaning 'executioner' and developing into either 'rapacious, gluttonous, ravenous (> beggar)' or 'hard,' is traced to a deformation of the adjective *arbi* (= 'Arab') caused by a popular tendency to exploit the ethnic term as a pejorative means of qualifying the disdainful valets of aristocratic houses. (2) *Vingt-deux*. Examples of slang vocabulary from other nations are cited to show the visual significance of the ciphers used in expressions meaning, like this one, 'Watch out!' *Vingt-deux* is probably a doubling of *onze* (= 'prenez vos jambes au cou, détalez'), in which the ciphers in *11* stand as a metaphor for the human legs. A German parallel for this metaphor is "seine langen Elfer."

326. "French *veule* 'weak, effete.'" *Lg* 20 (1944): 242–45.

Veule is a Pic. variant of *aveugle*.

327. "*Charade*." *PQ* 23 (1944): 77–83.

OFr. *charai(t)*, *charaie*, *charaut*, *charaude*, *charact(e)*, and *charat* > modern Fr. *charade* are all more or less popular modifications of *charácter*.

328. "Fr. *mièvre*." *MLN* 60 (1945): 52–54.

Derives from MHG *mürwe* (OHG *mur(u)wi*, NHG *mürbe*) (= 'tender, soft, weak, brittle'); *murwi* > **muirve* > *mivre* > *mièvre*.

329. "*Turlupin*." *MLN* 61 (1946): 104–08.

Affirming L. Sainéan's hypothesis of a root **turelup-*, Spitzer notes that it was originally a popular euphemism designating the sexual practices of the 14th-c. heretical sect it identifies.

330. *"Faire la combrecelle."* *RR* 37 (1946): 360–61.

Attested in Rabelais (*Pantagruel*, ch. 22), this expression is a representative of a word family for which Thomas (*Rom* 41 [1912]: 452) rightly postulates the etymon **coopercellum* (< *cooperculum*).

331. "Un apax anc. fr. expliqué par l'anglais?" *Rom* 69 (1946–47): 388–89.

OFr. *costis* < **costif* < *costive* < Lat. *constipare* (= 'constipated'). In view of the development of Eng. *costive*, adj., originally 'constipated,' then 'reticent, reserved, niggardly, hard and impervious, stiff,' OFr. *l'orage costis* = 'a stiff wind.'

332. *"Courir la calabre."* *FM* 16 (1948): 165–66.

Attested in 1698, this expression has the sense of 'to live a life of debauchery' and derives from a euphemistic use of archaic *calabre* (= 'catapult').

333. "Anc. fr. *cha(i)ele(s)*, *cheles*, *chieles*, *qu(i)eles*, 'S'il vous plaît.'" *MLN* 63 (1948): 240–44.

These terms may represent the petrified imperfect indicative voice of OFr. *cha(d)ler* (= 'command, govern, lead') < *cha(d)el* < *capitellum* (= 'head').

334. *"Triolet."* *RR* 39 (1948): 146–55.

Triolet was originally **criolet* (< Gk. *kyrie eleison*), a particular metrical form of the rondeau containing *kyrielles*. Parallel deformations of *kyrie eleison* are noted.

335. *"Réveillon."* *FM* 17 (1949): 84.

Rebellio (< Lat. *rebellare*) (= 'rebellion') > 'joyful noise' > 'joyful meal' survives in *réveillon*, originally in the feminine gender as attested in 14th-c. examples (Godefroy, s.v. *reveilloner*).

336. "Français *s'emberlucoquer*, *s'emberlificoter* 'entangle oneself, tangled up.'" *Rom* 70 (1948–49): 523–56.

OFr. *embireliquoquier* (= 'séduire, tromper,' *Roman de Fauvel*, 1314, v. 21114) is the earliest representative of this series and is related to It. *biriccocola*, *bericocola* (= 'apricot').

337. *"Semelle."* *FM* 18 (1950): 241–43.

Rebuts Wartburg's explanation (s.v. *lamella*: *semelle* is a Picard reflection of OFr. *lamelle*) and reinforces earlier findings with reference to non-Picard evidence.

338. "*Vanter* 'citer.'" *FM* 22 (1954): 36.

Vanter in this sense must be a calque in juridical language of a similar use of Lat. *laudare* (= 'to cite, to name [as witness]').

339. *"Interlocuteur."* *FM* 22 (1954): 89–95.

First found in Clément Marot's French translation of Erasmus's *Colloques* (1526), *interlocuteur* appears to be based on a Latin model. Analogues are cited. Chalcidius's translation of Plato's *Timaeus*, reedited in Paris in 1520, is a possible source. It begins: "Interloquuntur Socrates, Timaeus, Hermocrates Critias."

340. "A propos d'*interlocuteur*." *FM* 22 (1954): 267.

Spitzer's hypothesis is confirmed by P. Kristeller in examples from early 15th-c. translations of Lucan. Also, the existence of *collocutores* in the sense of 'partners in a dialogue' is attested in patristic texts (Tertullian, Augustine) and in humanist Lat.

341. "Ancien français *dalier*." *Rom* 75 (1954): 390–95.

AS *dal* (< proto-Germanic **dailo*) (= 'part, division, portion') would have been borrowed by AN and given a Romance suffix (*-ier*, *-oyer*, cf. *charrier*, *charroyer* <

char), and the semantic development would be as follows: (1) 'partager, faire partie'; (2) 'être en rapport avec quelqu'un, le traiter d'une certaine façon'; (3) 'converser, jaser, s'amuser avec quelqu'un'; (4) 's'engager dans une querelle'; (5) 'muser, tarder,' a development from 's'amuser,' the former being the usual meaning of modern Eng. *to dally*. According to Spitzer, the latter meaning appears for the first time in *La vie de Ste. Marie l'Egyptienne*, "Ore n'ad talent de dalier / Ne ele ne set en ki afier."

342. "Latin médiéval *brocard(ic)a* > français *brocard*." *MLN* 70 (1955): 501–06.
The proposed legal etymon **pro-contra* presents too many difficulties (*p* > *b*; *contra* > *c*-; -*ard*). Lat. vulgarization *brocarda*, attested in Pillius's *Liber disputatorius* (1182), is more likely the root.

343. "*Etendard*." *Rom* 76 (1955): 84–89.
The form *standale* (< VLat. **standa-lis*) is proposed, a derivation from Ger. *Stand* with the addition of the Lat. suffix *-alis*. The Fr. form ending in *-ard* is a backformation, a variant which stresses the 'straight' or 'upright' position of the *étendard*.

344. "*Roörs* (*Saint Léger*, v. 203)." *Rom* 76 (1955): 103–08.
OFr. *roörs* cannot be VLat. *rotor* because intervocalic -*v*- in OFr. often disappears before -*o*-, -*u*-. *Roörs* is a hapax, probably from *rubore*.

German

345. "Nochmals mundartl. dtsch. *schlamassel*, *schlamast(ik)* 'Verlegenheit, Unannehmlichkeit.'" *ANS* 138 (1919): 234–36.
Colloquial Ger. *schlamassel* and *schlamastik* (= 'embarrassment, unpleasantness') are not from *Schlamm* (= 'mud, slime') + *Grammatik* (= 'grammar') but from *schlimasel* < Yid. *schlimm-masel* (= 'bad star, fate').

346. "Volkstümlich-dtsch. *mackes* 'beating.'" *ZRP* 40 (1919–20): 703–04.
< Heb. *makkâh*.

347. "Österr.-deutsch *assentieren*." *GRM* 10 (1922): 180–83.
19th-c. Austrian *assentieren* (= 'to enlist, draft') was replaced by *mustern* (= 'to muster') during World War I. However, Austrian usage, reflecting an erroneous etymology, associated the term with the enlistee's medical examination. In fact, *assentieren* < It. *assentarsi* (= 'to enlist'), not from Lat. *assentiri* (= 'to approve').

348. "*Tachinieren*." *GRM* 11 (1923): 373–77.
This Austrian term was in common use among Hungarian and Austrian soldiers, though its origin is unknown. *Markieren* (= 'to feign sickness so as to avoid work') < *tachinieren*. Although these two terms were interchangeable in Austro-Hungarian army parlance, *markieren* replaced *tachinieren* in Ger.

349. "Rebuttal to L. Jordan's 'Von der Fassung des Problems, dem Beweisgang, *Wirklichkeit*, *Möglichkeit* und *Irrtum* in der Sprachwissenschaft.'" *A Rom* 9 (1925): 298–99.
Jordan's article appears in *A Rom* 9 (1925): 292–98.

350. "*Puxi*: Eine kleine Studie zur Sprache einer Mutter." *JbP* 3 (1927): 35–54, 101–15, 170–83.
In this study of his wife's language with their son during his first four years, Spitzer shows how the boy's assimilation of his own name depicts the essence of

a child's acquisition of the mother tongue. His wife's inventiveness with pet names is not an example of actual word genesis. It shows instead a unique and intense drive to regenerate language. The birth of a healthy, much loved child engenders a burst of optimism that emerges linguistically as an impulse toward language-play. A central thesis here is that language also is the creation of a person's "attentive fantasy" [19].

351. *"Bersilieren."* *NM* 34 (1933): 41.
The verb *bersilieren* (14th-c. Ger.) < Fr. *brésillier.*

352. *"Tipse."* *NM* 36 (1935): 48–52.
Tipse originated in the 1920s in banking and student circles in Berlin. It replaced *Steno-Typistin* (= 'female typist'). The word derives from the verb *tippen* (= 'slight touching of keys') and was probably modelled on the Yid. word *Schickse* (= orig., 'Christian girl'), later used by Christians to mean 'Jewish girl.'

353. "Nochmals *Tipse.*" *NM* 37 (1936): 301–03.
A letter to Spitzer from a Viennese friend explains the disappearance of the term *Tipse* from Viennese usage: words with *-epp-*, *-ipp-* sound Prussian to the Viennese ear; the *-se* ending calls to mind words like *Hexe* and *Nixe.* Both circumstances create unfavorable associations.

354. *"Kathole."* *MLN* 53 (1938): 433–39.
Kathole, the pejorative form of *Katholik,* is comparable to *Jude* (< *Juden*) in that its negative connotations derive from phonetic distortion. It seems likely, however, that the two developed independently, since their precise connotations are so different (*Jude* suggests 'greed' and 'shrewdness,' while *Kathole* connotes 'disloyalty' and 'stupidity'). *Kathole* was probably created by analogy with names of other national groups considered stupid yet sinister, for example, *Pole, Russe, Grieche.*

355. *"Schadenfreude."* *MDU* 34 (1942): 357–61.
It is incorrect to assume that *Schadenfreude* describes a typically German characteristic simply because the word is taken as is from Ger. Expressions having the same meaning in Gk., Lat., and Fr. are cited in support of this argument [in 28].

356. *"Muttersprache."* *MDU* 36 (1944): 113–30.
A discussion of L. Weisgeiber's view that *Muttersprache* derives from a Ger., not a Lat., root [in 28].

357. "Wienerisch *Remassuri.*" *MLN* 59 (1944): 100–04.
Several definitions of *Remassuri, Remassori* (= 'noise, fuss') are given. The *-u-* form is more current. The term derives from MLat. *litterae remissoriales.* In Viennese dialect, the expression originally signified the transfer of a dispute to another court, which was considered to be an annoyance. It thus came to mean 'uproar, unruliness.'

358. *"Nazi-spezi."* *GR* 21 (1946): 114–17.
Spitzer refers to his articles with F. Mauthner (*MLN* 59 [1944]: 93; *FM* 2 [1934]: 263–69) in which the source of the word *Nazi* is discussed not only as an abbreviation of *National-Sozialist* but also as a SGer. pet name for *Inatz* (= 'buffoon, dunce'), just as *Sozi* is not only an abbreviation of *Sozialdemokrat* but also a SGer. diminutive of *Socius* (= 'brute, boor'). *Spezi* is considered here to be analogous to *Sozi* as an abbreviation of *Spezialfreund.*

359. "Deutsch *marode*." *RF* 62 (1950): 417–23.
A discussion of the advantages of looking first within the language for a word's etymon, rather than seeking foreign sources.

Italian and Latin

360. "Zur Bildung romanischer Kindernamen." *ZRP* 36 (1912): 233–36.
SIt. *pichoun* derives not from *pipio* but from *petiot*, contrary to evidence adduced by Alice Sperber. An analysis of certain forms of *petit* shows that intervocalic *-t-* can develop into *-ch-* as in *pichot*, the original form of this nickname.

361. "Über italienisch *così*." *ANS* 130 (1913): 335–55.
Spitzer summarizes the uses of Ger. *so* as follows: (1) *so?* questioning the correctness of a previous utterance; (2) *so* as an acknowledgment of receipt of an announcement or a report; (3) *so!* in response to a question one doesn't wish to answer (cf. Fr. *parce que*); (4) *so so* in response to a question about one's health. This discussion is the basis for an explanation of It. *così*, which can be used in all four situations. Other nuances are described with reference to examples from literary texts [in 6].

362. "Aretin. *baruccabá* 'Verwirrung' = hebr. *baruch habbah* 'gesegnet sei, wer kommt im Namen des Herrn.'" *WS* 5 (1913): 124–28.
Heb. *baruch habbah* (= 'blessed be he'), the opening words of the Judaic liturgy, > It. *baruccabá* (= 'confusion, noise') because of the noise made by Jews praying in the synagogue. The latter term is closely related to It. *badananai* (= 'confused noise') and Port. *badaual* (= 'disorder'). All contain Heb. *adanaj* (= 'eternal one'), a word repeated in Psalms and by people praying aloud together.

363. "Ital. *lazaretto*–ital. *ghetto*." *WS* 6 (1914–15): 201–05.
Santa Maria di Nazaret, a hospital outside Venice's city wall, was the location of a leper colony, the first ghetto. Spitzer proposes that *ghetto* comes from Egypt. *ghezzo* (= 'Moor') through assimilation with Venet. *giudecca* (= 'Jew').

364. "*Escole* 'Schar.'" *ZFS* 41 (1915): 199.
As evidence adduced from OFr. *Meraugis* shows, this term means 'company,' not 'battle ranks.'

365. "Ital. *taranai, tananai* 'Wirrwarr, Lärm.'" *ANS* 136 (1917): 164–65.
The It. form is related to Rom. *dăndănăe* and Turk. *tantana* (= 'loud celebration, noise, fracas').

366. "Umbr. *nuo matre*–Deutsch *mutter(seelen)allein*–Franz. *Dieu possible*." *ZRP* 39 (1917–19): 630–35.
This bold construction cannot be analyzed syntactically.

367. "Zum REW Nr. 1117: *birrus* 'rot.'" *ANS* 137 (1918): 74–75.
Birrus (= 'red') is related to It. *birro* (= 'sheriff's officer'), OVenet. *beretin* (= 'gray'), and Gk. *byrrus*. There is another word family meaning 'cap': It. *berretta*, Fr. *béret*, Port. *birreto*. These are related to another *birrus* (= orig., 'a silk or wool coat collar or coat with cap'). The fact that these words never mean 'a red cap' indicates that there are two etyma at work here. The origin of the second is perhaps the Celt. word **birsos*, showing up in OIr. and Bret. as *berr* (= 'short').

368. "Kors. *ghjamberluccu, jam-* 'tonto, dappoco.'" *ANS* 138 (1919): 109–10.
This word is linked with Alb. *jamuti* (= 'saddlecloth, carpet material'), which derives from Turk. *jemenli.*

369. "Berichtigung." *ANS* 139 (1919–20): 97.
Spelling corrections for *ANS* 138 (1919): 109–10.

370. "Ital. *-ette.*" *ZRP* 40 (1919–20): 704–05.
The suffix *-ette* derives from Lat. *et.*

371. "Tessin. *papadú* 'Kesselhaken.'" *ZRP* 40 (1919–20): 706.
Meyer-Lübke (*REW* 6214) shares Schuchardt's doubts about the derivation of Tessin. *papadú*, Trevig. *papador*, Venet. *papaor* (= 'pot hook') from *pappare* (= 'to eat'). Schuchardt proposes instead Istr. *papo, pampo* = *pampano* (= 'shoot, tendril'). Spitzer cites It. *pappo* (= 'thick bristly appendage of certain plants') and follows Schuchardt's method of returning to an object's description to find the derivation of its name. That the flat hook was spoon-shaped (cf. It. *pappatoio*) supports a derivation from *pappare.*

372. "Ital. *indarno* 'umsonst.'" *ANS* 141 (1921): 135.
Meyer-Lübke handles the literature on *indarno* (*REW* 9145) critically. It is perhaps linked with *adarnir* (= 'to stun') and *dardeyé* (= 'to stumble like a drunkard'), both from **darnos* (= 'confused'). There are also possible connections with Ger. *Tarnkappe* (= 'cloak of invisibility') and its family. Lat. *dardanarius* (= 'grain speculator') is probably unrelated.

373. "Ital. *farfalla* 'Schmetterling.'" *ANS* 141 (1921): 146–49.
It. *farfalla* and *papilio* (= 'butterfly') are related. In other Romance languages there are intermediary forms like Fr. *parpaillot* and Franche-Comté *pafiro*. Ar. *farfar* (= 'foolish, gossipy') probably exerted an influence through words like Neap. *farfariello* (= 'devil') and Fr. *farfadet* (= 'goblin'). It is not surprising that a word meaning 'butterfly' should have connections with words meaning 'devil' and 'goblin,' because the butterfly is associated with the supernatural in popular mythology.

374. "Spätlat. *iotticus.*" *GRM* 9 (1921): 60–61.
Ludwig Radermacher (*Wiener Sitzber* no vol. [1918]: 97) assumes that this term refers to a kind of character mask having a local or regional meaning. Spitzer connects it with Lat. *idioticus* (= 'uncultured, uneducated').

375. "Varietà e aneddoti." *A Rom* 7 (1923): 386–96.
(1) It. *asolare* 'frische Luft schöpfen,' Neap. *ansoliare* 'horchen.' Contrary to *REW* 3011, Spitzer shows that **usolare* (= 'to peek or overhear through a crack') + *ansula* (= 'crack, opening') > *asolare* (= 'to get fresh air'). (2) Fr. *frôler* (= 'to graze') and It. *folata* (= 'gust of wind') < It. *folla* and not from the unattested **flabulare.* Includes a discussion of the onomatopoeic effect of *fr-, br-, pr-.* (3) It. *scaltrire* < Lat. *cauterire.* (4) *REW* 3075 errs in claiming that It. *sciocco* (= 'stupid, tasteless') < *exsucus.* Rather *sciocco* < *sciò* (= 'a comical term to scare away hens'). (5) The suffix in It. *sentinella* (= 'sentry') is explained by the soldier's effort to make light of his unpleasant situation through the playful use of the diminutive. (6) Venet. *úguolo* (= 'simple') = *uno* + *mígnolo* (= 'little').

376. "Italienische Etymologien." *ZRP* 43 (1923): 691–700.
It. *scilecca, cilecca* < Ger. *schleck*, not from OGer. *scileh*. Spitzer considers a variety of etymologies for *pitocca* and the word family It. *truffare*, Sp. *trufar*, and Fr. *tromper* to support his thesis: It is not always necessary to seek out the oldest etymon.

377. "Ital. *falbalà*, frz. *falbala*; tosk. *tarpano, tarpagnuolo* 'Bauer, Grovian,' *tarpare* 'beschneiden.'" *A Rom* 8 (1924): 144–46.

(1) Contrary to *REW* 3162, Spitzer shows that It. *faldo* < Fr. *falbala*. The Fr. term originated in courtly circles and belongs to the SFr. word family *farbello, ferbelho* (= 'fringe, tatters'), *se farboulha* (= 'dress oneself ridiculously'), *farbustel* (= 'badly dressed person'). (2) Tusc. *tarpano* (= 'peasant, yokel') < *tarpare* (= 'to weaken, to clip the wings of'), not from ONorse *thorpari* (= 'village dweller'). Spitzer cites (a) the back-formation It. *sterpare* (= 'to eradicate, destroy') < Lat. *extirpare* (*REW*), (b) formal parallels, such as *sterpagnuola/tarpagnuolo*, and (c) semantic parallels, such as *sterpone*(= 'bastard')/*tarpano*. This leads to a discussion of back-formations suggested for It. *strappare*, which has been linked to Ger. *streifen* (**streipjan*) (*REW* 8295). Spitzer's conclusion is that the entries for *thorpari, streipjan*, and *extirpare* in *REW* should be combined under the latter entry.

378. "Kalabr. *skantare* 'sich bräunen: Brot beim Backen, Fische beim Braten und Rösten.'" *A Rom* 9 (1925): 207–08.

Meyer-Lübke's etymology deriving Calabr. *skantare* (= 'to brown') from *candidus* (= 'soft') is problematic: it isolates the word and does not explain its original meaning, which was probably 'to blanch.' The word more likely is related to It. dialect verbs corresponding to It. *schiantare* (= 'to burst, to jump' or, secondarily, 'to have a sudden fear'). The shift from *schi-* to *sc-* is documented in Cors.

379. "Zu *Zeitschrift* 46, p. 74, Abruzz. *skupina* 'Dudelsack, urspr. *schlauch*.'" *ZRP* 46 (1926): 764–65.

Spitzer disagrees with Rohlfs on the root of this word meaning 'bagpipe.'

380. "Zu Sizil. *vasu* 'Kuss.'" *ZFS* 49 (1927): 199.

A note on an earlier article (*ZFS* 48 [1926]: 378) that corrects a misunderstanding of *vasu*, confusing its real meaning, 'kiss,' with a word meaning 'chamber pot.'

381. "Abermals 'Kuss' im Sizilianischen." *ZFS* 50 (1927): 154–55.

A rebuttal of Rohlfs's response (*ZFS* 49 [1926]: 346ff.) to Spitzer's comments. The issue is whether the Sicil. word *vasu* (= 'kiss') has been displaced by *vasu* (= 'chamber pot'). Spitzer upholds his interpretation (*vasu* = 'kiss') and maintains that linguists should avoid sparring fruitlessly.

382. "Ital. *(af)fattucchiare* 'bezaubern,' *fattucchiere, -in* 'Zauberer, -in'; ant. ital. *etterno* 'eterno.'" *A Rom* 13 (1929): 194.

(1) From Lat. *fare* (= 'to conjure'), **fattuchio* > *fattucchiare* (= 'to charm, to bewitch'). (2) Spitzer explains how this spelling variation occurred.

383. "Zu *Arch. Rom.* 13, p. 392." *A Rom* 13 (1929): 592.

A. Levi's clarification of It. *-ette* is the same as that offered by Spitzer in *ZRP* 40 (1920): 704.

384. "Zu *Zeitschrift* 51, 466." *ZFS* 52 (1929): 128.

Adds support, gained during a recent trip to Italy, to his study of the bird image evoked by words in the new field of aviation.

385. "Ital. *aggio*, Frz. *agio*." *ZFS* 53 (1930): 284–88.

Amplifies Meyer-Lübke's explanation for *aggio*, which he claimed to be a contraction of *vantaggio* (= 'advantage') from the language of commerce. More evidence is necessary for this derivation to be psychologically plausible. It is unlikely that a word is shortened by dropping its first syllable.

386. "Log. *pisómina*, bonorva. *posomina* 'Nachgeburt.'" *ZRP* 51 (1931): 298-99.
Log. *pisómina*, Bonorva. *posomina* (= 'afterbirth, placenta') < *post omnia* (= 'after everything').

387. "Ital. *lezio* 'Ziererei'; Ital. *gruzzo(lo)* 'Sparpfennig,' ait. *gruzzolo* 'Gruppe von Personen,' 'Herde Vieh,' 'Haufen Geld.'" *ZRP* 51 (1931): 707.
(1) It. *lezio* (= 'airs, affectation') < *electio* (= '[good] taste'). (2) It. *gruzzo(lo)* (= 'nest egg'), OIt. *gruzzolo* (= 'group of people, herd of cattle, hoard of gold') is related to and semantically derived from It. *gruzzolo* (= 'groat, a coin used in Europe').

388. "Zu *Zeitschrift* 52, p. 578, 'Ital. *gruzzolo*.'" *ZRP* 52 (1932): 831.
Brüch was amused by Spitzer's attribution. Citing Pied. *grüs* and Lomb. *grussolo*, Spitzer insists on his derivation. The word is also related to Austrian *gertschl* (= 'last saved penny').

389. "*Cemento* = *cimento*." *A Rom* 17 (1933): 410–14.
(1) It. *cemento* = *cimento* (= 'test, trial') is related to Fr. *cêment* > *cimenter* and to Sp. *cimentar*; all derive from Lat. *caementum* > *cimentum* and not from Lat. *specimentum* (= 'test'). (2) It. *pedante* is from It. *piede*, *pedata* (= 'footprint'), *pedant* (= 'pedestrian'), *pedant* (= 'lackey, footman') and not from Gk. *pedagogo*. (3) OIt. *querula* (= 'seagull') owes its name to the querulous sound the bird makes. Ger. *Möwe* comes from the sound a cat makes, as does Catal. *meuca* and Mall. *meular*. The bird is called the *mercatte* (= 'seacat').

390. "Zu neap. *vernacchio*." *VKR* 6 (1933): 274–75.
Max Wagner explains that a Neapolitan gesture imitating the noise of a fart derives from a Roman custom documented in Petronius. This lends support to Spitzer's claim that MFr. *tromper de quelqu'un* (= 'to make fun of someone') is derived from a similar gesture, which also imitated the sound of passing wind.

391. "It. *sollo* 'weich (vom Erdreich, Brot, etc.).'" *A Rom* 19 (1935): 436.
This word is related not to Fr. *souple* but to Lat. *suillus* (= 'of or concerning swine,' orig., 'fat').

392. "Ital. *madrigale* 'Madrigale.'" *ZRP* 55 (1935): 168–70.
It. *madrigale* (= 'madrigal') derives from *materiale* in the sense of 'bastard' (*filius materialis*), since the madrigal was considered a bastard genre, either because it lay midway between music and poetry or because it was originally of very low quality.

393. "Altital. *ripitare*." *ZRP* 55 (1935): 170–71.
OIt. *ripitare* (= 'lament, bewail') < *reputare* (= 'reckon, ponder'), perhaps by way of OProv. *reptar* (= 'reproach').

394. "*Cananaeus* 'Kananäer.'" *ZRP* 56 (1936): 71–72.
The reflexes of *cananaeus* (= 'Canaanite') are semantically interesting. Through folk etymology with *canis*, Neap. *kananea* acquired the meaning of 'ghetto, house full of noise and confusion.' Log. *Kananen* (= 'avaricious') is due to the fact that Canaanites were primarily businessmen.

395. "Romanesco *sisema* 'nervosismo, stizza, preoccupazioni, collera repressa.'" *A Rom* 22 (1938): 136.
Sisema derives not from Heb. *sciscim* or from *fisima* but from Lat. *scisim* (= 'worry').

396. "Venez. *marántega* 'beffana, spettro che appare la notte; riflesso di luce che cade su uno specchio.' " *A Rom* 22 (1938): 376.

Marántega < *mara* + *antico*, as *pregantego* < *praecantare*.

397. "Neapolitan *pernacchia*." *Lg* 14 (1938): 289.

Louis F. Solano's etymology of Neap. *pernacchia* (= 'Bronx cheer') < *vernaculum* (= 'act of a slave'), although correct, is not new (*Lg* 14 [1938]: 60). The change *v-* > *p-* is phonetically regular, so there is no need to assume a blend with *pireto* (= 'fart').

398. "Florentin *savia*." *A Rom* 23 (1939): 94.

Relates this word to *in issa via* (= 'immediately') < *ipsa via* rather than to *s'a via* (= 'if there is a possibility').

399. "Lat. *mentula*." *BSLP* 40 (1939): 46–47.

The Greeks and Romans differentiated between the animal spirit associated with the genitals and the mental spirit associated with the mind. However, there is no proof before the Renaissance that the meaning of *mentula* reflected this distinction.

400. "R. Hall, 'W. von Wartburg, *La posizione della lingua italiana nel mondo neolatino*,' *Lg* 14, 154." *MLN* 54 (1939): 237–48.

Spitzer defends Wartburg's idealist tendencies, such as trying to explain linguistic differences between two languages on the basis of cultural differences, against Hall's accusations of subjectivity. Language is a part of culture, not an isolable entity.

401. "*Fimare* in Isidore." *AJP* 61 (1940): 357–58.

There is evidence that Isidore's *fimare* means 'to fertilize with dung' and is a late derivative of *fimus*, *-i* (= 'dung').

402. "Italian *piagnisteo*." *A Rom* 24 (1940): 95–99.

Giovanni D'Alessio is correct (*ZRP* 59 [1939]: 244): *piagnisteo* derives from *piangere* + the suffix of *ministerium*. Like Sicil. *futtisteriu* and Tusc. *frignisteo*, it is a semilearned formation with a comical element produced by two contrasting attitudes given by the word's root and its suffix. The rigid distinction in Romance languages between learned and common expressions is a source of parody denied to naturally hybrid languages like Eng.

403. "Ital. *rifiutare*." *Ital* 17 (1940): 148–49.

Spitzer contests the *REW* explanation for *rifiutare* = *refutare* + It. *fiutare*. He agrees instead with Diez: *rifiutare* < Lat. *refugitare* < *fugita* (= 'to evade'). The It. verb, applied to a horse that refuses the bridle, is paralleled in Fr. *futer* = 'refuser (d'un cheval)'.

404. "R. A. Hall, 'Italian Etymological Notes,' *Lg* 15, 34–42." *MLN* 55 (1940): 79–82.

An attack on Hall and his ideas, methodology, and these etymologies.

405. "Due parole lucchesi antiche." *Ital* 18 (1941): 193–96.

(1) 13th-c. *corcibaldo* related to OFr. *courtiban* (var., *curcinbaldus*, *curieboldus*, *cortiballus*, *cortibaudus*, Du Cange, Lacurne de Sainte-Pelaye) means 'short ecclesiastical or royal garment'; it is related not to *bald(e)rich* but to Ger. *Kurzebolt*. (2) *Intrazacto*, parallel to *ad ogni baratto* (= 'a qualcunque costo'), means 'immediately.'

406. "Ancora *corcibaldo* 'veste corta' [*Ital* 18, 193]." *Ital* 19 (1942): 42.

In support of Fanfani's discussion of an apparently unique occurrence of this term, Spitzer cites another 13th-c. example where *corcibaldo* appears as *churcivaldo.*

407. "Trevigiano *denti spaísi* 'denti allegati.'" *Ital* 19 (1942): 168.

Denti spaísi is an echo of VLat. *dentes expavescunt* and shows the popular tendency to attribute psychological properties to parts of the body.

408. "*Parlascio-perilasio.*" *AJP* 64 (1943): 330–32.

In *AGI* 26 (1934), D. Olivieri traces Flor. *parlascio* and *perilasio* (= 'place where the municipal council sat') to It. *parlare.* Spitzer suggests the Gk. etymon *perielauno* because of the lack of convincing evidence in attestations offered by Olivieri.

409. "Anc. sienese *aciare* 'respirare,' *acio* 'fiato.'" *Ital* 20 (1943): 196–97.

Acio is a borrowing from OFr. *ache* 'h' and originally meant the letter name 'h'; *non aver acio in bocca* meant 'to be unable to pronounce an 'h',' a letter which exists in Lat. but which is never pronounced in It. *Acio* could refer to 'a minimum of breath.' *Aciare* may be a *t-are* from a word bearing the imprint of the 'h-aspiré,' such as Fr. *haleter.*

410. "Additional Remark to Professor Nitze's Article, *AJP* 66 (1945), p. 281." *AJP* 67 (1946): 267.

Spitzer admits he has erred in attributing *gradales* to a 12th-c. etymologist. Rather, it is first attested in 1010. Still, he maintains his correction of a line in the *Ecbasis.* He holds that *nec biberam cratum* should be amended to *nec biberam acratum,* which can be read in verse only as *nec biber(am) acratum.*

411. "It. *vogare, voga.*" *Ital* 23 (1946): 23–29.

Voga (= 'comando ritmico') and *vogare* (= 'to row rhythmically and with coordinated force') are shown to be related through comparison with the development of other marine terms, such as *ciloma* and *ciurma,* and described as the predecessors of the Fr. word family *vogue, voguer.*

412. "*Sbaglio, abbaglio, (ab)bagliare, bagliore, barbaglio.*" *Ital* 24 (1947): 69–72.

The sense of the root **bagl-* (= 'oscillate') is a semantic derivation of VLat. *bajulare* (= 'to carry a baby'). The family **bagl-* reflects a popular phonetic treatment and semantic trajectory.

413. "*Spavaldo.*" *LN* 14 (1953): 101.

Spavaldo is a gallicism related to Ger. *Sperber.* Its semantic development is: (1) 'sbigottire i piccoli uccelli, detto dello parviere'; (2) 'sbigottire'; (3) 'trattare inconsideratamente.'

414. "*Far filecca.*" *LN* 15 (1954): 13.

First attested in the 14th c., *far filecca* may be the first appearance of *far cilecca* (*scilecca*). *Filecca* would be a contamination of *scilecca/cilecca* < MHG *schleck!* with *fica* (in *far le fiche*).

415. "Parole di Dante: *caribo.*" *LN* 15 (1954): 65–66.

The development of this term, found in *Purgatorio* 31.132, is traced here: *garîb* (= Ar., 'jargon, unintelligible discourse'); *garip* (= Catal., 'whistle, strident cry'); *garip* (= Prov., 'musical components [without words], discordant dance accompaniment'); **discordo* (= 'a type of lyric with its melody'); *caribo* (= It., 'discord [Giacomino Pugliese], dance, or dance melody [Dante]').

416. "Parole vuote (a proposito di *blittri, LN* 13, 70)." *LN* 16 (1955): 1.

As noted by Zsigmond Simonyi (*Magyar Nyelvör* 42 [1913]: 285), the Lat. scholastic term, probably Gk. in origin, signifies 'vain or empty words.' Spitzer cites a modern Jesuitical occurrence (K. Frick, S.J., *Logica in usum scholarum,* Friburgo in Brisgovia: Herder, 1908, 42), as well as a Romance example (Gracián, *Criticon* I), and notes that *Titivilitius* as the name of a character in a dialogue by Luigi Vives appears to derive from the form found in Plautus, *tittibilicio.*

417. "*Ranuzzare.*" *LN* 17 (1956): 120.

The phrase "si *ranuza* il suo sermone" is found in lines 56-60 of an anonymous *canzone* from the codex Vat. 3793 (*Crestomazia italiana: nuova ed. riveduta e aumentate per cura di F. Arese,* Roma: Dante Alighieri, 1955, 115). The verb is derived from *ranuzza* (= 'frog') in the sense of 'to croak.'

Romanian

418. "Rumanian *gruĭŭ* (*gruñŭ*) 'Hügel.' " *ANS* 134 (1916): 138.

Grumus is not the source for *gruñŭ,* since intervocalic *-m-* rarely changes to *-n-*. Because *corolla* > *curull* and *cerebellum* > *creer, corona* > *cunună,* then *gruĭŭ* > *gruñŭ.*

419. "Rum. *porumb* 'mais.' " *ZRP* 40 (1919-20): 108-09.

Porumb is related to a word meaning 'dove-colored,' from the same root as Sp. *paloma* (= 'dove').

420. "Rum. *mire* 'Bräutigam.' " *Revue Internationale des Etudes Balkaniques* 1 (1934): 270-72.

Peter Skok (*Archiv für Slavische Philologie* 37 [1918-20]: 85) suggests that Rom. *mire* (= 'bridegroom') is a loan translation from Slav. *vojno* (= 'spouse, [orig.] brave, soldier'). Spitzer cites several 17th-c. biblical passages where "war hero" and "bridegroom" are connected and points out the Bible's general influence on word choice. Given the relation in Christian sacred language between military expressions and the sacramental nature of marriage as a symbol for the union of Christ and the church, the bridegroom who overcomes the temptations of the flesh in Christian marriage can be viewed as a soldier of Christ. Rom. *mire* represents this association.

421. "Arom. *mamă* 'Kinderpapp,' rum. *mămăligă* 'polenta.' " *Dacoromania* 8 (1936): 131-32.

Theodor Capidan (*Dacoromania* 7 [1935]: 153) traced this word to ORom. *mamă;* the Lat. root is *mamma* 'breast.' Spitzer shows that *mamma* is applied to several foods as well as to 'mother' and 'father.' Lists many Romance examples.

422. "La famille de mots *mattus* en roman." *BInst* 5-6 (1937-38): 231-34.

Mattus < Lat. *madidus* (= 'drunk').

423. "*Cătelin, Cătinel.*" *BInst* 5-6 (1937-38): 234-35.

Cătelin, cătinel = Lat. *cautela.* Both derive from **cătel.* The suffixes *-elin, -inel* are often interchangeable in Rom.

424. "Roum. *ateia*—afrz. *atillier.*" *BInst* 5-6 (1937-38): 235-37.

Both Rom. *ateia* and OFr. *atillier* derive, via different paths, from a common root, Lat. *tilium.*

Spanish, Portuguese, and Basque

425. "Val. *pa y formage*." *ZRP* 36 (1912): 724-25.
Valen. *pa y formage* turns out to be a game of skipping stones.

426. "*Baruch habbah* [sc. beschem adanaj]." *WS* 5 (1913): 126-28.
Development of this word for 'confusion' from Heb. through Port. *badanal* > *badanaj* and *taranai* > *tananai*.

427. "Altspan. *curiar* 'schützen.'" *ANS* 135 (1916): 420-21.
OSp. *curiar* (= 'to protect') is related to OFr. *curer* (= 'to guard').

428. "Katl. *tramitar* 'weitergeben,' *tràmit* 'Instanz,' span. *tràmite* 'Instanzenweg.'" *ANS* 136 (1917): 162-63.
The semantic development of this Sp. word family parallels the development of Fr. *canal* 'paths of influence' in the 18th c.

429. "Zu span. *zara* 'mais.'" *ANS* 136 (1917): 165.
This word for corn derives from early Latin American Sp. *mais zarazo* = 'corn that is neither fresh nor completely dry.'

430. "Altspan. *deçir*, port. *descer*, 'herabsteigen.'" *ANS* 136 (1917): 296-98.
Descidere > *descendere* > *deçir*. Includes many examples of similarly shortened derivatives of these verbs.

431. "Span. *esconce*; span. *escolimoso, escolimado*." *ZRP* 39 (1917-19): 496-97.
(1) Ernest Weekley (*English Studies* 40 [n.d.]: 316) traces Eng. *askance* to OFr. *à escons*. According to Spitzer, Sp. *esconce* also derives from *à escons*. (2) Gk. *cholē* > Sp. **colema* > Sp. *escolimoso* (= 'grouchy, morose, grumpy, fault-finding'), Sp. *escolimado* (= 'sickly, weakly'). Here he opposes Diez, who groups the two terms with Gk. *scolymos* (= 'a kind of artichoke').

432. "Span. *dibujar* 'zeichnen' = afrz. *deboissier*." *ZFS* 45 (1919): 375-79.
Sp. *dibujar* (= 'to draw') < OSp. *debujar* following the sound change *e* > *i*. OSp. *debujar* < Lat. *debuxare* < Lat. *buxus*. The origin of the prefix *de-* is problematic. Rufino J. Cuervo (*REW* 1430) fails to note the OFr. *debo(u)issier* (= 'to carve') = Sp. *dibujar*.

433. "Zur Wortgeschichte." *ZRP* 39 (1917-19): 617.
The Spanish Academy dictionary (*Diccionario de la lengua castellana, por la real academia española*, Madrid: Hernando, 1914) errs in its derivation of *de soslayo* (= 'askance') from *latus*. The term is equivalent to *de vislay* and is related to OFr. *besloi* (= 'to fool, deceive').

434. "Mall. *ell*." *NM* 21 (1920): 130-32.
To end his debate with Tallgren over the derivation of Mall. *ell*–from *ellum* or from *illud*–Spitzer shows that the impersonal subject "it" is used in Mall., therefore *ell* < *illud*.

435. "Hispanistische Wortmiszellen." *NM* 22 (1921): 44-49.
An examination of the following: (1) Lat. *ilex* in Sp.; (2) Sp. *ajar* (= 'to humiliate'); (3) Port. *entejar* (= 'to cause disgust'); (4) Port. *entertimho* (= 'connective tissue'); (5) Sp. *espolique* (= 'servant walking beside his lord, who is riding a horse'); (6) Sp. *fultriquera, faldriguera* (= 'jacket pocket'); (7) Sal. *hacientes* (= 'knowingly');

(8) Sp. *maleta* (= 'illness'); (9) Arag. *pusar maleta* (= 'to have a bad experience'); (10) Galician Sal. *solene* (= 'imbecile, idiot'); and (11) Sp. *soltero*, Port. *solteiro* (= 'not married').

436. "*Arribota*." *RFE* 8 (1921): 58–60.
Sp. *arribota* (= 'way up [there]') < *arriba* 'up' + *-ota* augmentative suffix; cf. *encimita, cerquita, derechito*, etc.

437. "Vieil esp. *poridad*, esp. *puridad*, port. *puridade* 'secret.'" *RFE* 8 (1921): 176–78.
OSp. *poridad*, Sp. *puridad*, Port. *puridade* < *puritate* (= 'purity') developed the meaning 'secret,' for example, *fablar en poridad* in the context of medieval vows between lord and serf, in which 'purity' was interpreted as 'fidelity,' an integral part of which is the duty to maintain confidentiality.

438. "Judeo-esp. *meldar*." *RFE* 8 (1921): 288–91.
The Jewish practice of teaching reading through the study of religious texts explains the semantic development between Judeo-Sp. *meldar* (= 'learn, read prayers in a synagogue') and its etymon, Heb. *melmed* (= 'teach').

439. "*Soccus* en español." *RFE* 8 (1921): 403–04.
The following corrections should be made to the article by V. García de Diego on Lat. *soccus* (= 'light shoe, slipper') in Sp. (*RFE* 6 [1919]: 127ff.): (1) *chocar* 'strike' < onomatopoeic root; (2) *zoco* 'left-handed' < *zoguete* 'dolt'; (3) *zurdo* 'left-handed' < *zoco* X *palurdo* 'country bumpkin'; (4) *chancla* 'slipper' < *choclo* 'clog' X *zanca* 'shank'; and (5) *socarrón* 'crafty' < onomatopoeic root.

440. "Zu *NM*, 22, 113–7." *NM* 23 (1922): 31–33.
Mermella = *melatella* = *melimellu*; *faltriquera* > *la que salta*; *maldisson* > *maudissons* > *mau-dich*.

441. "Wortmiszellen: *enclenque, escuelh, recancanilla*." *NM* 23 (1922): 85–90.
(1) Sp. *enclenque* > Catal. *enclenc* > OFr. *esclenc* (= 'sickly'). (2) OProv. *escuelh* (= 'attitude') is not from *scholium* but from Catal. *escull* (= 'good aspect'). (3) Sp. *recancanilla* > *canca* > *cancaneta* > *squenata* > *casquenata*.

442. "Santander *borcil* 'cubil.'" *RFE* 9 (1922): 67.
Sp. *borcil* (= 'lair of wild beasts') < **porcile* (= 'pigsty').

443. "Port. *gíria* 'calao,' 'argot' = esp. *gerigonza*?" *RFE* 9 (1922): 178–79.
Port. *gíria* (= 'slang, jargon') < Fr. *girie* (= 'trick, silliness').

444. "Esp. *vanistorio*." *RFE* 9 (1922): 390–94.
Sp. *vanistorio* (= 'ridiculous or affected vanity') owes its formation to a popular ironic parody of certain high-flown ecclesiastic terms, such as *consistorio* (= 'municipal council'), *faldistorio* (= 'bishop's seat'). The learnedness of the ending is belied by the mundane meaning of the root (*vano* = 'vain'), cf. *vejestorio* (= 'peevish old man').

445. "Etymologische Miszellen." *NM* 24 (1923): 150–57.
(1) Sp. *garduna* (= 'housemarten') < *escarcuñar* < *escarduñar* < *scrutiniare*. (2) Port. *caçapo* = Sp. *gazapo* (= 'young rabbit'). (3) Sp. *befa, bifa* = Fr. *biffe* (= 'woolen') > *bufarinheiro* > *bifferie*.

446. "Esp. *terco*." *RFE* 10 (1923): 70–72.
Sp. *terco* (= 'stubborn, hard [said of marble]') < **integricus*.

447. "Notas etimológicas." *RFE* 10 (1923): 167–72.

(1) Sp. *engurrio* (= 'sadness, melancholy') as well as *engurria* (= 'wrinkle') < _*engurullar_, a retrograde form meaning 'wrinkle, get old, be sad,' itself akin to Sp. *garulla* (= 'leftover grape skins'). (2) Sp. *esperiega* (= 'pippin [apple]') < _*hesperiaecus_, a combination of *Hesperia* (= 'Spain') and *-aecus*, a geographic suffix. The pippin is indigenous to southern Europe. (3) Catal. *pernoliar* (= 'administer last rites') < _*per-m-oleare_ < _*per-oleare_ X _*inoleare_ (in reference to the oils administered in the ceremony).

448. "Notas etimológicas." *RFE* 10 (1923): 373–79.

(1) Sp. (*echarse*) *pullas* (= 'make innuendos') < *púa* (= 'point') < *pulla* (= 'idem'). (2) Sp. *lacra* (= 'scar, sign of disease, defect') < Port. *lacre* (= 'red sealing wax [in reference to the color of the wound]'). (3) Sp. *colodra* (= 'milkpail') < *cucumus* (= 'cucumber, gourd') X *cylindrus* (= 'cylinder'), with the intermediate meaning 'measure of wine.' (4) Catal. *anyorar*. The derivation from Catal. *entranyorar* was first proposed by C. Michaëlis de Vasconcellos.

449. "Hispanistische Wortmiszellen." *NM* 25 (1924): 120–23.

Comments on *huero* (= 'rotten egg') and *pajarillo* (= 'spleen').

450. "Port. *choscar, chuscar* 'clignoter.'" *RFE* 11 (1924): 69–70.

Port. *choscar, chuscar* (= 'wink') < onomatopoeic root *klask-*, *klisk-* (= 'sound of blows').

451. "Santand. *asubiar*; esp. *sobaco*; esp. *sobón*." *RFE* 11 (1924): 70–72.

Santand. *asubiar* (= 'protect oneself from the rain') < _*ad-sub-obviare_. Sp. *sobaco* (= 'armpit') < Sp. *sobar* (= 'scrub') + *-aco* (e.g., *furaco* 'hole'), because it is often scrubbed. Sp. *sobón* (= 'sluggard, idler') < *sobar* (= 'to massage, to pummel someone').

452. "Esp. *zángano*, port. *zangão*." *RFE* 11 (1924): 183–86.

Sp. *zángano*, Port. *zangão* (= 'drone bee') < onomatopoeic root *zang-*, representative of a buzzing sound.

453. "*Masculillo*." *RFE* 11 (1924): 187–88.

Sp. *masculillo* (= '[game in which one receives a] blow to the hips') < *baculum* (= 'rod [for whipping]').

454. "Murc. *dedo margarite, margarín* 'petit doigt'; esp. *carrillo*; port. *carrilho* 'joue'; esp. *carrillera* 'mâchoire.'" *RFE* 11 (1924): 314–16.

(1) Murc. *margarite, margarín* (= 'little finger') < OFr. *Margariz* (= 'renegade'; also, 'small idol'). (2) Sp. *carrillo*, Port. *carrilho* (= 'cheek'); Sp. *carrillera* (= 'jaw') < *carro* (= 'cart') through the humorous metaphoric comparison of the act of eating with that of hauling goods in a cart, cf. It. *carreggiare* (= 'eat').

455. "Anc. esp. *priego*, port. *prego* 'clou'; *farmalio, farmario, faramalla*." *RFE* 11 (1924): 412–17.

(1) OSp. *priego*, Port. *prego* (= 'nail') < *plicare* (= 'fold, lay or wind together'), with the intermediate semantic stage = 'fix.' (2) Sp. *farmalio, farmario, faramalla* (= 'pact, contract') is a reflex of _*firmalia_, perhaps through OProv. *fermalha* (= 'treaty').

456. "Hispanistische Wortmiszellen." *ZRP* 44 (1924): 81–91.

(1) A discussion of the relationship between Sp. *chamorro* and *flamma*. (2) The light diminutive character of Sp. *chamuscar* and its *-u-i* vowel shift point to Lat. *coruscare* as the root. (3) *Llamarada* cannot be related to *rapidus* because of the

-ar- infix. (4) Since Mall. *baxest, bexest, bixest* are related forms of *bissext*, the term *baxest* goes back to *bissextus*, not to *bassus*. (5) A discussion of the term *polletón*, which occurs in an Andalusian folk tale regarding the destiny of women who die unmarried.

457. "Zu *Ztschr.* 43, 344." *ZRP* 44 (1924): 768.

Sp. *rigodón* (= 'rubble, flint') is not to be confused with Fr. *rigaudon* (= 'dance of Provençal origin, in vogue in the 17th and 18th centuries').

458. "Notes étymologiques." *RFE* 12 (1925): 229–51.

(1) Arag. *antiparte* (= 'notwithstanding') < *hazte parte* (= 'be informed'), which is a blend of *dar parte* (= 'inform') and *harcerse cuenta (cargo)* (= 'imagine, suppose'). (2) Sp. *bellaco* (= 'rogue, villain') < *vello* (= 'fuzz, hair') < *villus* (= 'shaggy hair') + *-aco*. OSp. *bellido* (= 'beautiful') < *vello* (= 'fleece, wool') through the intermediate meaning 'hairy, strong.' (3) Lat. *cingulum, -a* > Sp. *ceño* (= 'hoop [over the top of a horse's hoof]'), *cello* (= 'hoop used in cooperage'), *cellisca* (= 'fine rain, snow, or sleet blown by wind'), *cellenco* 'decrepit (orig. in reference to a disease of horses in the area of the cinch).' (4) Sp. *donaire* (= 'grace, gentility, witty saying') < **donarium* (= 'gift') possibly through Gallo-Romance. (5) Sp. *enconarse* (= 'fester, rankle [wound]') < *inquinare* (= 'befoul, stain, defile') contrary to *Lex. a. d. Kat.* 15 (*A Rom* 2 [1918]: 492). (6) Sp. *lacayo*, Fr. *laquais* (= 'lackey') < Catal. *l'al(a)cay* (= 'soldier') < Ar. *al-caid* (= 'leader').

459. "Vasc. *azurria*, esp. *zurriaga*." *Revue Internationale des Etudes Basques* 16 (1925): 146–49.

Both *azurria* and *zurriaga* derive from the same onomatopoeic Sp. root.

460. "Notes étymologiques." *RFE* 13 (1926): 113–28.

(1) Sp. *lagotear* (= 'flatter') < *lacus* (= 'lake') through a series of semantic changes: 'lake' > 'splash water (Béarnese *lagouta* = 'stir water')' > 'chatter' > finally 'flatter.' (2) Sp. *mostrenco*, Port. *mostrengo* (= 'vagabond, homeless') < *monstrum* (= 'monster') as claimed in *Lex. a. d. Kat.* 97, cf. Montañés *móstrico* (= 'mostrenco'). (3) OSp. *sençido* (= 'intact, undisturbed') < *sancitus* < *sancire* (= 'sanction, prohibit, protect'). (4) Sp. *sesgo* (= 'slant'), *sesgar* (= 'cut on the slant') < OSp. *sessegar* (= 'sit down') < **sessicare* (= 'sit'). (5) Sp. *sima* (= 'abyss,' previously, 'prison, grave') and Sp. *cimbria* (= 'fillet [architecture]') < **sedimen* (= 'ground, place'). (6) Sp. *tirria* (= 'ill will') < onomatopoeic interjection *trr!*, representing disgust or trembling. (7) Sp. *tomar* < onomatopoeic root *tomb!*, representing the sound of a blow or fall. (8) Sp. *turón* (= 'polecat, *ferret') < *taurus* (= 'bull').

461. "Encore une fois *ceño*." *RFE* 13 (1926): 279–80.

Sp. *ceño*, Port. *cenho* (= 'frown') < **cinnus* (= 'wink, sign') X *cilium* (= 'eyelid').

462. "Bask. *eskon*, sp. *azcona, ascona, escona* 'Wurfspiess'; sp. *ganzua*; bask. *eslata* 'vallado de madera.'" *Revue Internationale des Etudes Basques* 17 (1926): 94–97.

(1) Basque *askon* (= 'ash'). The Basque word does not derive from a Ger. root but is rather a borrowing from Castil. There are a number of Prov. words meaning 'spear' that are related: *ancona, ascona*. Gk. *agkor* (= 'elbow') and Lat. *ancon* (= 'anchor, brace, clamp') are probable sources. (2) Sp. *ganzua*. This word is probably not descended from a Basque word; it is instead related to Sp. *gancho* (= 'hook') and was originally used by swindlers. (3) Basque *eslato* (= 'slat'). Meyer-Lübke derives this word from Celt. *slatta* (= 'slat'); Schuchardt derives it from Eng. *slat*, which Ferdinand Holthausen derives from OFr. *esclat* (= 'splinter').

463. "Esp. *manga* 'osequio, presente'; 'trampa, negocio sucio.' " *RFE* 14 (1927): 69–71.

Sp. *manga* (= 'gift, trap') < *manga* (= 'sleeve') because (1) sleeves were actually used as gifts and gift wrappings in the Middle Ages, and (2) the sleeve is a symbol of deceit since it is used for such purposes by magicians and gamblers.

464. "Notes étymologiques." *RFE* 14 (1927): 243–55.

(1) Sp. *columbrar* (= 'perceive, descry, guess') < *colluminare* (= 'illuminate completely'). (2) Sp. *cundir* (= 'spread, extend') < *cundire* (= 'to season,' later, 'to infect'). (3) MexSp. *cuzco* (= 'prostitute'), Catal. *cusch* (= 'chaste'), OFr. *cuschement* (= 'respectfully') < **kusk-*, **gosk-* (= 'dog'). (4) Sp. *malrotar, marlotar, marrotar* (= 'destroy or squander') < **marla* (= 'marl, loam') < *margilia* (= 'marl, chalk, clay') with the intermediate meaning 'that which is wrinkled, rough, uneven.' (5) JudeoSp. *meldar* (= 'read Hebrew') < Gk. *meletan* (= 'read'). (6) Sp. *posma* (= 'sluggishness') < Fr. *pausmer* (= 'swoon'). (7) Sp. *pringue* (= 'fat, grease') < *pingar* (= 'drip'), *pendicare* (= 'hover, hang'). (8) Sp. *rabión* (= 'violent river current') < *rabia* (= 'anger') < *rabies* (= 'rage, madness'). (9) Santand. *rámila, rézmila, rosmil(l)a* (= 'stone marten') < *resmillar, rasmillar* (= 'scratch, clean grapes') < *racemus* (= '[stalk of] a branch of grapes'). (10) OSp. *regunçar* (= 'tell, recount'), MSp. *gonce, gozne* (= 'hinge') < *bucina* (= 'trumpet').

465. "Span. *ostugo* = bask. *ostugo*?" *Revue Internationale des Etudes Basques* 18 (1927): 634–35.

Sp. *ostugo* < Lat. **festucus*, not from Basque **ostugo* as Meyer-Lübke claims (*REW* 6120).

466. "*Zebro* 'onager.' " *RFE* 15 (1928): 375–76.

Corresponding to OSp. *zebro* (= 'onager') are the following Catal. forms: *atzebre* (1492), *quenzebra* (1495), *adzebruno* (1523).

467. "W. Meyer-Lübke, 'Misceláneas etimológicas,' *Biblios* (Coimbra) 3 (1927), 1–5." *RFE* 15 (1928): 389–400.

Detailed response to nine Port. etymologies.

468. "*Halacreta* 'arnés, loriga'?" *Revue Internationale des Etudes Basques* 19 (1928): 637.

This term is a borrowing from 15th- and 16th-c. Fr. *halacret*, *halacrète* and is not a derivative of Prov. *ala* + *creto*.

469. "Cas d'homonymie gênante en espagnole." *RFE* 16 (1929): 173–74.

Among the few cases in Sp. of true etymological homonymic disturbance are: (1) *traicionar* (= 'betray') created to clarify the confusion caused by *traer* (= 'bring') < *tradere* and *traer* (= 'betray') < *trahere*; (2) *reflecciónar* (= 'think over') created to avoid the ambiguity between *reflejar* (= 'reflect') and *reflejar* (= '*think over').

470. "Parallelen." *ZVS* 57 (1929–30): 63.

Contrasts the meaning of Ger. *Affen* (= 'ape') with Sp. *mono* (= 'beautiful, dearest,' also, 'monkey').

471. "Esp. *pícaro*." *RFE* 17 (1930): 181–82.

Sp. *pícaro* < Fr. *Picard* (= 'inhabitant of Picardy'). The borrowing may have gone through literary instead of military channels: some Picard farces of the 13th c. are quite similar in plot to *Lazarillo de Tormes*.

472. "*Estultar* 'ofender,' 'reñir, reprender.'" *RFE* 17 (1930): 183.
Sp. *estultar* (= 'offend, reprimand') < Lat. *stultus* (= 'foolish').

473. "*Requejo.*" *A Rom* 15 (1931): 596.
Vittorio Bertoldi's explanation of dialectal Sp. *requejo* (= 'steep terrain') (*A Rom* 15 [1931]: 407) contradicts Meyer-Lübke's (< *capseum* 'jaw'). The latter's derivation is substantiated by Sp. *quijedo* (= 'millrace slope') and testifies to the advantages of relying on indigenous Sp. explanations.

474. "E. G. Wahlgren, 'Franç. *surouest, surôit,* esp. *sur,* port. *sul,*' *Studier i Modern Sprakvetenskap* 11 (1931)." *RFE* 18 (1931): 185–87.
Wahlgren explains the phonetic development of these words. Spitzer explains why *norte* was borrowed by Sp. long before *sur, oeste,* and *este*: poets preferred it to the Lat. *septentrión,* and it was assigned the special meaning of 'north star.'

475. "Encore une fois *danga* 'coup de cloche.'" *Revue Internationale des Etudes Basques* 22 (1931): 241.
Does *danga* come from Lat. *tangere,* or is it simply an onomatopoeia? Spitzer offers a compromise: *danga* = *dang-ta(n)g* (< Lat. *tangere*).

476. "Span. *caraba.*" *VKR* 4 (1931): 168–69.
Suggests *caravana* > *carava* > *caraba* and describes several Latin American variations of this word.

477. "Span. *grandísima(zorra)* 'Hure.'" *VKR* 4 (1931): 169.
This word is related to the whore of Babylon in the Apocalypse.

478. "Span. *tafanario,* kat. *tafanari* 'Gesä.'" *ZRP* 51 (1931): 196–98.
Sp. *tafanario* (= 'buttocks, butt'), Catal. *tafanari* (= 'buttocks, vegetable garden behind the house') < It. *antifonario* (= 'buttocks') < Eccl.Lat. *antiphona* (= 'antiphon'), which gradually changed meaning from 'liturgical response' to 'bad news,' 'defecate,' and, finally, 'buttocks.'

479. "Nochmals sp. *carava.*" *VKR* 5 (1932): 243.
Links *carava* with *carrer las caravanas* (= 'to carry out a design or a job').

480. "Nprov. *gueissá* 'taller, drageonner.'" *ZFS* 56 (1932): 254.
Sp. *guájete por guájete* (= 'tit for tat') should be distinguished from Prov. *gueissá* since Sp. *¡guaj!* can be used as an interjection.

481. "*Pitoflero.*" *RFE* 20 (1933): 62–64.
Pitoflero (= 'musician of little ability') < *epitaphium* (= 'eulogy'). The etymon was poorly understood but definitely evocative of pejorative connotations. The phonetic effect of the word, together with its similarity to *mofletudo* (= 'chubby-cheeked, e.g., trumpet player'), may have affected the meaning.

482. "*Alrededor; arrobarse; melena;* anc. esp. *privado* 'vite'; anc. esp. *regunzar* 'raconter.'" *RFE* 20 (1933): 169–72.
(1) Sp. *alrededor* (= 'around') < OSp. *aderredor* (= 'idem') < **de retriore (loco)* (= 'from a place somewhat removed,' later, 'the area roundabout'). (2) Sp. *arrobarse* (= 'be enraptured') < *robar* (= 'ravish'), the meaning having arisen in the writings of religious mystics. (3) Sp. *melena* (= 'long lock of hair, lion's mane') < *miel* (= 'honey') + *-eno* (color suffix in *moreno*). (4) OSp. *privado* (= 'fast') < *privatus* (= 'private') through the semantic development indicated by OProv. *privat* (= 'in secret'), *perprivat* (= 'particular'), since private envoys invariably go fast (cf. Eng. 'express train'). (5) OSp. *regunzar* (= 'recount') < **re-cognit-iare* (= 'make known').

483. "Esp. *levente*." *Revue Internationale des Etudes Balkaniques* 1 (1934): 269–70.
Sp. *levente* means 'soldier of the sea' according to Rodríguez Marín (*Don Quijote* 3.175). Spitzer suggests a derivation from Ottoman *levend* < *levant(in)* (= 'volunteer soldier, sniper, vagabond, of proud appearance, bold'). The word has been borrowed by various Balkan languages, for example, Rom. *levent* (= 'Turkish marine soldier'), Bulg. *levén(t)* (= 'strong young man').

484. "*Z*." *BFL* 3 (1934–35): 318–19.
The speaker's hesitation is graphically represented in the shape of the letter *z* in *zig-zag*. However, phonetic and onomatopoeic determinants came first.

485. "Encore une fois *caritel*." *BFL* 3 (1934–35): 319.
Kaltere < *caracter* in the *Cartolario de San Vicente de Oviedo* (Oviedo, 1041) is linked with Port. *caritel* < *charactêle*, which is subject to similar consonantal substitution.

486. "*Estapafourdi*." *BFL* 3 (1934–35): 329–30.
Claudel uses this hapax, a Brazilianism, to emphasize the outlandish.

487. "*Milho, bagulho, maçaroca (galette)*." *BFL* 3 (1934–35): 400–01.
Disputes Abilio Roseira's findings on these numerical expressions (*BFL* 3 [1934–35]: 327). Here they are described as euphemisms for money. The association of grain with money and wealth renders this otherwise vulgar topic acceptable in polite conversation.

488. "*Estapafourdi* (additions à mon article, tome 3, p. 329)." *BFL* 3 (1934–35): 401.
This "monster" word is related to *estúrdio*, *étourdi*, and *estabalhado* and perhaps even to the interjection *patatrás*. These words signify both surprise and indecision.

489. "Astur. *xemes*." *RFE* 21 (1934): 279.
Ast. *xemes* (= 'one time'), *de xemes* (= 'once in a while') < *semel* (= 'once') + *-s* (plural suffix).

490. "*Bimbos; chape-chuga*." *BFL* 4 (1936): 183–84.
(1) *Bimbos* (Lisbon slang = 'rump'; Brazil = 'thigh,' fig., 'fool, idiot'). In several Latin American languages the onomatopoeic root *bimb-* = 'foolishness, childishness.' (2) *Chape-chuga*. The source of this onomatopoeic word for 'boat' is *sugar* or *sucer* (= 'to suck') as in *sanguexuga* and *sanguisuga* (= 'bloodsucker').

491. "*Baldraca*." *RFE* 23 (1936): 400–01.
OSp. *buffa de baldrac* (= 'insignificant play or game in gambling') can be associated with Sp. *baldraque* (= 'thing of little or no value'). Both are derived from Lat. *portulaca* (= 'purslane').

492. "*(En)soñar un sueño*." *VRo* 1 (1936): 49–63.
An extensive historical discussion of many Romance words meaning 'to sleep' or 'to dream' and having psychological and theological inferences.

493. "Encore *ensoñar un sueño*." *VRo* 1 (1936): 396.
The phrase "de sueños y ensueños" appears in a poem by Bécquer (Joaquín Casalduero, *Las* Rimas *de Bécquer*, Madrid: Cruz y Raya, 1935, 93). *Sueño* refers to a dreamed image, *ensueño* to a dreamy atmosphere.

494. "Sp. *ciclán*." *ZRP* 56 (1936): 72.

Sp. *ciclán* (= 'monogonadal') < *cyclamen, -inis* (Gk. *kycláminos*) = 'bush having a single knotty, disk-shaped rootstock.'

495. "Notes linguistiques." *RFE* 24 (1937): 24–36.

(1) The Sp. greeting *¿Adónde bueno?* (lit. = 'Whither good?') may reflect a primitive taboo regarding questions about the destinations of others: in order to disavow all demonic intent, the questioner appends the adjective "good," associated with God and blessedness. (2) The Sp. expression *echar de menos* (= 'to miss [a person]') replaced OSp. *hallar menos* (= 'idem') not through confusion with Port. *achar menos* but through a genuine switch within Sp. to *echar*; *hallar* having become too abstract, speakers chose *echar* (= 'count, calculate'), thus *echar de menos* = 'count less.' (3) Sp. *quejar* (= 'complain') may be traceable to **coactiare* (= 'compress, cause a difficult situation, complain') or **quassiare* (= 'shatter'). (4) Sp. *sabañones* (= 'chilblains') < **saban-ione* (= 'idem') < *sabanum* (= 'cloth'), through comparison of the ulcerous skin with a veil. (5) The attestations of Sp. *iñorar* (= 'not to know') in the sense 'to know' are due to the popular misunderstanding of the negative *no iñorar* (= 'to know'), whose combination of implicit and explicit negation was confusing to the uninitiated.

496. "Port. *calabrear* 'sophistiquer le vin'; a. port. *ergo* 'excepté.' " *BFL* 5 (1938): 376–79.

(1) Port. *calabrear*. This is identical to Sp. *calabriar* from the Italian area of Calabria, where it is believed that the expression referred to Judas, who was a Calabrian. The sophisticated wine thus is a 'perverted' wine. (2) Port. *ergo* (= 'except for') < Lat. *ergo* (= 'but, except for, thus').

497. "*Rejego*." *Investigaciones Lingüísticas, México* 5 (1938): 76–77.

A discussion of this word's opposing meanings throughout Latin America. It can mean 'tractable' or 'intractable.' It is a clear example of what is called *Gegensinn* or *enantiosemia*. Other examples are cited, including Lat. *altus* 'high' or 'low.'

498. "Sp. *cimarrón*; port., sp., *cisco, ciscar*." *Lg* 14 (1938): 145–48.

(1) Sp. *cimarrón* (= 'wild') < (*hacer*) *cimarra* (= 'play truant'), see *REW* 7563a. (2) There are two etyma for Sp., Port. *cisco, ciscar*: (a) in the meanings 'remove burning branches,' 'charcoal-dust,' 'little piece' < **cisicare* < **cisus* = *caesus* (= 'cut off') on the model of *occidere, incidere*; and (b) in the meaning 'row, hubbub,' 'defecate,' 'fart' < onomatopoeic stem *cisc-* (= 'defecate').

499. "Sp. *cansar* 'to weary.' " *Lg* 14 (1938): 205–06.

Sp. *cansar* (= 'to weary') < GrecoLat. *campsare* (= 'sail by') requires the semantic development 'deviate' (*campsare de via*) > 'cease, fail' > 'get tired.' There is no influence of the Gk. meaning 'bow down,' and, since this is unattested in Lat., it should be ignored.

500. "Glosarios latino-españoles (*MLN* 53, 145)." *MLN* 53 (1938): 554.

OSp. *alatitor* could simply be a misspelling of *glatitor*, Lat. for 'yelping puppies.' This verb has survived in modern Sp. as *latir* (= 'beating of a heart').

501. "*Estremunhado* 'estonteado ao acordar.' " *BFL* 6 (1939): 204.

From *turbinio* < Lat. *turbo*, possibly influenced by Sardinian *trumudzone* and other cases of assimilation like *termentina* = *terebinthus* < **ex-turbini-atus*.

502. *"Forca(da)s da língua."* *BFL* 6 (1939): 204.

Modern Fr. *barbillon* and MFr. *fourchillons* are related to the Port. *forca(da)s da língua*, contrary to Gunnar Tilander's view that only Port. has a word for this disease affecting birds' beaks.

503. "O. Sp. *regunzar* 'to narrate.'" *HR* 7 (1939): 75.

For OSp. *regunzar* (= 'to narrate'), the etymon **re-cognit-iare* is to be preferred to **re-comput-iare*, since *-iare* verbs were formed from participles and adjectives, never verbs.

504. "Sp. *bosar* 'to vomit,' *rebosar* 'idem,' 'to overflow.'" *Lg* 15 (1939): 50–51.

Sp. *bosar* (= 'vomit'), *rebosar* (= 'vomit, overflow') < *vulsare* < *vulsus* (= 'spasmodic, spastic').

505. *"Malevo < maleva 'engaño' < manu levare."* *RFH* 2 (1940): 177–79.

Arag. *malevo* 'evil' < Port. *maleva*, noun and adj. (= 'a bad, cruel [person],' orig., '*deceit, *deceitful person') < OPort. *mallevar* ('[ask to] swear') < *manu levare* (= 'raise one's hand'). The word *malévolo* 'malevolent' is irrelevant to the etymology.

506. *"Rebaño."* *RFH* 2 (1940): 389–90.

Sp. *rebaño* (= 'flock') < *rebañar* (= 'gather up completely [e.g., into a pile]') < *vannere* (= 'winnow [producing a pile of leavings]').

507. "W. D. Elcock, 'The Enigma of the Lizard in the Aragonese Dialect,' *MLR* 35 (1940), 483–93." *Anales del Instituto de Lingüística* (U.N. de Cuyo) 1 (1941): 182–84.

Unbeknownst to him, Elcock was not the first to suggest that Arag. *sa(n)gartana* 'lizard' and variants could have derived from *lacertus* 'idem,' with false identification of *la-* as a definite article and subsequent substitution through *sa-* from *ipsa*. Schuchardt addressed this question on various occasions and propounded a theory of multiple causation.

508. *"In-ossicare."* *RFH* 3 (1941): 271–72.

The etymon of *añusgarse* 'atragantarse, enfadarse' is **in-ossi-care* through the reduction *-sg-* > *-zg-*, for example, *conosco* > *conozgo*.

509. "Raza del sol." *HR* 10 (1942): 64–66.

The derivation of *raza del sol* is Port. *restea (del sol)* (= 'reed rope' > 'bar of sunlight') and Port. *raça (del sol)* (= 'aperture'), probably blended as the result of contamination of two firmly established Port. words *reste* + *raça*, not Lat. *restia* + *raça* as suggested by others.

510. "Port. *rilhar* 'to gnaw.'" *HR* 10 (1942): 344–45.

Spitzer rejects the etymology **rictulare* > *rilhar* in favor of **ringulare* > *rilhar.*

511. "Two Notes: 1. Port. *estâmago*. 2. Justification." *Lg* 19 (1943): 258–61.

(1) Port. *estâmago*. This well-documented variant of *estómago* accounts for the disputed spelling *estâmago* in Dom Duarte's *Leal Conselheiro*. The vocalic assimilation involved is traced to an assimilation in atonic syllables, *o - a - á* > *a - a - a*, which first took place in the verb form. The uncertainty of the stress in cases like *ámago, amàgo* is the origin of an *estómago* > *estámago* pronunciation. (2) Justification. Spitzer takes issue with an "antimentalistic" critic, R. A. Hall, Jr., and briefly reiterates with illustrations the view that "syntax and lexicology are more diaphanous to the human mind . . . [than] phonology."

512. "Portuguese *iguaria*." *Lg* 21 (1945): 160–62.

Proposes a derivation from OPort. *iguar* 'to make equal' < Lat. *aequare* formed with the aid of the existing Port. suffix *-aria*.

513. "*Lerdo* 'pesado, torpe en el andar,' (*bestias*) 'a tardo y torpe para comprender.'" *RFH* 7 (1945): 43–44.

Lerdo and *ledro* are the same word, both reflecting a fundamental consonantal instability. Spitzer posits **leldo* (< *lleldo*) > *lerdo* whose meaning descends ultimately from 'leavened bread, inflated.'

514. "*Enaziado, anaciado*." *RFH* 7 (1945): 160–62.

Enaziado, a synonym for *tornadizo* in the *Diccionario de autoridades: Diccionario de la lengua castellana* (Madrid: Hierro, 1726–39), is traced to an **ad-(in)-nati-atus* from the Lat. nominative *natio*.

515. "Etimológias hispánicas." *BICC* 2 (1946): 1–11.

Artesón is a loan word from MFr. *artuison* (14th c.), *artuson* (15th c.), derived from the adjective *artisonné* 'worked by the artisan'; *barahunda* is a composite, paralleling *barahuste* (< *vara-fuste*), *bara-hunda* (imperative + substantive) < **vara-hunda* (= 'lance-fronde'); *çeñiglo* (*Libro de buen amor*, st. 1008) is a semilearned form of *signaculum*, and *vestiglo*, like it, is a relatinization; in Catal. *migrarse*, the *-g-* is a secondary development of a *-u-* and points toward a radical **muir-* borrowed from OFr. *mièvre*.

516. "Portuguese *iguaria*, Judeo-Spanish *yegueria* Again." *Lg* 22 (1946): 358–59.

Rejects Y. Malkiel's etymon, LLat. *iecuaria* (= 'giblets'), maintaining that JudeoSp. *yeguaria, yegueria* (= 'a portion of food presented to a guest') is supported by his own etymology **aegu-aria* (= 'equal, [just] portion'), a derivative of *aequare*.

517. "Anc. prov. *aib*—anc. esp. *aleve*." *MLN* 61 (1946): 419–23.

Affirms Blondheim's thesis regarding an Ar. etymon for OProv. *aib* (= 'quality, customs') by showing that Sp. *alevoso, aleve* (= 'perfidious') and OSp. *aleve* (= 'betrayal') mean *al 'aib* and are parallel to OProv. *aiba* and Port. *eiva*. (A la mémoire de David S. Blondheim.)

518. "Salmantino *en íteles* y *véntiles*." *RFH* 8 (1946): 130–32.

Spitzer returns to his earlier discussion of this expression, for which he had suggested the Lat. *iter* (= 'road') as primary etymon, deformed by popular etymology. Here he points out that *item* (= 'again'), *interim, ínterin* may have lost the *-m*, which was replaced falsely through hypercorrection with an *-l*. In a phrase such as **en varios íteles se la ha ido toda la mañana*, common understanding perceived the notion of *ir*. Parallel examples are cited to support the popular derivation, *véntiles*.

519. "*Desmazalado; lerdo*." *NRFH* 1 (1947): 78–80.

(1) Classical Sp. *desmazalado* (= 'flojo') < Gall. Port. *desmazalado* and must be completely dissociated from JudeoSp. *desmazalado* (= 'disgraced') < Heb. *masal*. (2) *Lerdo* is not a postverbal adjective derived from *enlerdar* (attested, 1513). Much more probably *enlerdar* derives from *lerdo*, given (a) the scarcity of forms based on Lat. *-itare* in Romance languages in general, and (b) other postverbal adjectives in Sp. that show a different development, such as *manso, cuerdo*.

520. "*Rato*." *NRFH* 1 (1947): 177–78.

From the juridical Lat. *(pro) rata*, the masculine form in Sp., *rato*, may be explained by analogy with *tiempo*: **(por)rata de tiempo* > *(por)rato de tiempo*.

521. "Span. *mi oíslo* 'meine Frau.'" *RF* 61 (1948): 21–31.

A discussion of R. Marín's findings concerning 16th-c. Sp. usage of *oís* for 'wife,' and *oíslo?* or *!oíslo¡* for 'hörst du wohl?,' 'höre' (J. Gillet, *MLR* 25 [1940]: 60). Spitzer draws a parallel with Yid. *ziherstu* and NHG *hörst du zu* (= 'wife, spouse').

522. "On a Recent Criticism of Meyer-Lübke." *Lg* 26 (1950): 284–85.

Contests Malkiel's corrections of *REW* explanations for Port. *fechar* and Eastern Leonese *sojao.*

523. "Portugues *teima*, Castelhano *tema*, 'obstinacion.'" *RP* 15 (1950): 119–21.

Lat. *thema* > **theuma*, OFr. *t(i)eume*, Port. **teuma*. In Port. *-ei-* is a variant of *-eu-*, cf. *reima*, *reuma.*

524. "*Cobarde.*" *Estudios Hispánicos: Homenaje a Archer M. Huntington*. Wellesley: Wellesley College, 1952. 571–74.

Contrary to Gillet's theory (*NRFH* 3 [1949]: 377) that *couard* < *caudatus* 'con cola (= '*membrum virile*') truncado, impotente,' Spitzer proposes the addition of the augmentative pejorative suffix *-ard* to *coué* (= '*excaudatus*'), = 'cowardly rabbit.' *Couard*, *cobarde*, *coward* all refer to the rabbit who habitually (hypocritically) raises his tail as he flees and whose behavior has subsequently been used to represent cowardly acts.

525. "Nachtrag zu *mi oíslo* 'meine Frau' (*RF* 61, 21)." *RF* 66 (1954): 167–68.

Spitzer discusses new material brought to his attention by K. Lieberman in the newspaper *Yidishe Shprach* (Yivo 14 [1945]: 24), concerning the relationship between the Sp. *(mi) oíslo* and the Yid. *mein(e) Hörst-du-zu*. He traces the use of *horchstu* (= *horchst du?*) for husband and wife in Yid. in 19th-c. Russia. More important is the 15th-c. *Sefer Maharil*, in which the expression *mayn houz frou* is used instead of "my wife" and *hort ir nit* is used in place of the wife's name to call her. Spitzer reiterates his belief that the Yid. and Sp. use of these expressions in place of proper names resulted from polygenesis.

526. "Español *alrededor*." *Rom* 75 (1954): 245–49.

A return to an earlier analysis, with additional commentary: **de retriore (loco)* is parallel to *(in)aliore loco* > OFr. *ailleurs*, OProv. *alhor(s)*, following the explanation given by Rudolf Haberl and Gamillscheg. In response to Coromines and others, Spitzer reconsiders the term's grammatical and semantic development.

527. "Le sémantisme de l'a. esp. *redor* 'derrière' < 'autour.'" *Rom* 76 (1955): 108–12.

Riere in Swiss-Romansh (= orig., 'under the jurisdiction of, in someone's power') gradually evolved from the moral and expressive sense of protection to the meaning 'behind.' This is a retraction of the earlier explanation.

528. "*Yasi juro por la intemerata eficacia*." *QIA* 2 (1956): 483–84.

This is one section of a three-part oath found in Cervantes's short story "Celoso extremeño." *Intemerata* is an adjective, a traditional Marial epithet meaning 'immaculate' and here 'the efficacity of grace.'

529. "Español *tertulia*." *Omagiu lui Iorgu Iordan cu Prilejul Implinriri a 70 de Ani*. Bucaresti: Academici Republicii Populare Romune, 1958. 819–20.

Tertulia < *tractatorium* (= 'a meeting place [for discussion or conversation]'): **tractorium* > **tractolium* > **trechera* > **terturia* by analogy with *centuria*, *decuria.*

530. "Adición a *Filología*, II, págs. 80 y sigs." *Fil* 2 (1960): 343.

Notes two Lat. terms used by Gracián and points out their etymologies, absent in the article by Delfín L. Garasa.

Miscellany

531. "Miszellen." *ANS* 127 (1911): 153-61.

(1) Prov. *espérir* (= 'to waken'). Either *esperir* < *espert* (similar to *ouvrir* < *ouvert*) or < **experire*. (2) Prov. *escoill* (= 'manner'). If *escoill* < **scholium*, then the etymology includes either Fr. *escole* or a postverbal form of *escolhir*. (3) Prov. *veiaire, viaire* (= 'face, opinion') < OFr. *aviaire* < **avitarium* < **a(l)birarium* < Lat. *arbitrarium*. The *a-* in *aviaire* should be understood as a preposition. (4) Fr. *sémillant* < OFr. *semiller, semillens* < **seminicula* = OFr. *semille*, a problematic derivation because *semiller* is infrequently attested. (5) Fr. *s'ébarouir* (= 'to fall to pieces with old age'). Antoine Thomas (*Rom* 38 [1909]: 393) is mistaken to bring *s'ébarouir* together with OFr. *ébalouir*, Fr. *éblouir* since *l* > *r* cannot be justified. Rather *ébarouir* < OFr. *esbarir*. (6) Prov. *daurezi* (= 'goldsmith'). Prov. *daurezi* < **auricipem*, similar to *forcipe* < *forfice*. (7) Viennese *schlamassel* (= 'embarrassment, annoyance'). *Schlamassel* = Yid. *Schlimm Massel* < *Schlimm Masol* (Heb. *masol* = 'evil hour'). *Schlamassel* is the diminutive of *Schlamastik*. (8) Port. *fechar* (= 'to close'). *Fechar* < **fistulare*. Diez's derivation *fechar* < **factare* (= 'to set a date' > 'to close') does not bear out because Lat. *-ct-* > Port. *-it-*. (9) Sardinian *sicu*. *Sicu* < It. *seco* < Lat. *secum* where the *-i-* in *sicu* developed under the influence of *mimi, ti, si*.

532. "Zu Römisch *buggero* 'termine generico come caso, negazio.'" *WS* 6 (1914-15): 205-14.

A discussion of modern slang generic terms in Ger., Fr., It., and Eng., including *dingsda, thingamybob, machin-chose*. Quotes Goethe, Courteline, Guimerá, Daudet, De Roberto, Pous Pagés, and Pin y Soler.

533. "Albanisches." *IF* 39 (1921): 105-13.

(1) Zwei Tiernamen. G. Meyer is wrong: Alb. *hárdeje* (= 'lizard') is not a distortion of *lacerta*. Rather *hárdeje* = **sgord-* (*sg* > *h, rd* > *rd*) as other members of the same word family show. As Meyer-Lübke suggests (*REW*, s.v. **broscus* [= 'frog']), Alb. *bre[cir]ske* < Lat.: one need only assume a fusion of *ruspus* and *bruscum*. (2) Hiatustilgender *v*' im Albanischen? Spitzer agrees with Meyer-Lübke (*Mitteilungen des Rumänischen Instituts an der Universität Wien* 1 [1914]: 26) that Holger Pedersen (*Festskrift til Vilhelm Thomsen*, Kopenhavn: Hegel, 1894, 254; *KZ* 36 [1900]: 315) errs in his explanation of *v-* in Alb. *ve(cir)s* (= 'ear') as a grammatical hiatus. The *v-* < *u-*, and *u-* is the remains of a development of the long diphthong. (3) Ist lat. *e* im Albanischen zu *ie* geworden? N. Jokl's examples (*IF* 36 [1915-16]: 146) of Lat. *e* > Alb. *ie* are defensible.

534. "Aus Anlass von Gamillscheg's 'Französischen Etymologien.'" *ZRP* 42 (1922): 5-34.

Based on detailed criticisms of many of Gamillscheg's French etymologies, Spitzer disputes his positivistic approach to philology. Philology is more of a poetic enterprise – an intuitive creative process – than a matter of logical differentiation.

535. "Vermischtes zur Wortgeschichte." *ZRP* 42 (1922): 207-10.

An etymological and grammatical investigation of Fr. *sémillant* (= 'vivid, restless') and Liégois *sindresse*, an examination of the development and use of Lat. *ut* in contemporary Calabria, and a comparison of Apul. *ku* and Calabr. *mu*.

536. "Zu dieser *Zeitschrift* 49, 95." *ZVS* 50 (1922): 53.

The development of It. *nelle*, Catal. *-em* or *m* = *me*, and Austrian *in* = *n* = *den* from Lat. *-ne*.

537. "Varietà e aneddoti." *A Rom* 7 (1923): 155–64.

(1) It. *nicchiare* (= 'whine, shriek') < **hinnitulare* (= 'neigh'). (2) *Taffiare–pacchiare.* 17th-c. It. *taffiare* (= 'to eat greedily') is a manifestation of the onomatopoeic root *tapp-* (= 'blow'), cf. Ger. *zapfen* (= 'plug, tap'), It. *ziffe zaffe* (= 'series of short cutting sounds'); *pacchiare* (= 'eat greedily') may be derived from Gk. *pachys* (= 'thick'). (3) Port. *ovo chôco* 'bebrütetes Ei.' Port. (*ovo*) *chôco* (= 'incubating [egg]' > 'rotten egg') < Port. *chocar* (= 'brood'), which is in turn of onomatopoeic origin.

538. "Etymologien." *A Rom* 7 (1923): 512–16.

Pistoj. *bùrchio* 'Knäblein'; Pist. *ruciare*; Veron., Venez. *lampido*, Emil. *lampid*, 'rein'; It. *piaggiare* 'schmeichelnd betören.'

539. "Persönliches und Prinzipielles zu Gamillschegs Aufsatz." *ZRP* 43 (1923): 759–66.

A response to Gamillscheg's criticisms of Spitzer's review of Wartburg's work. In general, Gamillscheg's rejection of creative etymologies and etymologies based on onomatopoeia leads to a linguistic analysis that is inadequate to explain language's vitality.

540. "Etymologien." *A Rom* 9 (1925): 70–73.

(1) Prov. *ve(j)aire*, OFr. *viaire* (= 'way of seeing, opinion, appearance'). Defending his own etymology of Prov. *vejaire* against Carl Appel's criticism, Spitzer proposes *vide* + *-ariu* (> *-aire*) > *vejaire*, OFr. *viaire*. The coinage reflects a common tendency: popular stem + learned suffix. (2) Fr. *pouillé*. That *REW* ignores the Lat. derivation for *pouillé* proposed by Diez, inter alia, confirms the importance of linguists' analyzing indigenous roots before seeking further afield.

541. "Discussioni." *A Rom* 10 (1926): 291–94.

(1) *Violin*. The family *viola, viulu* presents certain problems, such as its relationship to Ger. *Fiedel*. One thing is certain: it originates in Provence, where there are a great many onomatopoeic words that have a terminal *-l*. *Viula* is an instrument that makes a *vi(u)* just as a *piulet* is an instrument that makes a *piu*. (2) *Rat*. Rats are relatively new animals in Europe, so it is surprising that they bear similar names in most Indo-European languages. Perhaps the same onomatopoeic force behind Eng. *rattle*, Ger. *rasseln*, and Prov. *rit* is behind the word for these animals. The rat is thus an animal that goes *rat-rat*.

542. "Ein neues 'Französisches Etymologisches Wörterbuch.'" *ZRP* 46 (1926): 563–77.

A damning critique of Gamillscheg's *Französisches Etymologisches Wörterbuch* (Heidelberg: Winter, 1926). A detailed dispute of items *b* through *e* follows a discussion of methodology. Gamillscheg has created a "word cemetery," because he has an unrealistic view of language development that consists of mechanical leaps, translations, inversions, and amputations. The study fails above all because it is built on outmoded conceptions of language, since Gamillscheg is concerned primarily with identifying sources instead of tracing developments.

543. "Etymologien." *A Rom* 11 (1927): 94–97.

(1) As noted in *REW* 7937, Lat. **sinefidicus* is not the root of OFr. *sen(z)fege*. Rather, *senzfege* < OFr. *sanc-fegié*. (2) Otranto *spara* < *parare*. (3) Fr. *garenne* < Fr. *garant* and OFr. *garanne, garande*, ultimately from OFr. *garir*. (4) All previous sug-

gestions regarding the etymology of Gallo-Roman **impeltare* (= 'to plug, graft') are unsatisfactory. The simple explanation is Lat. *pelta*.

544. "Etymologien." *A Rom* 11 (1927): 245–50.

(1) Fr. *frapper*. *Frapper* has an onomatopoeic explanation similar to Fr. *flap!* and Alb. *frap!*. (2) It. *cesso* (= 'abort'). There is no reason to derive *cesso* (= 'lavatory') from Lat. *cessus*, much less from *recessus*, *secessus*, when *cesso* derives from It. *cessare*. (3) It. *far greppo*. A brief discussion of the psychology of *far greppo* (= 'to distort the face by crying'). (4) Comelico. **kumpissó* (= 'worthless, miserable'). The meaning of the participle *kompisséda* is compared to Fr. slang *en pisser*, *en faire pisser*, and Ger. *beschissen* (= vulg., 'to be in a miserable situation'). (5) Lucca. *sconiato*. Contrary to Salvioni (*AGI* 16 [1923]: 468), Spitzer shows that *sconiato* (= 'killjoy') is the opposite of *uomo di conia*, whereas Flor. *conia* = 'fun.' He discusses the sexual meaning of *conia* and its similarity to SFr. *quoniam*, *conian* (= 'imbecile') and Catal. *coniam* (= 'fool, fop'). (6) It. *smargiasso*. Although the suffix indicates a South Tirolean origin, the etymology of It. *smargiasso* 'braggart' has yet to be found.

545. "Zu dem Wandel *Augenbraue* > *Rand, Furche, Gipfel*." *ZVS* 55 (1927–28): 23.

Discusses Rom. *genune*, It. *girone*, and Lat. *gena* > *Augenlied* > **Abhang* > *Abgrund*.

546. "Etymologien." *A Rom* 12 (1928): 159–60.

(1) The syntactic development *péter contre la rousse* > *rouspéter* (= Fr. slang, 'grumble before obeying, rebel') is an example of a verb formed from twin imperatives, as in *accusare* and *raccusepéter* (= 'to give notice, to denounce'), where such formations mean a turbulent, riotous activity. (2) According to Gregorio (*ZRP* 47 [1927]: 101), It. *ciurlare* (= 'non star ben saldo, tentennare') < *ci(golare)* + *urlare*, but this is problematic because of the perhaps unanswerable question whether such word combinations led to *-rl-* or whether the different variations (*pirl-*, *birl-*, etc.) first crystallized around the cluster *-rl-*.

547. "Kontamination-Analogie." *ZFS* 51 (1928): 325–37.

A defense against Kalepky's charge that Spitzer is "idealistic" in seeking to explain the reasons for particular phenomena in language change. Using examples from contemporary French novels, Spitzer traces the new formations to each author's "psychological disposition."

548. "Zu Ebelings Artikel 'Zur Bedeutungsentwicklung romanischer Partikeln,' *ZRP* 47, 644ff." *ZRP* 48 (1928): 236–40.

A discussion of the derivations and associated meanings of the following: (1) It. *tanto* (= 'anyway'); (2) Rom. *aşa* (= 'so, also, bravo'); (3) Sp. *ello* (= 'they are'); (4) It. *lo stesso*, Sp. *lo mismo*, Fr. *tout de même*; (5) CanFr. *pareil* (= 'nevertheless').

549. "Notes étymologiques." *RFE* 16 (1929): 148–53.

(1) Eng. *piss-pot* (= 'urinal, doctor [who makes diagnoses through urine samples]') < Port. *bisbote* (= 'urinal') and accounts for Port. *doutor* (= 'urinal'). (2) Catal. *estona* (= 'while, moment') < Catal. *estonarse* (= 'be amazed'). (3) The paradoxical meaning of Ecuadorian *latente* (= 'everything visible') can be understood if one considers that even hidden things must be visible in some way. (4) Sp. *a pasto* (= 'copiously') < *pasto* (= 'grazing,' orig., 'food [for men]'). (5) Sp., Port. *pauta* (= 'guidebook, ruled paper') < *pactum* (= 'pact, rules of a religious order'). (6) Sp. *ronía* (= 'ill will') < *ironía*.

550. "Zum *Sinn* einer Kontaminationsbildung." *ZFS* 52 (1929): 386–88.
A derivation explained by contamination must include the presentation of two linguistic histories that compose the language mix. Additions to a language are not abstract calculations. They are informed by the speaker's spiritual participation.

551. "Notes étymologiques." *RFE* 18 (1931): 235–38.
(1) Andal. *aciguatar* (= 'to watch,' orig., 'to seize') < **ad-secutare* (= 'to pursue [learned]'). (2) Montañ. *aticuenta* (= 'brandy') < *hazte cuenta* (= 'remember'). The anthropomorphized brandy spurs the memory of the drinker. (3) Sp. *enconar* (= 'to fester, to rankle [wound]') < *conari* (= 'to attempt') through the medical term *conationes egestionum* (= 'attempts at vomiting'), since an inflammation is the body's attempt to stop an infection. (4) Prov. *nonoy* (= 'small, weak, delicate') and Catal. *ninoi* (= 'child') both contain a "nursery suffix" *-oi*, produced by the child as an aid to remembering words in a series.

552. "Wortgeschichtliches." *ZRP* 53 (1933): 146–50.
(1) The apparently nonsensical name of a tavern in Brussels, *à la pie boiteuse* (= 'to the limping magpie'), may have resulted from a confusion of *boit* (= 'he drinks') < *boire* and *boite* (= 'he limps') < *boiter*. Another explanation: *pie* also = 'dapple-gray horse,' an animal whose limping is more likely to be noticed. (2) The final *-t* of the Fr. maritime exclamation *à Dieu vat* (= 'the ship [is in danger]') is the remains of an elided *tout*. (3) Catal. *arraulirse* (= 'to gather oneself together against cold, become shy') < **glirulus* (= 'dormouse [a hibernating animal]'). (4) Catal., Sp. *calabriar* (= 'to adulterate wine') is most likely derived from *Calabria*, the geographical region, because the inhabitants of the area were considered false.

553. "Wortgeschichtliches." *ZRP* 53 (1933): 287–303.
(1) Port. *caloiro* (= 'young student, fox') belongs to the same family as Tras-os-Montes *caloira* (= 'laziness'), Port. *caloiro* (= 'novice'), *calaça* (= 'laziness,' orig., 'pork ribs'), *caluga* (= 'pig's neck') < *collum* (= 'neck,' *REW*). (2) OFr. *creature* (= 'someone, no one') was also used for 'something, nothing,' since man is not alone among things that have been created. *Rien* and *chose*, used in reference to persons, indicate that the person is viewed as part of the hierarchy of things (usu. the highest level). Secularization accounts for the demise of *creature* in the latter usage. (3) Catal. *esglahó* (= 'step, stair, rung [of ladder]') < *esgrahó* (<*gradus*) X *escala* (= 'step'). (4) Lorraine *déplancié* (= 'loosely dressed, in disorder') < **palanca* (*REW* 6455, no. 2). (5) It. *fante* (= 'footsoldier') < *infante* (= 'young child'). (6) Sp. *goldre*, Port. *coldre* (= 'quiver') < *colorare* (= 'to give color to, to color reddish or brownish'), which was used in reference to leathermaking, cf. Fr. *coudrer* (= 'to color leather'), Sp. *cordovàn goldrado* (= 'colored leather'). (7) Alav. *golorito* (= 'goldfinch') < *color* (= 'color'). (8) Dialectal Port. *lapouça* (= 'young rabbit') < *lap-* (= 'burrow'). The suffix is common in place names referring to geological formations.

554. "Petite rectification à l'article de M. Pfandl, 'La palabra española *romance*.' " *Investigaciones Lingüísticas, México* 3 (1935): 203–07.
Is *Romance* or *Románica* the correct term in Fr., Sp., and Ger. to indicate "Romance languages"? The current usage is "Romance," one more example of how technical terms like this one change over time.

555. "Aprov. *romeu*, ital. *romeo*, afrz. *romier* 'Pilger.' " *ZRP* 56 (1936): 644–45.
These words derive from Gk. *romaios* (= 'Roman'), in reference to the Eastern pilgrim to Rome.

556. "Encore sur le mot *romance.*" *Investigaciones Lingüísticas, México* 4 (1937): 212–13.

In France, the establishment of the term *architecture romane* to describe the indigenous transformation of the *style romain* parallels the use of *langues romanes* for the languages derived from Lat.

557. "Romance **carestia* 'dearth.'" *Lg* 14 (1938): 144–45.

J. Ulrich (*Rom* 8 [1879]: 264) was right in establishing a hypothetical Romance **carestia* < **carestus* < *carere* (= 'lack').

558. "It. *bravo,* All. *Polier,* Fr. *camée,* All. *Schamotte.*" *MLN* 54 (1939): 633–34.

Review of and comment on a series of articles in *Zeitschrift für Indogermanische Sprachwissenschaft* pertaining to these terms.

559. "*Arrenquín.*" *RFH* 7 (1945): 281–82.

The inter-Romance family *arlequin* is studied here, and the semantic changes it undergoes in peninsular speech are noted. The original OFr. form *hernequin* (*Herlequin*) is due to the assimilation of *-l-* to the final *-n* and is derived from Ger. *Herla King* = 'Wotan.'

560. "Yiddisch *(t)schale(n)t* = Französisch *chaud?*" *MLN* 61 (1946): 101–04.

The term is traced to OFr. *eschaloigne* and MFr. forms *echalette* (15th c.) and *echalotte* (= 'shallot,' early 16th c.). NHG *Schalotte,* first in the forms *schelot, schelet,* springs from *echalotte.* Its use as the name of a sabbath meal stems from the fact that one of the meal's main ingredients is onions.

561. "Yakov Malkiel, 'Hypothetical Base in Romance Etymology,' (*Word,* 6/1, 42–73)." *RF* 62 (1950): 227–34.

Etymology has an instrumental value in the observation of language or in cultural or linguistic history, but it is not an end in itself. Spitzer stresses the importance of stylistics in etymology, which Malkiel does not emphasize in his own criteria for the correct use of hypothetical bases. Spitzer speaks in support of the work of previous scholars such as Meyer-Lübke, whose scholarship laid invaluable groundwork for contemporary studies.

562. "*Figl.*" *For Roman Jakobson: Essays on the Occasion of His Sixtieth Birthday.* Ed. M. Halle et al. The Hague: Mouton, 1956. 503.

Czech *figl* and Polish *figiel* derive from Ger. *vögeln.*

Grammar, Morphology, and Syntax

French

563. "Zu frz. *là*." *ZFS* 39 (1912): 107.

A response to T. Kalepky (*Vermischte Beiträge* 3 [n.d.]: 154ff.), who refers to A. Tobler's remarks on the use of *là*. In the latter's view, *là* indicates closure. In contrast, Spitzer sees *là* as an exclamatory particle designed to elicit the listener's attention [in 6].

564. "Über französisch *là*." *ZFS* 39 (1912): 276–78.

Fr. *là* is more rhythmical and expressive than Ger. *da*. Often *là* refers to an ideal place, known only to the speaker, which the listener must discover.

565. "Zur Syntax." *ZRP* 36 (1912): 717–23.

(1) Fr. *pourquoi faire*. Sometimes the phrase *pourquoi faire* actually means 'pour quoi faire' in the OFr. sense of 'pour ce faire.' The It. distinction between *perchè* 'why' and *per chè* 'in order to' sheds light on this problem. (2) *Entre causeurs à voix basse. Causeurs à voix basse* and *l'empêcheur de danser en rond* are two instances showing that *nomina agentia* based on the ending *-ator* survive in Romance languages. (3) *Toujours*. Certain instances of Fr. *toujours* and It. *sempre* mean 'as always' or 'still,' not just 'always.' (4) *La "moi*." In a passage from Maupassant there is an unusual occurrence of a feminine *moi*. In this and other examples, the referent is probably not the ego ('das Ich') but a specifically feminine being.

566. "Zur Stellung des frz. attributiven Adjectivs." *ZFS* 41 (1913): 105–07.

P. Phillipsthal errs when he claims (*ZFS* 40 [1912]: 104) that, when inserted, attributive adjectives in Fr. take on a more general or abstract meaning. The expressive value of these adjectives can only be determined on the basis of case-by-case analysis.

567. "Zu Kalepky's Artikel 'Il fait bon vivre ici.'" *ZFS* 41 (1913): 235–38.

Kalepky (*ZFS* 41 [1913]: 41ff.) is correct that there is a transition from the attributive to the predicative function of the object infinitive in phrases like this one. Spitzer adds examples from It.

568. "Frz. 'allons donc!'" *ANS* 133 (1915): 147–51.

Presents Hermann Soltmann's notion of a toned-down expression of will (*Syn-*

tax der Modi im modernen Französisch, Halle: Niemeyer, 1914), where the speaker chooses the first-person plural to voice his command. By including himself in the command, he softens its harshness. Spitzer offers another term for the same phenomenon, *plurale inclusivus*, where the speaker descends to the level of the person spoken to. This is not exclusively a French convention, as examples from other languages show.

569. "Frz. *plus tôt que plus tard* 'je eher je lieber.'" *ZFS* 43 (1915): 277–79.
Adds a third derivation of this phrase to the two suggested by Tobler.

570. "*Faire* mit dem Infinitiv zur Umschreibung des Verbum Finitum." *ZFS* 43 (1915): 279–85.
Paraphrasing a finite verb with *faire* + inf., for example, *faites-moi escouter* = 'écoutez-moi,' takes the verb function away from the main verb by assigning it to the helping verb. H.-F. Muller's *Origine et histoire de la préposition "à" dans les locutions du type "faire faire quelque chose à quelqu'un"* (Poitiers: Masson, 1912) shows the historical development of the theoretical considerations outlined in this article [in 6].

571. "Zu afrz. *si bele de li* 'so schön wie sie.'" *ZRP* 39 (1917–19): 630.
This construction derives directly from Lat.

572. "Attributive Anreihung von Substantiven im Französischen." *Literaturblatt für Germanische und Romanische Philologie* 39 (1918): 375ff.
A discussion of the psychological and stylistic origins of nouns used as attributive adjectives in modern Fr., for example, *ses yeux couleur de ciel*. Commercial and administrative language, which strives for brevity, and a literary trend toward precise observation and description set the stage for this development. Brief comparison with examples from Eng., It., and Sp. [in 20].

573. "'Une mouche naît à 9 heures du matin pour mourir à 5 heures du soir.'" *GRM* 7 (1915–19): 222–24.
The conflict between a logical analysis of syntax and the speaker's intentions is exemplified in this sentence from Stendhal. The phrase does not signify that the fly is born for the express purpose of dying; rather, it is born under the condition of death. *Pour* provides here a providential nuance similar to Ger. *um zu* (e.g., "er schlief ein, um nicht mehr aufzuwachen"), a usage common among historians [in 20].

574. "Zu *Archiv* 41, 111ff." *ANS* 143 (1922): 106–07.
A passage from *Les croix de bois* (1919) by Dargelès provides a nice example of the ambiguous boundary between the imperative and the future. It also illustrates the difficulty in distinguishing the categorical future from the suggestive future. The optative present is an intensification of the optative future, which suggests that the Ger. optative present is more "tyrannical" (Lerch's word) than the Fr. optative future. The passage shows that the use of the optative future in Fr. is as limited as the use of the future in general.

575. "Zur pronominalen Verwendung von *des* im Frz." *NS* 30 (1922): 169–71.
In Fr., Spitzer distinguishes between a nominalizing *des*, used in locutions that combine elements to form essentially one word, and *des et des*, used to describe an inexpressible amount. The former both individuates and categorizes within a group. In locutions such as "des cartes postales, des en couleur et des en noir," the latter betrays linguistic laziness as well as an avoidance of "morphological calamities" such as *des colorées* [in 20].

576. "Beiträge zur französischen Wortbildungslehre." *ZRP* 43 (1923): 641–56.

(1) Fr. *-ande*, It. *-anda*. These suffixes derive from Lat. gerundives. They still convey a sense of necessity or duty, but this sense is no longer as strong as it once was (*offrande* is no longer 'what should be offered' but 'the offering'). (2) Characteristics of nouns understood as feminine in Fr. Certain things are personified as women: weapons, which are seen as brides of the soldier, and inventions, the products of man's industry. Passive objects of male discovery, creation, and possession are regarded as feminine: plants, continents, business ventures. Collectives are frequently feminine, as are abstractions of qualities viewed as feminine. (3) The use of *-istre* in Fr. A relation might exist between *-astre* and *-istre* in OFr. but only when the two suffixes have corresponding meanings. Fr. *-âtre* does in fact often mean 'approximately' and has a deprecatory connotation, as do many words ending in *-itre*. That this is not a general rule, however, means that more than one etymon is involved.

577. "Frz. 'par exemple'–'peut-être'–'déjà.'" *GRM* 12 (1924): 50–56.

Many examples of these locutions' interchangeability and a comparison with the use of *déjà* for *peut-être* in the negative sense [in 20].

578. "Frz. *Il ne faut pas que tu meures*, 'du darfst nicht sterben.'" *GRM* 15 (1927): 69–73.

Tobler (*Vermischte Beiträge* 1 [n.d.]: 29) regards *il faut que tu ne meures pas* as more logical than *il ne faut pas que tu meures*. Lerch agrees (*Historische Französische Syntax* 1 [1925]: 274). The problem is that Tobler holds language to a logical ideal that, in the case of compound negative expressions, depends on the distinction between contradictory and contrary expressions. With certain verbs, this distinction collapses. It makes no difference which verb in the combination carries the negative. *Il ne faut pas que . . .* is no less logical than the other, but it has a different effect. This tendency to use the contradictory mode is analyzed from a psychological point of view [in 20].

579. "Spreizstellung bei präpositionalen Ausdrücken im Französischen." *IF* 45 (1927): 196–206.

In French prose since impressionism, prepositions are sometimes separated from the nouns they govern: "avec sur la figure grave un bon et doux sourir." This construction occurs most frequently with the prepositions *avec* and *sans*. The splitting of prepositional phrases sometimes takes place in colloquial language, where it is the result of sudden afterthoughts and unanticipated digressions. This way of speaking is surprisingly appropriate for modern thought: first, because it has a nervous feel to it that is in keeping with the modern mood; second, because it is synthetic and refuses to divide an idea simply for the purpose of clarity [in 20].

580. "Französische Tempuskontamination." *ZFS* 50 (1927): 148–53.

In response to several scholars (Kalepky, Tobler, H. Yvon), Spitzer shows how the future perfect is used to particular effect. It extends an action into the future where it can be viewed retrospectively. Such a grammatical maneuver allows for a prophetic or determinate tone, which can be found in some historical writing. Napoleon used this ploy when speaking to his troops.

581. "Frz. 'jeunes gens' Plural von 'jeune homme.'" *GRM* 16 (1928): 244–48.

Compares the plurals for *young man* and *young girl* in Ger., Fr., and Eng.

582. "Nachtrag zu 'jeunes gens.'" *GRM* 17 (1929): 316.
The Russ. equivalent for the Fr. shows the same construction.

583. "Frz. *i-* in *ici*." *ZFS* 52 (1929): 385–86.
Spitzer summarizes H. Kjellman's thesis on *i-* from Fr. *icest, icel*. He notes that he has published the same ideas and questions the plausibility of Kjellman's interpretation of *ihrec* as the result of a threefold "contamination."

584. "Frz. *vrombir*." *ZRP* 49 (1929): 708–09.
Fr. *vrombir* 'roar (of motor)' fits Schuchardt's phonetic formula for onomatopoeias of heavy, hollow sounds: plosive + *r* + *o/u* + *n/m* (+ *t, d/b*).

585. "Zum Problem des franz. Argot." *NMo* 1 (1930): 205–16.
Argot springs from daily speech; written down, it is immediately obsolete. This is true of street language everywhere; it cannot be captured or controlled [in 22].

586. "Frz. *aujourd'hui*." *ZRP* 50 (1930): 336–41.
Fr. *aujourd'hui* exemplifies two seemingly contradictory tendencies: (a) the morpheme for *day* in words meaning 'today' often becomes unrecognizable (*hui* < *hodie* < *hoc die*); (b) where (a) occurs, there is a tendency to restore the element meaning 'day.' The tendencies correspond to normal and emphatic usage. In normal discourse, all that is needed is a unified word for a certain span of time; in emphatic contexts, the word *day* is needed to highlight *today* as a distinct member of a series of days [in 22].

587. "Zum französischen historischen Infinitiv." *ZRP* 50 (1930): 533–47.
The infinitive differs from the finite verb in that it is less connected to reality: in signaling neither person nor tense it produces only an affective impression of action conceived as separate from reality. The historical infinitive introduced by *de* (e.g., "Et l'homme de répondre avec modestie . . . ") has an effect midway between the pure infinitive and the finite verb: the action is connected to reality by means of *de*, which, because of its causal-rational grammatical character, refers obliquely to a presupposed situation.

588. "Warum ersetzt frz. *-erie* (dtsch. *-erei*) das alte *-ie* (*-ei*)?" *ZRP* 51 (1931): 70–75.
The triumph of the Fr. abstract suffix *-erie* over *-ie*, the reflex of GrecoLat. *-ia*, is attributable to the richer semantic overtones of the former. While *-ie* is purely abstract, *-erie* is more concrete and person-oriented since it seems to be a combination of the agentive suffix *-arius* and the abstract *-ia*. Thus, while OFr. *diablie* suggests only devilishness, modern Fr. *diablerie* conjures up an image of a group of devils going about their work. The distribution of the corresponding suffixes in Ger. also obeys this criterion.

589. "*Mon vieux*." *NS* 40 (1932): 337–44.
This term of affection can be condescending; the use of the possessive pronoun puts distance between the speaker and subject. The discussion includes comparison with similar locutions in other languages, for example, *old chap, altes Haus*.

590. "A propos de *vache type*." *FM* 2 (1934): 161–62.
The semantic ambivalence of *vache type* 'wonderful fellow' and *type vache* 'disagreeable fellow' originates in the actual ambivalence of human emotions. It illustrates the syntactic principle whereby in Fr. preposed adjectives are figurative and often appreciative, while postposed adjectives are to be taken literally.

591. "Le rappel chez M. Céline." *FM* 3 (1935): 193–208.
Céline's novel *Voyage au bout de la nuit* contains numerous examples of the popular tendency to use pronouns in the first part of a sentence, antecedents in the second. The structure of such sentences is exclamatory-explanatory: "Elle travaillait dans l'éternel, ma belle." "Il était venu de Yougoslavie, ce brebis." (Rpt. in *Louis-Ferdinand Céline* 2, *l'Herne* 5 [1965]: 153–64.)

592. "B. Migliorini, 'Appunti sulla lingua contemporanea: Il suffiso *-istico*,' *Cultura* 10, 976–84." *FM* 3 (1935): 281–82.
A comment on the difference between *-iste* and *-istique* in Fr.

593. "Nfrz. *avec ça (que)* 'als ob.'" *ZFS* 59 (1935): 335–38.
Spitzer cites articles by K. Nyrop, Lerch, and Kalepky regarding ironic and nonironic uses of modern Fr. *avec ça (que)* (= 'as if'). His discussion centers on the ironic use of this locution in Maupassant, "avec ça qu'elles s'en privent, les honnêtes femmes," and focuses on the way it is used to present a central issue as merely peripheral. An obvious truth is "pushed into a corner" from which it must be retrieved by the reader. Underlying this kind of irony is the belief that, though treated in this fashion, truth will always shine through. Spitzer briefly compares *avec ça (que)* with *plus souvent*.

594. "Au sujet de la répétition distinctive." *FM* 4 (1936): 129–35.
Repetition of words in Fr., for example, "Ce n'est pas le béret-béret" 'It's not a real beret,' represents one way of combating the vagueness with which words are sometimes used. The noun is repeated, but the second member fulfills the role of an adjective, denoting the essence of the noun.

595. "*Depuis . . . que*." *ZRP* 56 (1936): 79–82.
Depuis . . . que can have either a temporal or a causal meaning, like *since* in English. The phrase probably developed its causal meaning because speakers and orators appreciated its compact power: "Depuis dix années qu'elle ne l'avait revu, elle chercha avec une sorte d'inquiétude . . . " gives strong emotional emphasis to the ten years during which she had not seen him.

596. "Syntaxe et sémantique: 'Elle en mange qu' c'en est dégoutant.'" *FM* 5 (1937): 13–15.
The second occurrence of *en* in this phrase denotes a resultant condition, suggesting the idea of becoming.

597. "Le suffixe 'gadzarique' *-s*." *FM* 5 (1937): 121–26.
In the argot of a certain lycée, it is common practice to add a semantically null *-s* to abbreviated nouns, for example, *professeur* > *profs*, *fromage* > *froms*. This is due to mock imitation of Lat. nominatives ending in -[s], such as *rex*, *dux*, *plebs*, *ops*, *fax*.

598. "Encore une fois . . . 'Elle en mange qu' c'en est dégoutant.'" *RR* 28 (1937): 268–72.
Robert le Bidois (*RR* 28 [1937]: 157–63) claims that in the phrase in question the element of vulgarity rests completely in the word *que*. In fact the causal *en* also contributes to this nuance because it is unexpected; that is, its antecedent would not normally be represented by *en*.

599. "Remarques sur *personne*, *aucun*, *rien*, *jamais*." *FM* 6 (1938): 51–55.
Although these words are used principally for negation in modern Fr., their

etyma are positive in thrust (*personne* < *persona*, *aucun* < *aliquunus, *rien* < *rem*, *jamais* < *iam magis*). This explains their occasional use as positive negatives: Fr. "Il parle le français mieux que personne," like Eng. "He speaks French better than anyone," suggests that one could perhaps, but only with difficulty, find someone who can speak Fr. better.

600. "P. Falk, *'Se Jhesu en bonne le met* ou la mise en point d'une définition,' *Studia Neophilologica* 10 (1937), 54-61." *FM* 6 (1938): 280–82.

Tobler had thought that *bonne* here was a feminine neuter, but Falk shows that it actually refers to "semaine." Falk had the example right, but the neuter feminine phenomenon is real, both in Fr. and other Romance languages.

601. "Frz. *des et des*." *NS* 36 (1938): 612–13.

A comparison between this locution and *les et les*, with quotations from Flaubert and others.

602. "*Faire une scarlatine (une typhoïde)*." *RR* 29 (1938): 170–72.

Physicians often prefer phrases of the form "faire une scarlatine (typhoïde)" to the more popular "avoir la scarlatine." The grammatical differences reflect a difference in attitude toward the illness. For the ordinary person, an illness is a particular demon (definite article) that possesses its victim (*avoir*). For the physician, each case is just another occurrence (indefinite article) of a physiological process (*faire*).

603. "A. François 'Suffixe littéraire *-ance*' (*VRo* 4, 20–34)." *FM* 7 (1939): 276–78.

The learned suffix *-ance*, which forms nominal abstract from present participles, has the effect of suggesting the prolongation of a brief and ephemeral act, for example, *souvenance*, *repentance*, *attirance*.

604. "'Il a de l'argent plein la poche.'" *FM* 7 (1939): 329–34.

In expressions such as "Il a de l'argent plein la poche" and "gagner sa cause haut la tête," there is no adjective agreement, because the apparent adjectives are actually adverbial holdovers from Lat. *plene, *alte, and so on.

605. "'Fermez donc votre porte.'" *RR* 30 (1939): 63–68.

In this phrase the possessive pronoun fulfills a polemical function, that is, it expresses the anger of "Fermez donc la porte, vous!" without the latter's degree of directness. This usage is also found in Eng. and Port.

606. "Français pop. 'question de,' 'comme' = 'en fait de.'" *FM* 8 (1940): 19–26.

The popular use of *question de* with the meaning 'en ce qui concerne,' 'quant à' (e.g., "Question de femmes, d'abord, il était terrible mon père") originated in scholastic milieux, where the single *question* is isolated from the many that pertain to a particular problem. The omission of the definite article, characteristic of lists in Fr., indicates this specificity to the hearer. When *comme* is used in this same acceptation (e.g., "Comme érudition, Lanson n'a pas de rival"), its effect is to make a general statement seem more relativistic, since only a single characteristic is named.

607. "Il a de l'argent plein la poche (P.S.)." *FM* 8 (1940): 117–19.

An expansion on a detail in the previous article (*FM* 7 [1939]: 329–34) regarding abstract expression such as "n'avoir pas un sou vaillant," where *vaillant* is the substantivized present participle of *valoir*. Such a derivation is admissible in Fr., so there is no need to go back to Lat. neuter *valens*, as does S. Lyer (*ZFS* 58 [1934]: 27).

608. "*Vous* et *nous* régimes atones de *on*." *FM* 8 (1940): 323-43.

The lack of an oblique counterpart of *on* in Fr. led Tobler to suppose that *vous* and *nous* fulfill this function (e.g., in "Et ne se sent-on pas certains mouvements doux, quand on vient à songer que cela sort de vous?"). For semantic reasons, it is necessary to conclude rather that there simply does not exist an oblique counterpart of *on* and that the oblique counterpart of *vous* or *nous* must be used instead, with a consequent change in meaning from general and impersonal to intimate.

609. "J. Jeanjaquet, 'Formules archaïques de négation renforcée dans les patois suisse romands,' *Mélanges Duraffour*, 59–79." *FM* 8 (1940): 374–77.

The use of *diable* in an expression such as "diable l'oiseau que j'ai vu" 'je n'ai vu aucun oiseau' reflects merely the speaker's desire to curse. Feeling frustrated at being unable to find a certain thing or person, the speaker suggests that the devil has taken it.

610. "'Le manque d'argent qui se fait rare.'" *MLN* 55 (1940): 332–38.

The phrase "le manque d'argent qui se fait de plus en plus rare" illustrates the common tendency to try to reinforce an inherently negative word with a negation. This produces a logical meaning that is contradictory to the one intended. The phenomenon occurs in many languages and is due to the logical difficulty of negation, imperfect understanding of learned words, and etymological opacity.

611. "*Aujourd'hui* et *jour*." *SP* 37 (1940): 565–84. (This article is an expansion of the information in *ZRP* 50 [1930]: 336–41.)

The triumph of *aujourd'hui* 'today' over OFr. *hui* 'today' (< *hodie* 'today' < *hoc die* 'this day') is due to several forces: (1) the need for an etymologically transparent word meaning 'day' in terms used in series (e.g., *le jour d'hier*, *le jour d'hui*, etc.); (2) the imprecision of *hui*, which sometimes meant 'nowadays'; (3) the need for a precise term for juridical use (a use more preponderant in northern France than elsewhere in Romania). As for the victory of *jour* over *di* in OFr., it can be attributed to an opposite tendency, the preference for an expressive term (*jour* < *diurnu* 'time of light') over a petrified, official one (e.g., *lundi*, *tandis que*) [in 22].

612. "*Comme quoi*." *MLN* 59 (1944): 454–60.

Like *comme c(el)a*, *comme quoi* is a popular expression substituting for the more synthetic *comment* (= 'ainsi'). This tendency accords with the general development of modern Fr. The original psychological nuance of astonishment survives in contemporary usage, where *comme quoi* is grammatically equivalent to *que*.

613. "La particule *mon*." *PMLA* 61 (1946): 605–19.

The OFr. term, attested as late as the classical period in France and conserved in some modern Fr. patois, is traced to a first-person present form of a Gallo-Roman derivative of *monere*. Abundant examples of semantic and syntactic parallels are included.

614. "Suffixes masculins dans les prénoms féminins en français." *RR* 37 (1946): 127–49.

A history and morphology of feminine names ending in the masculine suffixes *-on*, *-ot*, and *-in* with comparative reference to Ger., It., and Sp. Spitzer attributes particular developments to the psychological basis of certain linguistic phenomena, but stresses that the modern French-speaking community considers these developments as irrational events, which it has refined.

615. "Le genre de 'la Nouvelle-Orléans.' " *MLN* 65 (1951): 571–72.

"La Nouvelle-Orléans" reflects the influence of popular speech, which the Abbé Prévost tried to attenuate with "le Nouvel-Orléans." The confusion is attributed to the uncertainty of gender of Fr. nouns beginning with vowels and the influence of feminine *ville* on the gender of cities.

616. "La particella 'si' davanti all 'aggettivo nel romanzo stendaliano *Armance*." *SFr* 3 (1959): 199–213.

A discussion of L. Maranini's study "Monologo interiore e movimenti stilistici nel primo romanzo di Stendhal" (*Letterature Moderne* 7 [1958]: 42–61), addressing the use of *si*. A refutation of Maranini's thesis—that *si* preceding an adjective is used especially to indicate a psychological tension in the characters—is based on an analysis of the general use and meaning of *si*: it is most often used to solicit the interlocutor's agreement with the speaker. Additional examples are cited and compared.

German

617. "Wucherndes *und* im Schlesischen." *GRM* 8 (1920): 369–72.

There are several unconventional Silesian uses of *und*: (1) a single action is divided into two verbs joined by *und*; (2) a proleptic use of *und* effects a tonal emphasis on the second part of a compound sentence by dropping the verb from the first, for example, "Gelt, dass Euch d'r Jäger und kriegt Euch so pack'n"; (3) there are similarities between these usages and forms common in MHG.

618. "Als er das hörte, war er überrascht." *GRM* 15 (1927): 152–54.

In common speech "ich bin überrascht" is preferable to "es überrascht mich." The former expresses a lasting condition, while the latter is a more direct expression of fleeting emotion. Likewise, one cannot say "er wurde überrascht," because "wurde" only indicates a passing condition.

619. "MHD *ein* in auffälliger Verwendung (mit romanischen Parallelen)." Für Ernst Gamillscheg zum 70. Geburtstag. *NM* 67 (1956): 285–315.

A discussion of the use of the definite article follows three basic constructions in which popular usage parallels obsolete legal usage: (1) instances in which no comparison with *ein* and the definite article comes into question; (2) instances in which definite and indefinite articles are placed together because two thoughts or ideas are being considered; (3) instances in which the older language makes use of the indefinite article, whereas the modern uses the definite article. Includes comparison with similar usage in the Romance languages.

Italian

620. "Italienische und portugiesische Parallelen zu verschiedenen Gebrauchsweisen von frz. *là*." *ZFS* 40 (1912–13): 230–36.

Drawing examples from D'Annunzio's work to illustrate the rhythmical and expressive effects of *là* in It. (as in Fr.), Spitzer shows how stylistic effects are achieved through the use of particular expressions. He compares examples in Port.

621. "Zur romanischen Syntax." *ZRP* 36 (1912): 679–704.

(1) "Er hat es ja getan!" und verwandte Redensarten. An examination of the different uses of It. *sì* and *no*: *ora sì, ora no* used to describe something that might or might not work; *sì e no* 'almost, possible'; *sì o no*; *egli sì che l'ha fatto* 'yes, he did it, indeed.' *Sì* is also used in a valid statement or in connection with a polite title. *Sì che, no che* is a related expression. The different uses of OPort. *não que* are also included. (2) *Pazienza*. A study contrasting the semantic trajectory of *pazienza* in classical, Christian, and modern usage [in 6].

622. "Zur Syntax des italienischen Possessivpronomens." *ZRP* 37 (1913): 221–25.

In It., the possessive pronoun is occasionally used in apposition to the noun to which it refers, for example, "Ma che furia è la vostra!" Such constructions, which place added emphasis on the possessive element, are impossible in Ger., where the idea of possession is either excluded, made attributive, or realized as a personal pronoun [in 6].

623. "Umbr. *nuo matre*–deutsch *mutter (seelen) allein*–frz. *Dieu possible*." *ZRP* 39 (1917–19): 630–35.

Nuo matre (It. *nudo madre* < *nudo come mi fece la madre*) parallels Ger. *mutternackt* < *nackt wie aus der Mutter* 'naked as a newborn babe' and Ger. *mutterallein, seelenallein* 'utterly alone.' The expressions' brevity creates a suggestive syntactic relation by combining the two meanings. Fr. *Dieu possible* conjoins the concepts of the wonder of God and the gift of God. This is a profane expression similar to Fr. *Dieu merci* 'God's mercy' > 'Thank God!' [in 20].

624. "Über Personenvertauschung in der Ammensprache." *GRM* 10 (1922): 247–48.

Spitzer examines a syntactical peculiarity of Abruzzese described by Meyer-Lübke (*Literaturblatt für Germanische und Romanische Philologie* 15 [1894]: 236). When the mother calls her son, she says *mammasé* 'his mother' instead of 'my son.' In this locution the third-person pronoun is used instead of the pronoun appropriate to the person spoken to. Apparently this derives from nursery language; its use indicates an anticipation of what the child would say. This is adult "baby talk" [in 20].

625. "Nochmals 'Personenvertauschung in der Ammensprache.'" *GRM* 12 (1924): 247–51.

Unlike the person-reversal of nursery language, where the adult speaker anticipates what the child would say, examples found in CanFr. represent true baby talk, not adult imitation. There are parallels in Rom. and other languages where parents address each other as "Mother" and "Father." The tendency to pluralize one's child is universal. This pluralization sets the child in his or her place; it can also be a mark of tenderness or expansiveness [in 20].

626. "Bemerkung." *ZRP* 44 (1924): 767.

Viver èo in "come viver èo sanz'amor" is not the imperfect subjunctive, contrary to Gamillscheg's contention (*ZRP* 43 [1943]: 727), but a *dubitativen Infinitivs*.

627. "Zu *Ztschr.* XLV, 292ff (siz. *caminari campagna campagna*)." *ZRP* 45 (1925): 640.

Rohlfs is wrong: the accusative of movement and of traversed space for verbs of motion is not lacking in Sicil. Many examples are cited.

628. "Zu *Arch. Rom.* 13, p. 392." *A Rom* 13 (1929): 592.

E. Levi's clarification of It. *-ette* (*ZRP* 40 [1920]: 704) is the same one offered by Spitzer in 1920.

629. "B. Migliorini, 'Il tipo *radiodiffusione* nell'italiano contemporaneo,' *AGI* 27 (1935): 13–39." *FM* 4 (1936): 180–83.

Resumé of an article on technological affixes such as *electro-*.

630. "B. Migliorini, 'I nomi italiani del tipo *bracciante*,' *VRo* 1 (1936)." *FM* 4 (1936): 281–82.

A look at nominalized present participles derived directly from nouns: *braccio* 'arm' > *bracciante* 'laborer.' Spitzer would like to see a similar study of Fr. participles.

631. "Una locuzione giudeo-italiana." *A Rom* 23 (1939): 469.

The Hebrew-Italian expression *fare bugnoth chiuse* 'to get angry within oneself' corresponds to It. *fare i pugni chiusi*. The Heb. feminine plural ending *-oth* is incorrect since *pugni* is masculine in Heb. The suffix is perhaps explained by the It. archaic plural *le púgnora*.

632. "Un intéressant exemple du langage-écho." *BFL* 6 (1939): 180–81.

When asked whether he was a prophet or an artist, Mussolini replied with one word, "Artist." Ordinarily a speech echo signals passivity; here it represents a strong affirmative.

633. "*Usare* fraseologico." *SFI* 14 (1956): 594–600.

A critical look at Franca Ageno's explanation of 15th- and 16th-c. use of the periphrastic or modal *usare* (*usò di dire* = *disse*) as tautological.

634. "La particola *s'* nei canti popolari del Piemonte." *AGI* 43 (1958): 97–107.

Spitzer's response to B. Terracini's *Pronome impersonale e stile epico nei canti popolari del Piemonte* (Torino: Atti dell' Accademia delle Scienze di Torino, n.d.) adduces linguistic and stylistic evidence to show that *s'* and *si* develop from *sì*.

Romance and Indo-European

635. "Vermischtes. Zur Syntax." *ZRP* 37 (1913): 476–83.

(1) "Sans la Bataille de Chéronée, Démosthènes eut sauvé la Grèce." This phrase is a textbook example of the uses of *sans* to mean 'if not for.' It. *senza* can be used the same way. (2) *Se mai*. Originally this meant 'if ever.' It later acquired the meaning 'if somehow.' (3) "Il guardare ch'egli ha fatto qui dentro 'sein Hereinschauen.'" *Il guardare* and *sein Hereinschauen* are infinitival constructions meaning 'his looking in.' The Ger. infinitive construction emphasizes the action, whereas in It. the possessive pronoun is the construction's striking feature. (4) "Caro il mio amico." This vocative construction is especially common in colloquial language. (5) "Non la vedo da otto giorni." As E. Herzog points out, the distinction between the durative and perfective verbs is murky in It. An example is the verb *to see*, which in Eng., Ger., and It. has (A) a perfective meaning: 'to catch sight of,' and (B) a durative meaning: (a) 'to see poorly' and (b) 'to see someone,' meaning 'to consort with him.' In It., unlike Ger., *to see* in sense (B)(b) can be used in all tenses: "I haven't been seeing him for three months." The same holds true for the durative meaning

of *to speak, to hear,* and *to write.* (6) *Pare di vedere* 'it seems that one sees.' This phrase can be compared with similar LLat. vulgarisms like *potest, debet,* and *dicit.*

636. "Syntaktische Beiträge." *Mitteilungen des Rumänischen Instituts an der Universität Wien* 1 (1914): 56–78.

(1) A discussion of Romance parallels to the Rom. construction of the type *primblă-mi-se primblă* in which a verb is repeated pleonastically. (2) In the ORom. sentence "kaft-auá, kaft-akló dédiro tuto kasa di pade, ma di flurĭi ritsi un semne" (= 'she seeks here, she seeks there,' 'they turned the whole house upside down, but there was no trace of the gold pieces'), the change from third-person singular to third-person plural is problematical. A discussion of similar examples in It., Prov., modern Gk., Bulg., and Rom. follows. *Kaft-auá* and *kaft-akló* are instances of second-person-plural imperatives. Probably such expressions originated in actual cries that were uttered or thought to have been uttered. Discussion also of (a) Romance substantivization of the double imperative, (b) the use of punctuation between the imperative and the following clause, and (c) the meaning of the imperative phrase, that is, repeated or continued action [in 6].

637. "Nachtrag zu Artikel II der Syntaktischen Beiträge." *Mitteilungen des Rumänischen Instituts an der Universität Wien* 1 (1914): 386–400.

A list of examples of imperative constructions used in Catal. to continue a narration (e.g., Imp. + *que* + Imp. or second-person future; or simple imperative). Several notes to specific points and examples in the previous article are included [in 6].

638. "Persona pro re." *ZFS* 44 (1917): 240–45.

In this response to Kalepky's observations about reflexive forms (*ZFS* 41 [1913]: 257ff.), Spitzer points out that the kind of contraction permitted by use of the reflexive is not restricted to Fr., as Kalepky claims. Ger., It., Rom., and probably OFr. and Prov. share this tendency [in 6].

639. "Kritische Bemerkungen zu E. Metis' 'Der Gebrauch von *duplu* als Ersatz für Proportionalia in den romanischen Sprachen.' " *ZFS* 46 (1923): 323–25.

An addition to E. Metis's study of the use of the *duplu* root in Romance languages to represent "several" or "more."

640. "*Singen und sagen–Schorlemorle.*" *ZVS* 54 (1926): 213–23.

In all Indo-European languages there are many words built with the vowel pattern *i-a,* for example, *singen und sagen, zigzag, krikkrak, klingklang.* There are also words based on the pattern *u-a,* e.g., *buffa-baffa, puf-paf.* Within the vowel series, *a* is generally viewed as normal and nonextreme, while *i* and sometimes *u* are exciting and noteworthy and therefore placed first. Words constructed on this pattern refer to a series of one kind or another. The alternation between the extreme and the nonextreme vowels conveys onomatopoeically a sense of enumeration [in 20].

641. "Nachtrag zu *Singen und sagen.*" *ZVS* 54 (1926–27): 311.

H. Jacobsohn argues that the labials have the most onomatopoeic powers (*ZVS* 54 [1926–27]: 102) and therefore occur in a word like *csiribiri.* It seems more likely that they occur because they are comfortable and easy to pronounce; they seem normal to the speaker, like the vowel *a* [in 20].

642. "Attributives Gerundium im Portugiesischen, Spanischen, Rumänischen und Französischen?" *ZFS* 50 (1927): 464–69.

Contrary to Kalepky (*ZRP* 46 [1926]: 630), Spitzer argues that there is no organic development within Romance languages dictating the preference of gerund verb forms over participial forms.

643. "Rum. *p(r)e* und span. *á* vor persönlichen Akkusativobjekt." *ZRP* 48 (1928): 423–32.

Rom. *pre* has a wider range of meaning than Sp. *á*. The prefix *ad-* is used in Sp. when there is no direct connection with the verb. Generally, these prepositional constructions create a distance between verb and object.

644. "Vergangenheitstempus im futurische Sinn." *IF* 48 (1930): 45.

Justification for an earlier thesis in his book *Stilstudien* on the correct meaning of the verb tenses in several languages.

645. "*Volaverunt!*" *RFE* 17 (1930): 37–39.

In Sp., Port., and OFr., Lat. verbs in the past tense are sometimes cited with the ending *-averunt*, regardless of the person or number of the subject. The bizarre structure of the form was apparently used to add jocularity.

646. "De Hitler–l'hitlérisme." *ZFS* 57 (1933): 451–52.

References to Hitler illustrate a general law: emphasis follows the sound of the root and not that of its derivations. Adjectival derivations indicate a shift of semantic emphasis from the individual denoted to his or her general significance, which can result in phonetic negligence of the root.

647. "Zu Nhd. *-tsch-* als Laut niederer Sprachschicht." *Revue des Etudes Indoeuropéennes* 1 (1938): 452–56.

Probably all sound change in a language is originally stylistic. An unusual sound begins in the "lower regions" of the spoken language and may spread, but, because it remains a relatively uncommon sound, it maintains a high degree of expressivity.

648. "La conjonction romance *si* vient-elle du latin *sit?*" *Rom* 65 (1939): 289–311.

Nicholson (*Rom* 56 [1930]: 3ff.) is mistaken in tracing Romance *si* (*se*) 'if' to *sit*, for the following reasons: (1) there is no attestation of *sit* with the meaning 'if' in Lat.; (2) the theory proposes an unlikely primitive petrification of *sit* as 'if,' since the form that prevailed in Romance is *siat* (e.g., Sp. *sea*); (3) the medieval graphies *set, sed* are due to scribal confusion of *si* and *sed*; (4) certain examples cited by Nicholson in which *si* seems to be derived from *sit* are actually traceable to *sic*.

649. "'H. Mihaesai, Despre începuturile sufixului romanic *-mente*,' *Buletinul Institutului de Filologie Romîna Alexandru Philippide*." *FM* 8 (1940): 189–91.

The use of *-mente* to form adverbs is of learned, not popular, origin.

650. "Feminización del néutro (rumano *oasele*, italiano *le ossa*, ant. francés *ces brace*, español *las visceras*)." *RFH* 3 (1942): 339–71.

The feminization of certain neuter formations is attributed to a general early Indo-European tendency to make collective nouns feminine. (The earliest example given here is from Vergil: *victricia arma*.)

651. "G. Bonfante: 'The Romance Desiderative *se*,' (*PMLA* 57 [1942]: 930–50)." *MLN* 60 (1945): 211–14.

Spitzer contests Bonfante's documentation and conclusions regarding Lat. *sic* and judges that the construction *si m'aït Dieus* (and not *se Dieus m'aït*) testifies to the survival of the Lat. desiderative *sic*. Generally *si* = *sic* and *se* = *si*.

652. "Lokaladverb statt Personalpronomen." *RF* 62 (1950): 158-62.

A review of discussions about the substitution of adverbs of place for personal pronouns in Rom. and Sp. is followed by an analysis showing the connection between the use of *acá*, *aqui*, and an accompanying gesture. The avoidance of personal pronouns is attributed to psychological reasons.

653. "Sur quelques emplois métaphoriques de l'impératif: Un chapitre de syntaxe comparative (I)." *Rom* 72 (1951): 433-78.

A composite study of the gerundive and desiderative-imperative construction, widely used in Romance languages to replace the third-person indicative. Examples are drawn from Skt., Russ., Lat., New Gk., Lithuanian, and Hung.

654. "Sur quelques emplois métaphoriques de l'impératif: Un chapitre de syntaxe comparative (II)." *Rom* 73 (1952): 16-63.

Four general categories produced the descriptive imperative: (1) instances in which the imperative form is addressed to a character in a story that is being recounted to us; (2) instances in which the imperative is addressed to "someone" (*sauve-qui-peut*) who might intervene in a situation in which the narrator takes an interest; (3) instances in which an impersonal order is given by an authority or authorities (e.g., military or nautical commands); (4) cases where an individual speaks to a single interlocutor who represents the public and is called on to become an agent in the story being told. The third category, the oldest, is the most significant in the development of the descriptive imperative, since it implies the automatic accomplishment of a spoken order.

655. "Le type moyen anglais *I was wery for wandred* et ses parallèles romans." *NM* 60 (1954): 161-77.

The development in Romance languages of adjectives and participles following a preposition (*pour, por, pur, für*) is an international phenomenon. The discussion focuses on *de, da* + adjective or participle. The disappearance of this and similar formulations in Eng., for example, *for dry*, is attributed to the efforts of Renaissance and baroque grammarians who viewed a phrase containing a preposition followed by an adjective or participle as an aberrant form.

656. "Alphons Nehring, 'Das Wesen der Fragesätze' (*IF* 61, 40-54)." *RF* 65 (1954): 422-24.

According to Nehring, supplemental questions do not show a specific raising of the voice, whereas verification questions do. He attributes this to a tone of uncertainty in verification questions. Nehring's school of thought stresses the priority of the indefinite function of the "who" pronouns. Spitzer, however, opts for the priority of the "question function" of these pronouns.

657. "The Actor-Infinitive Construction in Russian and Other Indo-European Languages." *Word* 10 (1954): 442-56.

The evolution of the descriptive-infinitive construction is traced with reference to many examples. Spitzer notes in conclusion that it is emotionality that leads the speaker to use "unhewn blocks . . . of subject and predicate, the latter being expressed in the most rudimentary form (e.g., as infinitive)."

658. "Zur 'Inversion' beim Komparativ." *ZDP* 77 (1958): 63-65.

A discussion of the difference between an "intensifying inversion" and a "balanced inversion" in comparatives (cf. H. Renicke, *ZDP* 74 [1955]: 68ff., 280ff.) with reference to contrasting usage in Fr. and It.

659. "Zum Warum der Lautentwicklung." *Mélanges Salverda de Grave*. Genève: Slatkine, 1972. 306–11.

The rise of diphthongs is an example of a psychologically based sound shift. The conceptual pair "expression" and "communication" (going back to Croce and Vossler) helps explain the motivation behind sound shifts. Those who want to express themselves develop innovative ways of speaking; those who wish to communicate conform to the linguistic norms. The use of diphthongs may well originate in a desire for expression in the service of communication: hoping to emphasize their vowels, certain speakers ended up lengthening and distorting them. Such psychological considerations are probably always behind sound shifts; but to determine precisely why they occur when they occur, one must also study the entire linguistic system in which they take place and understand the general psychological state of the language community.

Romanian

660. "*Duceţi-vă-ţi, duce-vă-ţi*." *BInst* 3-4 (1936): 180–82.

The repetition in this imperative construction emphasizes that it is second-person plural. It is also a stylistic device (*chiasma*) used to create symmetry in the phrase, a frequent device in popular speech.

661. "L'expression 'a făgădui marea cu sarea.'" *BInst* 5-6 (1937-38): 190–95.

Like other folk idioms, for example, Ger. "das Blaue vom Himmel versprechen," It. "promettere Roma e toma," Fr. "promettre monts et merveilles," and Port. "prometer mundos y fundos," this one cannot be explained by semantics alone. Alliteration, paradox, and the unexpected blend of the real and the imaginary combine to give such locutions their force.

662. "Quelques parallèles turcs pour des phénomènes syntaxiques roumains." *BInst* 5-6 (1937-38): 237–38.

Certain aspects of Romanian syntax resemble Turkish usage: partitive *la* in Rom. is used like the suffix *-da* in Turk.; to indicate in polite usage where something or someone is found, the first-person plural is substituted for the singular in certain verb forms. In some cases in Turk., the dative replaces the accusative, as occasionally happens in Rom.

663. "Sur 'a făgădui marea cu sarea.'" *BInst* 5-6 (1937-38): 238.

A French form of this Romanian saying occurs in Ronsard's ode to Odet de Colligny.

664. "'Vine el tata.'" *BInst* 5-6 (1937-38): 245–58.

A reversal of the usual syntax here conveys a threatening note, because in Rom. the verb in first position carries unusual emphasis. In certain French phrases, the inversion of noun and verb is used for emphasis.

665. "Rumanian *un prieten al mieu* 'a friend of mine.'" *Word* 6 (1950): 141–59.

The Romanian construction is placed within a European framework. Parallels cited show that the possessive pronoun here signifies an absolute possessive, not an anaphoric possessive, and that *a*, first accepted as a simple demonstrative (or article), in Rom. has a partitive meaning before possessive pronouns originating in cases such as *membra ad duos fratres* 'limbs of two brothers.'

Spanish, Portuguese, and Catalan

666. "Stilistisch-Syntaktisches aus den Spanisch-Portugiesischen Romanzen." *ZRP* 35 (1911): 192–230, 257–308.

This article deals with verb tenses, articles, prepositions, conjunctions, spelling variations, and principles of style.

667. "Zur Syntax: Span. *como que*." *ZRP* 37 (1913): 730–35.

This locution is merely an interpolation, which diminishes the impact of the sentence.

668. "Über Span. *que*." *ANS* 132 (1914): 375–94.

In this study of the various uses of *que*, Spitzer opposes Louis Weigert (*Untersuchungen zur spanischen Syntax auf Grund der Werke des Cervantes*, Berlin: n.p., 1907) on most counts and adds examples drawn mainly from modern Sp. Weigert's view to the contrary, *que* is a conjunction, not a relative pronoun [in 6].

669. "Syntaktische Notizen zum Katalanischen." *Revue de Dialectologie Romane* 6 (1914): 81–138.

In this study of Catalan syntax in literary language and colloquial speech, Spitzer details its uniqueness by comparing it with syntax in Prov. and other Ibero-Romance languages.

670. "*Es* im Portugiesischen." *ZRP* 38 (1914–17): 713–18.

Karl von Reinhardstoettner (*Grammatik der portugiesischen Sprache auf Grundlage der lateinischen und der romanischen Sprachvergleichung bearbeitet*, Strassburg: Trübner, 1878, 198) states that Port. has no impersonal *it*. Here Spitzer points out that the demonstrative pronouns *aquillo* and *isso* are not often used as demonstrative pronouns; instead they take on the function of *it*.

671. "Das Gerundium als Imperativ im Spanischen." *ZRP* 42 (1922): 206–10.

Lists examples in which the Sp. gerundive is (a) like Ger. *schnell* and the imperative *schnell!*, (b) used as a finite verb in colloquial expressions, and (c) used to express duration and a so-called occasional imperative.

672. "Zu *Arch. Rom.* 7 (129ff.)." *A Rom* 8 (1924): 467.

The plural *los padres* means 'the elders,' just as *brothers* can mean 'brothers and sisters.'

673. "Der Dual im Katalanischen und Spanischen." *A Rom* 9 (1925): 129–53.

Los padres is a true dual, original in Sp., not a borrowing from Ar. Specifically, it is called an elliptical dual because it is based on a proper name. Other examples, from Lat., include *castores, quirini, patres, fratres.* Admittedly all these words are late constructions, but the frequent occurrence of duals in Indo-European languages indicates that they are a genuine Indo-European phenomenon.

674. "Beiträge zur spanischen Syntax." *Homenaje ofrecido a Menéndez Pidal: Miscelánea de estudios lingüísticos, literarios e historicos* 1. Madrid: Hernando, 1925. 49–62.

(1) Grammatische Rückdatierung im Spanischen. The Spanish occasionally put present-tense sentiments into the past tense. Some maintain that modesty motivates this usage, while others assert that it is caused by a strong desire to see something as a fait accompli. Both schools of thought are right. The use of the imperfect

indicates modesty and politeness, suggesting that the speaker awaits the listener's approval. Thus the imperfect is frequently used at the beginning of a speech. The perfect is used when the main idea is presented, and the present is used when a plan's accomplishment is described. (2) *Al volver que volvió.* This phrase is an admixture of *Al volver que volvió (a Italia)* 'while returning (from Italy)' and *Al volver que hizo* 'during the return trip (which he made).' The catchiness of the repeated sounds is the stylistic motivation for this contamination [in 20].

675. "Arag. *estuque* 'me parece que . . . , creo yo . . . , es mi opinión, parecer.' " *RFE* 12 (1925): 72–75.

Arag. *estuque* 'I think . . . ,' comparable to the colloquial Sp. elliptical phrase *estoy que* 'I am (in a situation) that,' 'I think . . . ,' owes its creation to the grammatical incompetence of the speaker to express him- or herself fully in an emotional situation.

676. "Pourquoi *granadino*, mais *sevillano*?" *RFE* 13 (1926): 375.

The suffix *-ino* replaces *-ano* in place-name adjectives whose stems are dominated by the vowel *a*, for reasons of euphony.

677. "*Fait-accompli*–Darstellung im Spanischen." *JbP* 2 (1927): 270–92.

Sp. has many expressions and words suggesting that a merely possible event has in fact already taken place or that an opinion is actually truth. In an analysis of certain constructions that, in his view, reflect aspects of Spanish national character, Spitzer analyzes many examples. All the features he discusses have different historical origins but constitute nevertheless a single, more or less unified *Sprachstil* [in 20].

678. "Les diminutifs basques avec *-ch-*." *Revue Internationale des Etudes Basques* 25 (1934): 353–59.

The Basque diminutive *-ch-* used in proper names and some adjectives has a direct relationship to the same sound used in everyday speech in Spain and in Spanish America. The sound reflects a reversion to baby talk to express affection or even anger.

679. "Mauricio Schneider, 'El colectivo en latín y las formas en -a con valor aumentativo en español' (*Boletín de la Academia Argentina de Letras* 2 [1935], 25–92)." *Rom* 62 (1936): 397–99.

Page-by-page critique of Schneider's discussion of Lat. neuter plurals that become augmentative feminine plurals.

680. "Du langage-écho en Portugais." *BFL* 5 (1938): 165–69.

In Port. this device reflects an antiintellectual and antigrammatical tendency, a kind of affective primitivism. Examples of the device of repeating part of a question as its answer are cited in Fr., Ger., It., and Lat. and are compared with those in Port.

681. "Du langage-écho en Portugais." *BFL* 5 (1938): 374–76.

Colette's use of this device is an occasion for an amplification on earlier observations.

682. "*Não se há não preguntar.*" *BFL* 6 (1939): 179–80.

This is simply an emphatic negative, as additional examples show in support of earlier comments.

683. *"Falei de si."* *BFL* 6 (1939): 181–85.

The reflexive pronoun *si* here replaces the personal pronoun. The same construction occurs in Fr. This is either a new usage or a return to an archaic usage, neither of which is unusual.

684. *"Falei de si."* *BFL* 6 (1939): 204–05.

The use of *soi* in Fr. implies a harmonious sense of self, whereas the use of *lui* implies a sense of alienation.

685. "Omission of Object Pronouns in Portuguese." *HR* 8 (1940): 58–62.

A reply to R. Abraham (*HR* 7 [1939]: 248), in which Spitzer shows again (first in *ZRP* 36 [1912]: 683) that Portuguese affirmations by verb repetition – for example, "Tu gostas d'ella?" "Gosto" – are primitive constructions harking back to the stage when Lat. lacked a word for "yes." Abraham (following Williams, *Lg* 15 [1939]: 205) thought that such verbs had once been followed by object pronouns, which were later assimilated.

686. "Paralelos catalanes y portugueses de *ello*." *RFH* 3 (1941): 272.

Further examples of the emphatic use of *ello* are added to those adduced by P. H. Ureña (*RFH* 1 [1939]: 209–29).

687. "Notas sintáctico-estilísticas a propósito del español *que*." *RFH* 4 (1942): 105–26, 253–65.

In this two-part study Spitzer examines two general uses of *que*. In part 1 he analyzes what he calls the narrative *que*, for example, "Que muerto se quedó en la calle / que con un puñal en el pecho / y que no lo conocía nadie" (García Lorca, *Obras completas* 4, Buenos Aires: Losada, 1938, 88), whose significance he defines as a mark of the narrator's reluctance to accept responsibility for the truthfulness of the narration. Part 2, a study of repetitive phrases that use *que*, for example, "noche que noche nochera" (García Lorca), suggests that this *que* helps to effect an enrichment process through intensification.

688. "Las expresiones temporales *a lo que, a la que*, etc., en España y América." *RFH* 6 (1944): 394–95.

(A) lo que is a neutral expression indicating indeterminate duration. *A la que*, on the contrary, makes reference to a precise lapse of time. The form of the first expression may be patterned on the second. Parallel and variant locutions are examined.

689. "El sintagma *Valencia la bella*." *RFH* 7 (1945): 259–76.

OFr. syntagmas such as *Alde la belle, Babyloine la grande*, for which there exist parallels in the *Poema del Cid* (e.g., *Bavieca el corredor, Valencia la grant, la mayor, la casa, la clara*), are explained as proper nouns that, though unique in themselves, are modified by a substantive adjective and article in order to enforce the psychological effect of affective isolation. Although such proper nouns are not part of a series or group, they are treated as though they were. This study includes analysis of usage and a commentary on the almost total disappearance of such expressions in modern Fr. and Sp.

SEMANTICS

690. "Hans Sperber, *Über den Einfluss sexueller Momente auf die Entstehung und Entwicklung der Sprache.*" *WS* 5 (1913): 206–15.

Working with ideas formulated by O. Jespersen and Noiré, Sperber develops the thesis that the sublimation of sexual desire is responsible for the creation of language and tools. There are many objections to Sperber's hypothesis: (1) The sexual connotations associated with tools are only documented in literary works from highly civilized cultures. (2) The instinct for self-preservation was no doubt as strong in primitive peoples as the sex drive: surely it was responsible for the creation of tools. (3) The theory is pleasing because it is logical, but it has no relation to facts: in particular, the idea that the words used by two individuals in a sexual act would be applied by an entire community to tools is dubious.

691. "Altfrz. *oz* als Imperativ." *A Rom* 3 (1919): 375–76.

Although OFr. *oz* 'hear!' is etymologically indicative (< *audis*), it is sometimes used as an imperative. This semantic shift must have taken place through an intermediate, interrogative stage: 'you hear' > 'you hear?' > 'hear!'

692. "Altfranzösisch *clamer*, altprovenzalisch *clamar* 'anklagen' und einiges Prinzipielles aus diesem Anlass." *WS* 9 (1919): 69–81.

OFr. *clamer* and OProv. *clamar* mean 'to cry out' and 'to accuse.' A study of the two meanings of this word leads to speculations about the nature of semantic borrowings. Meyer-Lübke asserts that the OFr. and OProv. words acquire the meaning 'to accuse' because OHG *karen* and *klagen* have the same double meanings. Alfred Schulze, however, points out that even in classical Lat. the same word means both 'to cry out' and 'to accuse in court.' Three possibilities exist in this sort of situation: (1) a concept takes a similar form in two languages because of similar cultures, not because one language borrows from the other; (2) analogous legal practices produce analogous words; (3) the less cultured society imports technical terms from the more cultured society. It is almost always difficult to tell whether the Ger. words are autochthonous or borrowed.

693. "Spanisch *pues.*" *ANS* 142 (1921): 270–75.

Pues has an astonishingly wide array of meanings and is used in a large number of contexts. The basic meaning is 'therefore' or 'hence.' It is also used as the introductory word in an answer to a question. Although it is frequently translated as 'indeed,' 'true,' or 'admittedly,' the actual sense is more like 'since you ask, I say. . . .' It is often used as a filler word to soften a response—not only in answers to questions but in all utterances that might seem too harsh. Comparisons are drawn with Hung. *hát.*

694. "Romanisch **facit* 'er sagt'–Zur Bewertung des 'Schöpferischen' in der Sprache (Zwei Musterfälle)." *A Rom* 8 (1924): 349–85.

(1) Romance *facere* 'to say.' The French use "il fait" to mean 'he says.' Some argue that this form developed because "je dis," the present of the preterite of *dire*, is ambiguous. This seems improbable. In any case, "il fait" is quite as ambiguous as "je dis"; moreover, the use of *facere* to mean 'to say' is a phenomenon that occurs in many Romance languages, even in ones where the present and the preterite of *dire* are not the same [in 20]. (2) Wall. *savoir* as *pouvoir*. In Wall. there is a confusion between *savoir* and *pouvoir* analogous to the *können-wissen* confusion in Ger. It is conceivable that Ger. "ich kann lesen" 'I know how to read' influenced Fr. "je sais lire" and "je peux lire."

695. "Zur Wortgeschichte '*Polaina!*'" *ZRP* 44 (1924): 576–89.

In Coloma's *Pequeneces*, "Polaina!" is a curse that stands for something too coarse to be uttered in the presence of ladies. Since *polaina* means nothing but 'legging' or 'spat,' Spitzer uses it as the basis for a number of speculations concerning bowdlerizations and euphemisms. A harmless word can replace a sacred or an offensive word if both words share just one linguistic trait or two. *Polaina* is a particularly complex example. Its etymology reveals that euphemisms and bowdlerizations are fantastic examples of popular creativity. This essay includes a list of bowdlerizations based on *coño*, *cojones*, *carajo*, *puñeta*, *Cristo*, *diablo*, *demónio*, *dios*, and *hoder*.

696. "Vom Küssen." *ZFS* 48 (1926): 371–78.

(1) Rohlfs (*ZFS* 48 [1926]: 131) does not accurately trace the displacement of Fr. *baiser* 'to kiss a woman,' a vulgar expression by the 17th c., by *embrasser* 'to embrace.' (2) To dispute, as do Rohlfs and Lerch (*Festschrift für Oskar Walzel*, Potsdam: Akademische Verlagsgesellschaft Athenaion, 1924, 110), whether a term originates in popular or learned sources is usually to falsify the situation. With the development of abstract constructions (e.g., *baisage* 'fornication'), the popular use of substantivized infinitives (e.g., *le baiser*) fell off but never disappeared. Both Lerch and Rohlfs are mistaken to separate the history of *le baiser* from other similar constructions. (3) Rohlfs is in error to claim that Ger. for 'give me a kiss' prevails over 'kiss me.' *Küsse mich* is the lover's expression, not that of parents and children. *Küsse mich* and the substantivized infinitive *Küssen* express duration and the reciprocity of joy, unlike the finite, less ceremonial *Kuss*.

697. "Über französisch *gros*." *ZFS* 57 (1933): 67–76.

In his effort to explain the influence of social class on the development of language, L. Jordan wrongly characterizes contemporary literate society's distaste for Fr. *gros* as evidence of the chivalric ideal of beauty. Lat. *grossus* > *crassus* is a precedent for the alliterative semantic transformation *gros* > *grossier*. Contrary to Jordan's simplification, *gros* has always had its place. It connotes materiality and fleshiness more than does *grand*, and it lends itself to the pejorative as well as to the affectionately exaggerative.

698. "Une faute d'ortographe trahissant la détresse sémantique." *FM* 5 (1937): 15–16.

A contemporary writer consistently wrote *chaos* 'chaos' for *cahot* 'jolt,' thus revealing that the two terms have become confused–semantically telescoped–in his mind.

699. "Eugen Lerch, 'Histoire et influence des mots *distractus* et *distrait*,' *RLiR* 12 (1936), 270–83." *FM* 6 (1938): 280.

Distractus in scholastic Lat. meant 'confused, double-minded,' as does Eng. *distracted*. In Fr. it has evolved to a quite different meaning in *se distraire* 'amuse oneself.'

700. "Frz. 'voter socialiste.'" *NM* 39 (1938): 73–81.

The French socialist party utilized the term "voter socialiste" rather than "voter pour le parti socialiste" in the 1936 election campaign. This locution is modeled on "parler français" and is meant to suggest to the French voter that voting for the Socialist party is as natural as speaking French. The question of whether the French modeled their construction on English usage "speak English" or "buy English" is raised but not resolved.

701. "Eugen Lerch, '*Sinn, Sinne, Sinnlichkeit*,' *Archiv für die gesamte Psychologie* 103 (1939), 446–95." *FM* 8 (1940): 89–90.

Because of the Christian rejection of the senses, Fr. *sensuel* and Ger. *sinnlich* 'sensual,' 'sensualist' are now pejorative.

702. "'Ça fait distingué'; 'elle fait espagnole.'" *RR* 31 (1940): 44–51.

In phrases such as "ça fait distingué" and "elle fait espagnole," the use of the word *faire*, rather than the expected *être*, effectively shifts the semantic focus from essence to appearance.

703. "*Chez Vandamme sont venus*." *MLN* 47 (1942): 103–08.

Citing parallel examples from western Fr. patois and CanFr., Spitzer avers that such expressions originally emphasized the group (family) symbolized by the house itself, thus detracting attention from individuals. *Chez*, whose rudimentary sense is 'house' (< *casa*), is not necessarily, as earlier suggested, Pic. *ces*, but retains, albeit in an attenuated way, the sense of 'house (of).'

704. "*Milieu* and *ambiance*: An Essay in Historical Semantics." *Philosophy and Phenomenological Research* 3 (1942): 1–42.

Milieu and *ambiance* are used to trace the classical organic notions of a harmonious universe through medieval cosmology to the Newtonian universe of human isolation and insignificance, where humankind's *ambient medium* becomes an infinite, chilly cosmos and the individual is no longer the measure of all things [in 28].

705. "Español y portugués *decorar* 'apprender, recitar de memoria.'" *RFH* 6 (1944): 176–86.

A discussion of the dual semantic trajectory of this verb surveys classical, medieval, and Golden Age usage.

706. "Adición a *decorar*." *RFH* 6 (1944): 283–84.

Mnemonic learning designated as 'learning by memory (by heart)' appears in Hugh of Saint Victor (*De tribus circumstanciis gestorum*) as *cordi imprimere, in corde disponere*, and *cordetemus affirmare*.

707. "L'étymologie d'un 'cri de Paris.'" *RR* 35 (1944): 244–50.

The formation of a Parisian vender's cry (in Proust's *La prisonnière*) is traced to a variant of the medieval lyric *reverdie*, which accompanied or commemorated the gathering of certain spring plants. The analysis is based on variant forms of a key refrain word, *verdure* [in 34, 35, 44; trans. 724].

708. "Classical and Christian Ideas of World Harmony: Prolegomena to an Interpretation of the Word 'Stimmung' (I)." *Traditio* 2 (1944): 409–64.

A survey of the semantic field of the "untranslatable" *Stimmung*. Spitzer points out a movement from the Pythagorean-Platonic tradition of the musical and mathematical correspondences of the "World Soul," to the "polarity" of Ambrose's invention of the Christian hymn and Augustine's "spiritualization of the instrument of the soul," to the development of medieval and pre-Renaissance musicology and some of its parallels, for example, rhyme [40].

709. "'Nom de Dieu!'" *MLQ* 6 (1945): 243–61.

The popular repeated expletive developed from the moment the semantic value of the preposition *de* was no longer understood, giving rise to the tendency to new formation that followed the loosening of the original formula's meaning. Examples and parallels demonstrate that the most imaginative lexical innovations can be grafted on to simple traditional motifs rooted in Christian civilization and culture.

710. "Classical and Christian Ideas of World Harmony (II)." *Traditio* 3 (1945): 307–64.

The analysis continues here with an examination of the semantic development of *temperare*, **accordare* in order to pursue further the modern concept of *Stimmung*, which is a composite of different etyma [40].

711. "The Gentiles." *JEGP* 45 (1946): 444–47.

A historical semantic study of the word *gentile* and its use particularly in America [in 28].

712. "*Soy quien soy.*" *NRFH* 1 (1947): 113–27.

Returning to an earlier discussion of this locution (*ZRP* 54 [1934]: 563), Spitzer examines and differentiates Latin and Hebrew formulations of God's speech to Abraham rendered in Lat. as *sum qui sum*. The Spanish locution, in its general sense equivalent to Polonius's admonition to Laertes, "To thine own self be true," is viewed as a particularly significant representation of a trait of Renaissance thought. How divine self-definition came to be applied to human beings is analyzed in the context of the Judeo-Christian biblical tradition and the Christian-stoical tradition.

713. "Adición a *soy quien soy.*" *NRFH* 2 (1948): 275.

Differentiates between the 16th-c. Béarnaise motto *Gratia Dei sum, id quod sum* and *soy quien soy*. The former is closer to the medieval sense of Sp. *ser algo*, whereas the latter has the Renaissance connotation *ser alguien*.

714. "*Nate que nate.*" *Rom* 70 (1948–49): 74.

Identifies others who offer the same interpretation as A. Henry (*Rom* 69 [1946–47]: 174), that is, "nate (est) que nate (est)" 'Nature est ce que nature peut être.'

715. "*Mesturar* y la semántica hispano-árabe." *NRFH* 3 (1949): 141–49.

Although many Sp. words cited by Castro (*España en su historia: Cristianos, moros, y judíos*, Buenos Aires: Losada, 1948) seem clearly to derive from an Ar. semantic base, others, such as the word family *mesturar* 'delatar calumniosamente,' do not. This word family is examined in the light of other Romance analogues, such as OFr. *mesler* 'brouiller' and OProv. *mesclar* 'brouiller' (< **misculare*).

716. "La danse macabre." *Mélanges de linguistique offerts à Albert Dauzat par ses élèves et ses amis*. Paris: d'Artrey, 1951. 307–21.

The *danse macabre*, a variant of the *chasse sauvage*, is traced to a blending of the ecclesiastical and the popular, a blending by means of which Judas, considered popularly to be a heretic, takes the place of Wodan as the chief *chasseur sauvage*.

717. "*Pucelle*." *Rom* 72 (1951): 100–07.

Traces the semantic development from a feminine derivation of *pulex* > VLat. *pulicella*, originally signifying the humble station of a maidservant, finally coming to designate 'a young noble girl.' Suggests that from within the context of Christian humility, the term was taken over by the feudal system, which guaranteed its evolution toward this meaning. Parallel examples are cited.

718. "*Silvas* = 'formes.'" *BHi* 65 (1953): 383.

The appearance of *sylvas* in the place of 'formes' in two 16th-c. Spanish translations of Lucan is traced to the semantic use of this word in Lat., the general sense of which is 'material (of a work of poetry but not of philosophy).' The Spanish Latinism indicates this sense of 'material' = 'species,' equivalent to "forms" and opposed to "ideas."

719. "*Insignifiant* dans le titre d'un journal américain." *FM* 22 (1954): 253–57.

A history of the use of *petit* in newspaper titles in France describes its appearance following the end of the Second Empire and notes the absence of this epithet in American newspaper titles (attributed to an American aversion to diminutives except in affective language). Spitzer cites the counterexample of the New Orleans *Picayune* (the *Times-Picayune-States*), which came into existence in 1837, thirty years before the French *Petit Journal*.

720. "Auf keinen grünen Zweig kommen." *MLN* 69 (1954): 270–73.

This refinement of his discussion in *Essays in Historical Semantics* traces the negative form to the 12th and 13th centuries. The medieval moral example became a sentimental representation of helplessness. The expression formerly meant 'never again to sit on a green branch' but now meant 'never again to come upon a green branch.'

721. "Auf keinen grünen Zweig kommen." *MLN* 69 (1954): 620.

Two examples are given relating *wither'd bough* and *leafless tree* to the *dürren Ast* mentioned in the preceding discussion (*MLN* 69 [1954]: 270–73).

722. "Prolegomena ad una interpretazione della parola *Stimmung*: Il concetto di 'armonia universale' nell'antichità classica e cristiana (I)." *Conv* 24 (1956): 257–74; (II) *Conv* 24 (1956): 513–29 [trans. of 708, 710; see also 40, 42].

723. "*Situation* as a Term in Literary Criticism Again." *MLN* 72 (1957): 124–28.

The replacement of *assiette* by the word family *situer*, *situé*, and *situation* in 17th- and 18th-c. French texts is attributed to a proliferation of Latinisms in Renaissance scientific writings. *Situation*, originally associated with astronomy and astrology in the Middle Ages, prevails over *assiette* because of its scientific connotation 'a conjunction (of stars),' a meaning that is transferred into the fictional use of *situation*.

724. "L'etymologia di un 'grido di Parigi.'" *Palatina* 1 (1957): 5–12 [trans. from 707; also in 34, 35, 44].

Literary Criticism and Theory

Comparative Literature

725. "Goethe et Racine." *Revue d'Histoire de la Philosophie et d'Histoire Générale de la Civilisation* 1 (1933): 58–75.

In response to Denis Seurat, for whom Goethe's oeuvre is dead – except for *Iphigenia*, which owes a substantial debt to Racine – Spitzer sets out to demonstrate Goethe's originality and enduring greatness by focusing on the differences between Goethe and Racine. Comparing tragedies by the playwrights, he concludes that Racine's classicism is based on his adaptation of traditional language and an inherited moral and poetic repertory. Goethe has reinvented the classical tradition using the language he has inherited.

726. "Remarque sur la différence entre 'poesía popular' et 'poesía de arte.'" *RFH* 23 (1936): 68–71.

The distinction between "popular poetry" (poetry continually reworked by the "people") and "artistic poetry" (poetry written by a single author) is artificial when applied to medieval literature. The process of text transmission guaranteed that even a particular author's poetry would be continually reworked by scribes, popularizers, censors, et al. Both types therefore evolved toward the same "popular" ideal.

727. "Le lion arbitre moral de l'homme." *Rom* 64 (1938): 525–30.

In medieval literature the lion is often portrayed as a moral judge or barometer of human character; he kills the proud, shows mercy toward the meek, and is tamed by the great.

728. "Albert Henry, 'Góngora et Paul Valéry, deux incarnations de Don Quichotte,' Tirada aparte de la revista *La Flambeau*, Bruselas, abril 1927, 24 págs." *RFH* 1 (1939): 178–80.

Any similarity between the two poets is due to a common Latin heritage.

729. "Rassisch-nationale Stilkunde." *MLN* 55 (1940): 16–24.

In his article "Nationale Sinnbilder und lyrische Sprachgestaltung" (*NMo* 8 [1937]: 449–62), Edgar Glässer compares the horn symbol in Vigny's "Le cor" with the blood-red cloud symbol in Wildenbruch's "Siegfried's Blut." This comparison is unjustified and politically motivated, since (1) stylistically speaking, Vigny's poem is incomparably more aesthetically pleasing than Wildenbruch's, and (2) the horn is a natural, sincere symbol of the French heroic spirit, while the blood-red cloud is capable of representing the German spirit only because Wildenbruch clumsily forces it on the reader.

730. "Le style 'circulaire.'" *MLN* 55 (1940): 495–99.

The *Perlesvaus* is stylistically "circular" in that its author tends to begin and end thoughts with the same words. This is no idiosyncrasy, but an example of the interrelatedness of style and thought. The circular style seems to predominate among all mystical thinkers (e.g., Paul, Augustine, Dante, Hegel) who view life as a circle beginning with God. In contrast, rationalist thinkers (Plato, Aristotle) have a pyramidal structure of thought and style, in which the particular leads to the general [in 35].

731. "Additional Note on 'Wool and Linen' in Jerome." *AJP* 64 (1943): 98–99.

The opposition of wool (earth and death) and linen (life) noted by J. Quasten in Jerome's letter to Fabiola is extended by another patristic passage (Augustine, "Sermo" 37.5: Migne, 37, 224) in which the contrast is mixed with another, exterior vs. interior life.

732. "Note on the Poetic and Empirical 'I' in Medieval Authors." *Traditio* 4 (1947): 414–22.

Because medieval literature dealt with humankind and not the individual, the poetic "I" had more liberty than it has today and is not to be confused with the empirical or pragmatic "I." Consequently it is erroneous to apply modern standards of plagiarism to medieval texts, especially since the medieval public construed the poetic "I" as a representative of humanity. Cites Marie de France and Dante among others [in 35].

733. "L'archétype de la ballade *Mioriţa* et sa valeur poétique." *Cahiers Sextil Puscariu* 2 (1953): 95–120.

A critique of Ovid Densusianu's idea, which separates "epic material" from "lyric material" as a means of tracing the ballad's development. A more sensible approach is to compare *Mioriţa* with other European examples of the ballad—such as the epico-lyric Spanish romances—rather than seek to establish links between the Romanian poem and a presumably earlier epic. English, Catalan, German, Italian, Portuguese, Romanian, Scottish, and Spanish examples are cited to support this argument [in 35].

734. "The Poetic Treatment of a Platonic-Christian Theme." *CL* 6 (1954): 193–217.

Du Bellay's sonnet 3 of *L'Olive*, with its "anaphora of progression and ascension" uniquely conveying the notion of "wings of the soul," is a centerpiece for tracing the Platonic theme of the soul's striving toward beauty. Latin, Italian, and German examples are cited to illustrate the poetic treatment of this Platonic idea from the classical period to the Renaissance [in 35].

735. "The Problem of Latin Renaissance Poetry." *StRen* 2 (1955): 118–38. (Published version of a lecture delivered at the meeting of the Columbia University Seminar on the Renaissance, 19 April 1955.)

A consideration of neo-Latin poets, such as Petrarch, Poliziano, and Pontano, who attempted to infuse the Latin idiom (considered "remote" in atmosphere) with the "warmth" of the "unique, immediate, personal emotions" they sought to express [in 35].

736. "'A New Synthetic Treatment of Contemporary Western Lyricism,' H. Friedrich, *Die Struktur der modernen Lyrik von Baudelaire bis zur Gegenwart*, Hamburg: Rowohlt, 1956." *MLN* 72 (1957): 523–37.

Friedrich's achievement with respect to European poetry is akin to Diez's with respect to the Romance languages. He has convincingly shown that the origins of modern lyricism, as well as the unity of subsequent 20th-c. traditions, lie in 19th-c. France.

English and American Literature

737. "Explication de Texte Applied to Walt Whitman's Poem 'Out of the Cradle Endlessly Rocking.'" *ELH* 16 (1949): 222–49.

Whitman's poem offers a significant new blending of age-old motifs centered on a conception of world harmony [in 38].

738. "Spenser, 'Shepheardes Calendar, March' ll. 61–114, and the Variorum Edition." *SP* 47 (1950): 494–505.

An analysis of the sources and textual analogues helps to show how Spenser has succeeded in revealing the transformation of a verbal mythological reality into a living reality [in 38].

739. "Explication de Texte Applied to Three Great Middle English Poems (I)." *ArL* 3 (1951): 1–22.

The poetic emphasis on perfection is achieved through repetition in the 13th-c. "Blow, northerne wynd" [in 38].

740. "Explication de Texte Applied to Three Great Middle English Poems (Continued)." *ArL* 3 (1951): 137–65.

"Of a rose, a lovely rose" and "I sing of a maiden" show how the individual's closeness to God is conveyed through the representation of the Nativity and how the miracle of Christ's coming is rendered through the treatment of natural renewal [in 38].

741. "Understanding Milton." *Johns Hopkins Review* 4 (1951): 17–27.

Using Milton's sonnet "Methought I saw my late espousèd Saint" as a point of departure, Spitzer criticizes interpretations that indiscriminately use facts drawn from a poet's biography. Such interpretations detract from or falsify the artistic coherence constructed by the poet [in 38].

742. "A Reinterpretation of the 'Fall of the House of Usher.'" *CL* 4 (1952): 351–63.

In a discussion of Poe's concept of "atmosphere," Spitzer emphasizes the ideas associated with *milieu* and *ambiance* that were developing during Poe's time [in 38].

743. "'Tears, Idle Tears' Again." *Johns Hopkins Review* 5 (1952): 71–80.

According to this reading, "some divine despair" means literally "the despair of some god," the god of "Death in Life" named at the poem's conclusion. The dual principle "Death in Life" supports the poem's structural and thematic unity. Ovid's *Tristia* is cited as a source in this and other treatments of the theme [in 37]. (Also in *Critical Essays on the Poetry of Tennyson*, ed. J. Killham, New York: Barnes, 1960, 192–203.)

744. " 'And prestes three . . . ' (*Canterbury Tales*, Prol., 164)." *MLN* 67 (1952): 502–04.

Prestes is a genitive singular, not a nominative plural: "and (the) priest's three" = 'and the (number, the sum total) three that is formed (achieved) by the priest.' This rare use of the genitive is consonant with the belief that a series' final item achieves the realization of the number it represents.

745. "On Yeats's Poem 'Leda and the Swan.' " *MP* 51 (1954): 271–76.

A response to Hoyt Trowbridge's Longinian exegesis (*MP* 51 [1953]: 118–29) in which Spitzer emphasizes the temporal and spatial treatment of the rape scene [in 38].

746. "The 'Ode on a Grecian Urn,' or Content vs. Metagrammar." *CL* 7 (1955): 203–25.

In a rebuttal to Earl Reeves Wasserman (*The Finer Tone: Keats' Major Poems*, Baltimore: Johns Hopkins UP, 1953), Spitzer uses the explication de texte to show how the text works as a "verbal transposition of sensuous experience" [in 38].

747. " 'Runaways Eyes' and 'Children's Eyes' Again." *NMo* 57 (1956): 257–60.

Contesting Tauno Mustanoja's thesis (*NMo* 56 [1955]: 250–58) that these Shakespearean phrases are "objective genitives," Spitzer maintains that "children's eyes" (sonnet 9) is a normal construction signifying that the children's eyes are " 'a form of thee' left behind by the father for the widow to behold." The "runaways" (*Romeo and Juliet* 3.2) are elopers who are in sympathy with Romeo's stealthy flight to visit Juliet and who blink so as not to see him.

748. "Marvell's 'Nymph Complaining for the Death of Her Faun': Sources versus Meaning." *MLQ* 19 (1958): 231–43.

"Imagistic positivism" does not work to explain a poem like this. Through stylistic contrasts Marvell succeeds in capturing both disillusionment and metamorphosis. The combination of Christian and pagan elements is traced to the medieval lay tradition of blending the worldly with the unworldly [in 38].

749. "Herrick's 'Delight in Disorder.' " *MLN* 76 (1961): 209–14.

There is neither ambiguity nor indirection in this sonnet. The poem is built on a tension between wildness and civility characteristic of the kind of classical art Herrick advocates. This tension is reflected in all aspects of the poem, including its syntax and rhyme scheme [in 38].

French Literature

750. "Corrections à *Yder*." *Rom* 40 (1914): 246–50.

Detailed corrections of Heinrich Gelzer's edition (*Der altfranzösische Yderroman, nach der einzigen bekannten Handschrift mit Einleitung, Anmerkungen, und Glossar. Gesellschaft für romanische Literatur*, 31, Dresden: Gedrukt für die Gesellschaft für romanische Literatur, 1913).

751. "Zu E. Richter's Ausgabe von Octavien de St. Gelais' Übersetzung des *Eurialus und Lukrezia*." *ZFS* 44 (1917): 237–39.

Detailed commentary on individual lines.

752. "Zur Motivgeschichte." *ZRP* 40 (1919–20): 112–13.

H. Patzig ("Berliner Programm," 1891) and Cecione (*Rivista Contemporanea*, 1889) could not have borrowed the motif of the "eaten heart" from French, where it occurs in Léon Bloy's "Sueur de sang" (Paris, 1894), because their works are earlier.

753. "Zur Texterklärung: Rabelaisiana (I)." *ZRP* 43 (1923): 611–14.

(1) *Touquedillon*. *Touquedillon* is probably related to Sp. *tocadillo* (= 'backgammon'). (2) *Capitoly*. In all probability this refers not to Rome but to the provincial capitals in France. (3) *Dronos*. In the phrase *faire dronos* (= 'to give a beating'), *dronos* is probably onomatopoeic; cf. Prov. *drin* (= 'a blow'), Ger. *dröhnen* (= 'to threaten'), Arag. *dorondón* (= 'hoarfrost'). (4) *Tenez*. Probably derives from OFr. *tes(ill)ier* (= 'to strive to be self-important') and OFr. *teseillier* (= 'to open one's mouth').

754. "Der Unanismus Jules Romains' im Spiegel seiner Sprache." *A Rom* 8 (1924): 59–122.

The consistency and unity of Romains's poetic vision in works like *La vie unanime* (1918) and *La mort de quelqu'un* are demonstrated in his language. Romains views life as a unified field in which birth and death, growth and disintegration are one. In life, unities and connections are constantly established, then dissolved to make way for new unities. This philosophy is mirrored in the vocabulary, grammar, and syntax of Romains's works examined in this study [in 20, 34].

755. "Zur Texterklärung. Rabelaisiana (II)." *ZRP* 44 (1924): 101–02.

(1) The name *Pantagruel*. *Panta* conveys a sense of suffocation and is related to *panteler* (= 'to pant') and *pantois* (= 'flabbergasted'). The second half of the name is probably related to Prov. *greùla*, *grieula* (= 'to whine loudly') and *greùle* (= 'strangled voice, difficult breathing'). (2) *Bauduffe*. This word refers specifically to oakum.

756. "Bemerkung zu *Ztschr.* 44, 747." *ZRP* 45 (1925): 128.

In opposition to Holbrook, Spitzer agrees with Pio Rajna (*Rom* 14 [1885]: 409) that *decliner* in the final verse of the Oxford version of *La chanson de Roland* can only mean 'to explain.'

757. "Ehrenrettung von Malherbes 'Consolation à Monsieur du Périer.'" *NS* 34 (1926): 191–96.

Contrary to Schulz-Gora (*ZFS* 26 [1903]: 92), Spitzer claims that Malherbe's poem owes nothing to Ronsard or to Montchrestien. Malherbe was more than a rhetorician, as his mastery of rhetorical figures reveals. In this poem his originality lies especially in his use of chiasma to reveal the correspondence between the individual and the universal [in 20, 36].

758. "Die klassische Dämpfung in Racine's Stil." *A Rom* 12 (1928): 361–472.

In the tragedies Racine uses several devices to evoke his characters' majesty: the indefinite article as a distancing device, the demonstrative to depersonalize, the third-person pronoun instead of the first, vague plural forms in preference to specific singulars, and others. Despite its lyricism, Racine's poetry may seem remote and cold. However, this restraint characterizes Racine's classicism and does not diminish the works' ardor [in 22, 44, 48].

759. "Vigny's 'Le cor.'" *GRM* 16 (1928): 399–414.

Though erudite, Schulz-Gora's article (*ANS* 53 [1874]: 67) is flawed in its aesthetic conception. The contradiction noted in Vigny's "Le cor" is stronger than he asserts, for he has not grasped the substance of the poem. Clarification of style must remain within the work itself, because a priori aesthetic views and biographical, geographical, and philological criticisms regarding the influence of other texts cannot reveal the work's own view [in 22].

760. "Notiz zu Péguy's Stil." *NS* 37 (1929): 503–05.

Péguy adopts a pattern from the antique style of Gorgias, who depicted the world in series of antitheses. In Peguy's use of antithesis the rhythm of his language becomes fragmented [in 20, 22, 34].

761. "Zu dem Aufsatz: 'Zur sprachlichen Interpretation von Wortkunstwerken.'" *Neue Jahrbücher für Wissenschaft und Jugendbildung* 6 (1930): 768.

The title of Jodelle's poem "A luy mesme" does not mean '(to the poet) himself.' In accordance with 16th-c. tradition, it refers to the dedicatee, that is, the Comte d'Alçinois, Nicolas Denisot [in 22, 23, 31, 32].

762. "Marie de France–Dichterin von Problem-Märchen." *ZRP* 50 (1930): 29–67.

Marie de France has been too much regarded as a mere storyteller and insufficiently appreciated as a poet. Storytelling is highly compatible with the aspirations of serious poetry, and Marie de France's achievement is to have combined the two. Her theses are neither simple nor one-dimensional; they resolve themselves in a dreamlike fashion and present a view of the contradictory, many-sided nature of the world. The poet's deft handling of tensions and ambiguities in these largely symbolic short narratives renders them lively and vivid [in 22].

763. "Erstellung des *Polyeucte* durch das *Alexiuslied*." *A Rom* 16 (1932): 473–500.

This spirited defense of Corneille's Christian tragedy shows that Corneille used the elements of legend to create a believable Christian martyr. Using *La vie de Saint Alexis* as an example, Spitzer shows that the Christian view encompasses both a withdrawal from the world and a militant search for heavenly glory. Corneille demonstrates in human terms and reasonable language how the higher value (Pauline's conversion) emerges from Polyeucte's struggle and death [in 48].

764. "Zu den Gebeten im *Couronnement Louis* und im *Cantar de mio Cid*." *ZFS* 56 (1932): 196–209.

The *Cantar de mio Cid* lends support to D. Scheludko's thesis (*ZFS* 55 [1931]: 447ff.), which claims that the confession and prayer typology in Old French epic derives from the *Couronnement Louis*. A detailed explanation of the prayer form's history shows how the pathos of a unified Christian worldview and the Christian epic style are interpolated into the secular epic.

765. "*Pape* im afrz. 'Alexius.'" *ZRP* 52 (1932): 769.

LLat. *papa* referred to bishops as well as to the pope, so the phrase *papa urbis Romae* was used to clarify. This explains why in *La vie de Saint Alexis* the word *pape* occurs exclusively in the phrase *pape de Roma*; in isolation *apostolie* is preferred.

766. "Interpretation einer Racine-Szene (*Bérénice* I, 4)." *NMo* 4 (1933): 87–95.

In *Bérénice* 1.44 Antiochus, an Oriental king, bares his soul to Bérénice. He is in love with her, but she loves Caesar Titus. Since the king's situation is hopeless–it is the eve of her wedding to Titus–his speech to her is a final "adieu." His speech is precious and stylized: Bérénice asks him to speak; he responds indirectly; she commands him to be silent. His love cannot change her mind, his deeds are futile, and his words, too, are of no avail. For Racine, both language and love are impossibilities, as illustrated in the tension between Antiochus's inner state and the language he uses ineffectively to express it.

767. "Dichterische Schönheit und Quellenstudium." *A Rom* 18 (1934): 561-66.
A work of art reveals more about the artist's intentions than does a study of its sources. This is true even in a poem like Malherbe's "Consolation à M. du Périer," which relies heavily on conventional and traditional imagery. In this poem, the use of the rose as a metaphor for a woman is traditional, as a study of rhetorical sources indicates. What matters more is how Malherbe redefines the metaphor in a new way, and a study of sources is only the beginning.

768. "Zur 'Passion' und zur syntaktischen Interpretation." *ZFS* 58 (1934): 437-44.
Spitzer questions Karl Ettmayer's interpretation of a line in the Old French *Passion* (*ZFS* 57 [1933]: 395ff.) and states that intrinsic criteria must always be examined in the assessment of a literary work. The literary critic and historian must guard against imposing modern views on medieval texts and must recognize and respect conceptual and linguistic differences.

769. "Zum Kommentar Villons." *NM* 36 (1935): 207-11.
In Villon's poetic world, in which contemporary criminal jargon frequently appears, macabre and sexual fantasies do not exclude each other. Furthermore, Villon tries to undermine and destroy the medieval connotations of martyrdom through sexual allusions.

770. "Victor Hugo's 'Le rouet d'Omphale.'" *NM* 37 (1936): 98-107.
This is not a "Hercules poem," as Hanns Heiss claims, but an "Omphale poem." Since Omphale overcomes the conqueror of the world by loving him, she stands higher than he in the Olympian hierarchy. Her superior position is expressed in the text's central symbol, the resting spinning wheel [in 35, 36].

771. "Zu Victor Hugo's 'Le rouet d'Omphale' (Nachtrag)." *NM* 37 (1936): 160.
The composer Saint-Saëns transformed Hugo's poem into a symphonic composition and emphasized the motif of the spinning wheel, thereby, in Spitzer's view, lending further support to his interpretation [in 35, 36].

772. "Zu *Florimont* 8673ff." *ZRP* 57 (1937): 597-98.
Schulze (*ZFS* 59 [1935]: 320) is ill-advised to change *avoir* to *amour* in *Florimont* 8673. *Avoir* is perfectly compatible with the context.

773. "*Lenguages* dans 'Li pélerinages Charlemagne,' v. 209." *MLN* 53 (1938): 20-21. "Correspondence." *MLN* 53 (1938): 553.
In line 209 of *Li pélerinages Charlemagne*, "car li lenguages i vienent de trestote la vile," *lenguages* means not 'people of many languages' but 'groups of foreign nationals.' In the letter, Spitzer later seems to admit that some of his critics are right in saying that *lenguages* refers to Europeans whom foreigners seek out in order to buy goods.

774. "Die Kunst des Übergangs bei La Fontaine." *PMLA* 53 (1938): 393-437.
La Fontaine's use of hidden transitions in the fables echoes Horace's art in the *Satires*. Cicero characterizes this quality of *suavitas* as a style appropriate to disputation, dialogue, and satire. The fables remind us of Horace both in their conversational form and in their satirical content. This wide-ranging study includes comparisons with works by Rabelais, La Rochefoucauld, Boileau, Hugo, and Valéry [in 31, 35, 44, 48].

775. "Pour le commentaire de Villon (*Testament* v. 447)." *Rom* 64 (1938): 522-23.

In Villon's lines (*Testament* 447-48) "Quant ilz voient ces pucelletes / Emprunter elles . . . ," *emprunter* is used in the sense of 'to imitate'; thus, the meaning is: "when they see the young girls imitate them" (the former prostitutes).

776. "The Name of Roland's Sword." *Lg* 15 (1939): 48-50.

The name of Roland's sword, *Durendal*, is a purely playful creation, based on an onomatopoeic root suggestive of dangling (cf. *dandiner* 'swing in the arms, dandle a baby'), with possible influence of *dur* 'hard.' The suffix of the variant *Durendart* is the same as that used for heroes, for example, *Escouflard*.

777. "Sur le v. 2015 du *Testament* de Villon." *Rom* 65 (1939): 101-03.

In opposition to M. Moldenhauer (*ANS* 171 [1937]: 212), Spitzer defends the sexual interpretation of lines 2014-15 in the *Testament* that he first offered in *NM* 36 (1935): 207.

778. "Verlebendigende direkte Rede als Mittel der Charakterisierung." *VRo* 4 (1939): 65-86.

Inserted direct speech is a tool for characterization in Montherlant's novel *Les jeunes filles* (1936). This device makes the character more lifelike. Through the parenthetical insertion of direct speech the author also gains a certain ironic distance from his characters.

779. "Die Branche VIII des *Roman de Renart*." *A Rom* 24 (1940): 206-37.

Léopold Sudre maintains that the eighth branch of the *Roman de Renart* is one of the oldest parts of the romance (*Les sources du "Roman de Renart,"* 1892, 206); Lucien Foulet is probably right when he points out that it is instead one of the most recent because it exhibits the most artistry (*Le "Roman de Renart,"* Paris: Champion, 1914, 372ff.). Both are wrong to deny the work's unity, for there is one overarching theme, namely, Renard's repentance [in 35].

780. "Le 'bel aubépin' de Ronsard." *FM* 8 (1940): 223-36.

M. C. Voile (*FM* 5 [1937]: 343-54), failing to recognize the importance of the final stanza of Ronsard's "Bel aubépin," misinterprets the tone of the poem as violent and militaristic. The forces of nature, seemingly at war, are in the long run necessary for the continuation of life.

781. "*Durendal* Once More." *Lg* 16 (1940): 213-14.

As pointed out by Dauzat, the name of Roland's sword is most likely a derivative of *Durand*, a proper name derived from *durare* 'endure,' 'be constant.' This is a retraction of *Lg* 15 (1939): 48-50.

782. "Etude ahistorique d'un texte: 'Ballade des dames du temps jadis.' " *MLQ* 1 (1940): 7-22.

Medieval literature should be studied for its aesthetic merits, not just as an exercise in literary history. Villon's "Ballade des dames du temps jadis," for example, is more than a monument in the development of French literature; it is a work of art. The interplay of strophe and refrain (the famous "Mais où sont les neiges d'antan?") creates a delicate equilibrium between the fear of death, as represented by the names of famous ladies now dead, and a quiet acceptance of it, depicted in the refrain's allusion to nature's cycles [in 35].

783. "Le prétendu réalisme de Rabelais." *MP* 37 (1940): 139-50.

Some scholars, most notably Abel Lefranc, maintain that Rabelais's works are realistic, since most of the places, persons, and events in them are based on historical fact. But the term "antirealist" would more accurately describe Rabelais's style, which consists of twisting and exaggerating facts in order to produce grotesque satire. This procedure is even reflected in the Rabelaisian lexicon, in the form of neologisms, for example, *Sorbonne* > *sorbonien, sorboniforme, sorbonisèque, sorbonisan, saniborsan,* and so on.

784. "A Linguistic and Literary Interpretation of Claudel's 'Ballade.'" *FR* 16 (1942): 134–43. (Published version of a lecture delivered at the MLA convention in Chicago, 1937.)

The author's "inner biography" is revealed in his style, a conjunction of the literary and linguistic features of this work [in 29, 34, 49].

785. "The Prologue to the *Lais* of Marie de France." *MP* 40 (1943): 96–102.

Marie views her book as another text that will be glossed according to the model of the church fathers' commentaries on the Old Testament. Aware that her tales have a Christian significance, Marie entrusts their doctrinal elucidation to the "subtlety" of future commentators [in 35].

786. "Etudes d'anthroponymie ancienne française." *PMLA* 58 (1943): 589–96.

(1) Olivier. Despite Albert Pauphilet's tentative attempt to establish a literary, not historical, basis for Olivier's existence in *La chanson de Roland* and also a well-established tradition of women's names taken from trees, bushes, fruits, and flowers, the derivation of masculine names remains obscure. Theoretically possible **olivarium* (= 'mont des oliviers') would have yielded **olivar-arius* and not **oliverius*, the latter formed from *oliva* > OFr. *olive* and *olivier* (in *Roland*) thanks to the common *-erius* (Emeterius, Desiderius). (2) The proper name, Pépin, is identified with the appellative *pépin* with which it shares both phonetic development (Lat. *pipinna* reflects a popular **pipinnus* or **pipinus* [= 'a small child']) and the hypothetical sense of 'small.'

787. "Le style de Ch.-F. Ramuz: Le raccourci mystique." *Agonia* 12 (1944): 12–26.

Anacoluth, the blending of tenses and modes of discourse, and repetition are features of "Salutation paysanne" that characterize Ramuz's tendency to evoke his search for a union with the All, "an earthly (nontranscendent)" mysticism [in 35].

788. "Des guillemets qui changent le climat poétique (Correction et commentaire à la première strophe du fragment d'Alexandre d'Albéric)." *PMLA* 59 (1944): 335–47.

A rearrangement of the quotation marks that punctuate lines 3–4 in the tenth edition of the *Chrestomathie de l'ancien français* (ed. Karl Bartsch and Leo Wiese, Leipzig: Vogel, 1910) brings the text into closer accord with medieval poetic values. This comparison of the Old French fragment and its Middle High German counterpart shows that d'Albéric, a medieval humanist, was more concerned with the general model exemplified in Solomon, whom he ostensibly quotes in these lines, than in an individualized representation of his own situation [in 35].

789. "La genèse d'une poésie de Paul Valéry." *Renaissance* 2–3 (1944–45): 311–21.

"La fileuse" (*Album des vers anciens*, 1920) represents a synthesis of elements drawn from Hérédia's sonnet ("La fileuse," 1905) and Mallarmé's "Sainte." Valéry transposes the idea of artistic creation through his treatment of symbolism and "la 'musicalisation' des idées" [in 35].

790. "Un *hapax* ne peut être expliqué par la linguistique seule: *Espacïun* dans *Gormont et Isembart*." *MP* 42 (1945): 133–36.

Proposes that *aspectio* > OFr. *espascïun* (**aspecïon*) could be the equivalent of

It. *cospetto* (= 'face, eye, appearance, presence'). It is not a "raw Latinism" but a Latinism with a long biblical tradition behind it, which has been adapted to Fr. [in 35].

791. "Notes aux 'Mots rares des *Faictz et Dictz* de Jean Molinet' (*Rom* 65, 9)." *Rom* 67 (1945): 372–76.

Corrections and some additional examples of four items detailed by M. N. Dupire: *boudrer, bucq, escorfant,* and *citoullet.*

792. "Le vers 830 du *Roland.*" *Rom* 67 (1945): 471–77.

It is Charlemagne's psychophysical process of maintaining self-control and reaching a difficult decision that is rendered in "suz sun mantel en fait la cuntenance." Classical, biblical, and other Old French examples are cited.

793. "Encore *espacïun* dans *Gormont et Isembard.*" *MP* 43 (1946): 129–30.

The expression "ne por tun Deu espacïun" must allude to an 11th-c. popular belief in a cure effected by looking on an image of Christ, an interpretation suggested by Menéndez Pidal in a letter to Spitzer pointing out the importance of the Veronica legend.

794. "Joinville étymologiste (*preu-home – preudome*)." *MLN* 62 (1947): 505–14.

J. Crossland's distinction between *preu-home* and *prodome* in Joinville is factitious. Instead the two terms designate the *miles christianus* and signify noble birth, exemplary character, valor, and moral generosity. The passage in question (ch. 559) shows the moralizing tendency of most medieval etymologies.

795. "Le vers 2 d'*Aucassin et Nicolette* et le sens de la chantefable." *MP* 45 (1947): 8–14.

A review of previous discussions of this controversial line (Gaston Paris, Mario Roques, M. A. Schulze, and Walther Suchier). Spitzer proposes that the line contributes to the *argumentum* offered in the *exordium* by drawing attention to the behavior (*desport*) of the young lovers' major obstacle (*viel antif* [= Garin de Beaucaire, Aucassin's father]) [in 35].

796. "La 'lettre sur la baguette du coudrier' dans le lai du *Chievrefueil.*" *Rom* 69 (1947): 80–90.

Spitzer reviews and contests other interpretations (Foulet, Gertrude Schoepperle) of this episode and advances the thesis that only Tristan's name appears on the hazelnut branch – sufficient evidence for Iseut, who, through the miraculous effects of her love, can interpret the spirit of the message [in 35].

797. "Patterns of Thought in the Style of Albert Thibaudet (I)." *MLQ* 9 (1948): 259–72.

In an analysis of Thibaudet's posthumously published letter on the League of Nations, Spitzer calls attention to the writer's associative talents, especially his use of simile in political writings. This letter represents a development away from the organicism of Thibaudet's early years [in 34, 35].

798. "Patterns of Thought in the Style of Albert Thibaudet (II)." *MLQ* 9 (1948): 478–91.

Spitzer discusses Thibaudet's essay on Boileau and compares the procedures used in Thibaudet's literary analyses with those in his political writing. The cultural totalities of the latter are represented in the former by Thibaudet's way of dealing with a particular phenomenon within the framework of all French literature. Thought processes are constant; however, the technique itself leads to contradictory results [in 34, 35].

799. "Tervagant." *Rom* 70 (1948–49): 397–408.

As suggested by L. Sainéan (*Les sources indigènes de l'étymologie française* 2, Paris: Boccard, 1925, 431–37), Tervagant, the name of one of the three Saracen gods in *La chanson de Roland,* is an epic invention, not an alteration of an existing pagan name. Additional examples of this participial name form are cited.

800. "Ronsard's 'Sur la morte de Marie.'" *Expl* 10 (1951): 1–4.

The second stanza of the sonnet should be printed in parentheses in order to give full importance to the first half of line 10, the dramatic center of the poem, which concludes the development of the epic descriptive simile that Ronsard creates in the preceding lines.

801. "*Aucassin et Nicolette,* Line 2 Again." *MP* 48 (1951): 154–56.

A reiteration of the earlier interpretation in which linguistic, stylistic, and semantic reasons are summoned to demonstrate that Old French words must not be combined according to the same liberties that underlie modern speech habits [in 35].

802. "Baudelaire's *Spleen.*" *Johns Hopkins Review* 6 (1953): 33–39.

Baudelaire is paraphrasing the physical experience of a headache in a tripartite treatment of the motif of claustration [in 35, 36].

803. "The Works of Rabelais." *Literary Masterpieces of the Western World.* Ed. Francis H. Horn. Baltimore: Johns Hopkins UP, 1953. 126–47.

This general appraisal of Rabelais's oeuvre includes a biographical sketch, a synopsis of all five books, a general characterization of Rabelais's style, and a lengthy discussion of Panurge who, according to Spitzer, is the work's true protagonist [in 43].

804. "Balzac and Flaubert Again." *MLN* 68 (1953): 583–90.

B. F. Bart's qualification of the two authors' styles, which contrasts Balzac's "energy" (*Les illusions perdues*) with Flaubert's "art" (*Madame Bovary*), is wrong.

805. "Les *Lettres portugaises.*" *RF* 65 (1953): 94-135.

By way of response to the question "Qui fut l'auteur des *Lettres portugaises?*" (M. F. C. Green, *MLR* 21 [1926]: 159ff.), Spitzer raises another question: "Quelle est la signification de ces lettres?" A description and analysis of the artistic value of the five letters begins with an explanation of their unity. A discussion of previous critical judgments, comparison with other *romans épistolaires,* and stylistic commentary follow. An appendix treats Rilke's interpretation of the *Lettres* and includes excerpts from his 1913 translation [in 35, 43, 48].

806. "A propos de *La vie de Marianne* (Lettre à M. Georges Poulet)." *RR* 44 (1953): 102–26.

Poulet's thesis (in *Etudes sur le temps humain: La distance intérieure,* Paris: Plon, 1952) that Marivaux's works reveal only a concern for the instantaneous is wrong. There are in effect two Marivaudian times, the instantaneous and the continuous ("la continuité au dessus des instants"), described in reference to *Marianne* [in 35, 43, 44, 49].

807. "Zu Marot's *Eclogue au roy, soubs les noms de Pan et Robin* (153)." *RJb* 9 (1958): 161–73.

The eclogue brings two worlds together: that of Pan – classical-antique – and that of Robin – popular-French. Marot, paraphrasing or borrowing from previous works, achieves originality and freshness through Robin's childlike qualities [in 36].

808. "Zu Ronsard's Sonett 'Je voudroy bien richement jaunissant. . . . '" With Wolfgang Spitzer. *RJb* 9 (1958): 194–98.

In a qualification of an interpretation offered by F. H. Friedrich ("Dichtung und die Methoden ihrer Deutung," *Festschrift zur Jubiläumsfeier der Albert-Ludwig-Universität*, Freiburg: n.p., 1957), Spitzer reviews the sonnet's final tercets with reference to the myth of Narcissus and cautions against hypermythologizing.

809. "Nochmals 'König David und der Diebsschlüssel.'" *ZRP* 74 (1958): 423–25.

On the basis of iconographic evidence, "roi David avoltre" and "clef avoltre" are shown to be associated.

810. "Nochmals zum Davidsschlüssel." *ZRP* 74 (1958): 428–29.

J. Mayr's reference to the Advent antiphon supports Spitzer's argument that Isaiah's phrase "clavis David" in the liturgy refers to an omnipotent messianic key or masterkey.

811. "Nota sulla favola di La Fontaine 'Les deux pigeons' (IX, 2)." *SFr* 3 (1959): 86–88.

A discussion of particular passages supports a new interpretation of the relation between the fable and its epilogue: the fable is about love, not about the transition from friendship to love [in 36].

812. "Rabelais et les 'rabelaisants.'" *SFr* 4 (1960): 401–23.

An eight-part article responding to those whose studies appear in *Travaux d'Humanisme et Renaissance* 7 (1953). The prevailing view of Rabelais as a realist is debated; the inherent artistic value of the work takes precedence over any historical theory imposed on it [in 44].

813. "Quelques aspects de la technique des romans de Michel Butor (I)." *ArL* 13 (1962): 171–95.

This discussion of *L'emploi du temps* focuses on the manner of narration and takes into account the treatment of time and place through which the protagonist's preoccupations are re-created. Butor uses a multilevel narrative time, which helps the reader live with the author, the novel's true protagonist, "le roman de son roman." (Spitzer was preparing this study at the time of his death; a note by Georges Poulet accompanies part 1.) [in 44]

814. "Quelques aspects de la technique des romans de Michel Butor (II)." *ArL* 14 (1962): 49–72.

A discussion comparing *La modification* and *Passage de Milan* with *L'emploi du temps,* particularly in regard to the treatment of time and place and the narrator's role and identity [in 44].

815. "Ancora sul prologo al primo libro del *Gargantua* di Rabelais." *SFr* 9 (1965): 423–34.

Rabelais's admonitions to the reader to seek the *substantifique moëlle* are tongue-in-cheek, contrary to assertions by Lefranc and others who have sought to discover the work's hidden meaning. This consideration of the prologues to *Gargantua* and *Pantagruel* leads up to a summary of two postulates underlying Spitzer's method: (1) The form and content of a literary work are one. Any attempt to analyze them as separate entities inevitably produces errors and distortions. (2) In works from the past, scholars must be very cautious in choosing historical data. Therefore, in the absence of evidence to the contrary, it is an error to interpret *substantifique moëlle* as evidence of the author's heretical attitude.

816. "Zur Auffassung Rabelais' (1931)." *Rabelais*. Ed. August Buck. Darmstadt: Wissenschaftliche Buchgesellschaft, 1973. 26–52. [in 22]

817. "Le portrait de Louis XIV par Saint-Simon." *Cahiers Saint-Simon* 7 (1979): 37–67. [in 22, 48]

German Literature

818. "Zum ältesten rätoroman. Sprachdenkmal." *ZRP* 36 (1912): 477–79.

A commentary on the translation of many of the terms in the first five lines of the oldest Rhaeto-Romanic text.

819. "Romanisches bei Oswald von Wolkenstein." *NM* 21 (1920): 72–77.

An examination of the use of Romance locutions in Wolkenstein's work. In the line "non mais plus disligaides," the phrase "non mais plus" stems from Catal., whereas the verb "disligaides" is a German borrowing from Fr. In general, Wolkenstein's use of Romance borrowings reflects a mixture of Arag., Catal., and Castil.

820. "Steigerungen von Adjektiven und Adverbien bei Goethe." *GRM* 18 (1930): 308–09.

Otto Pniower (*Euph* 30 [1929]: 189) refers to four kinds of comparatives in Goethe's *Faust*. While Spitzer accepts Pniower's analysis at the grammatical level, he questions Pniower's account of the comparatives' psychological origin. According to Spitzer, they evoke impressions; they do not name well-formed concepts.

821. "Das Nein des Märtyrers." *NM* 35 (1934): 159–61.

A parallel exists between poetic and visual creation, a prolific source of comparative study, provided that text and painting correspond aesthetically. A description of a painting of Saint Ursula found in a German magazine in 1934 supports this thesis.

822. "Die Sonne geht zu Gnaden." *MLN* 52 (1937): 506–08.

In the expression "Die Sonne geht zu Gnaden" 'the sun sets,' *Gnaden* signifies 'place of heavenly glory.' The phrase means 'the sun dies.'

823. "J. A. Walz, 'Nochmals "Die Sonne geht zu Gnaden."' *MLN* 54 (1939)." *MLN* 54 (1939): 236.

Walz tries to show that in the phrase "Die Sonne geht zu Gnaden" the last word means 'rest' rather than 'death,' as suggested by Spitzer. Walz has interpreted literally what should be viewed metaphorically: the overpowering connotation of 'rest' in this phrase is 'divine grace,' therefore, 'death.'

824. "Nochmals: Zur Interpretation von 'Wandrers Sturmlied.'" *GR* 20 (1945): 161–65.

The poem's conclusion is an ironic reversal of the ostensible celebration of genius in earlier sections (cf. W. F. Michael, *GR* 19 [1944]: 176ff.).

825. "*Neidgetroffen*." *NM* 48 (1947): 164–69.

In st. 9 of "Wandrers Sturmlied," Apollo's envy of the cedars is what is intended: *neidgetroffen* signals the suddenness of this effect on the sun god. (The term is a hapax legomenon in Goethe; cf. H. J. J. Weigand, *GR* 21 [1946]: 166–72.)

826. "Emilia Galotti–eine 'Gans' oder ein 'Ludechen.'" *GR* 23 (1948): 40-41.
Goethe's description of Emilia Galotti as a goose or a hussy is paralleled in 16th-c. Spanish sources, which refer to Lucrecia as "puta y necia" (cf. J. Gillet, *HR* 15 [1937]: 120-36). Goethe probably arrived at this expression independently.

827. "Note on Immermann's *Chiliastische Sonette.*" *GR* 25 (1950): 196-97.
What Karl Immermann had in mind in the third line of the first tercet is now known as *Banausentum*.

828. "Wiederum Mörikes Gedicht 'Auf eine Lampe.'" *Trivium* 9 (1951): 133-47.
The significance of the lamp's form, its symbolic importance, is noted by neither Emil Staiger nor Martin Heidegger, whose discussions are referred to here. The lamp has brought the poet to a definition of beauty traced in the poem through a representation of the lyric experience. (Staiger's response follows.) See also "A 1951 Dialogue on Interpretation: Emil Staiger, Martin Heidegger, Leo Spitzer," *PMLA* 105 (1990): 409-35.

829. "'Auf eine Lampe.'" *MLN* 68 (1953): 333-34.
Mörike's model was Theocritus's first idyll, "Thyrsis" (also paraphrased by Leconte de Lisle in "Le vase").

830. "Zu einer Landschaft Eichendorffs." *Euph* 52 (1958): 142-52.
Descriptive passages in Eichendorff's works are neither superfluous nor interchangeable (cf. Richard Alewyn, *Euph* 51 [1957]: 42ff.). *Viel Lärm um Nichts* is used to illustrate this view in a discussion of the relation between landscape and characterization [in 43].

831. "Matthias Claudius' *Abendlied.*" *Euph* 54 (1960): 70-82.
The first six lines must not be considered in isolation, for they set the scene for the rest of the poem– a pattern that shows up in other works by Claudius (cf. H. Broch, *Einige Bemerkungen zur Philosophie und Technik des Übersetzens*, Gesammelte Werke: Essays 1, Zurich: Rhein-Verlag, 1955, 277ff.) [in 43].

832. "Zum Rilke-Sonett 'Atmen, du unsichtbares Gedicht.'" *WW* 10 (1960): 52.
In response to J. Müller's interpretation of the sonnet's last tercet (*WW* 9 [1959]: 288ff.), Spitzer points out how the contrast it contains expresses the poet's transformation of language in the sonnet as a whole.

Italian and Latin Literature

833. "Matilde Serao." *GRM* 6 (1914): 573-84.
Literary naturalism is a product of the modern industrial city with its contradictions and disharmonious details. It arose in the overheated culture of Paris with Zola and Maupassant and moved south into Italy, where it was used to explore the unspoiled regional provincialism of the south. The Italians have no Zola. The closest Italian representative of naturalism is Matilde Serao, who differs from Zola in that she does not resign herself to a pseudoscientific objectivity. As a journalist and novelist, Serao never stops declaring her "j'accuse" and "je défends." She is not a great writer, perhaps, but like the great epic writers she can symbolically appropriate a type in a definitive way.

834. "Zu Tallgren, 'Les Poésies de Rinaldo d'Aquino.'" *NM* 19 (1918): 6-9.

Spitzer's commentary on Tallgren's interpretations includes linguistic corrections of the poems.

835. "Zu studi su la lirica siciliana del Duecento *IV*." *NM* 20 (1919): 1-4.

Translations and interpretations of these poems, including "Rinaldo."

836. "Bemerkungen zu Dantes *Vita nuova*." *Travaux du Séminaire de Philologie Romane* (Istanbul) 1 (1936): 162-208.

Detailed linguistic and stylistic commentary on most of the sonnets [in 47].

837. "Altital. *riviera*." *ZRP* 57 (1937): 90-91.

The phrase "Amor in gentil cor prende riviera" in Guinizelli's "Al cor gentile ripara sempre amore" means 'Love lingers in the noble heart,' not 'Love influences the noble heart' as suggested by Dimitri Scheludko (*Deutsche Vierteljahrsschrift für Literaturwissenschaft und Geistesgeschichte* 12 [1934]: 391).

838. "Una variante italiana del tema del 'condenado por desconfiado.'" *RFH* 1 (1939): 361-68.

The Hindu motif of the religious hermit who turns renegade upon seeing a thief saved (as in Tirso de Molina, "El condenado por desconfiado") appears in the Italian genre "dramma claustrale," but in slightly different form. Although the hermit does sinfully insist upon knowing God's plan for another, apparently less holy, man, he does not turn against God in a fit of egotistical rage when the man is saved. The plot is more idealistic than Tirso's but less powerful.

839. "Speech and Language in *Inferno* XIII." *Ital* 19 (1942): 81-92.

Stylistic devices in *Inferno* 13 are partly related to an evocation of the historical character Pier Delle Vigne. However, Dante uses these rhetorical devices to represent torture, schism, and estrangement, themes that dominate this canto. Dedicated to James Eustace Shaw [in 35, 47, 49]. (Also in *Dante: A Collection of Critical Essays*, ed. John Freccero, Englewood Cliffs: Prentice, 1965, 78-101.)

840. "Two Dante Notes." *RR* 34 (1943): 248-62.

(1) An autobiographical incident in *Inferno* XIX. *Inferno* 19.10-24 is discussed to show that seemingly autobiographical notes in Dante's work serve an artistic rather than a personal end. Traces the trajectory of *suggel* < *sigillum* (= 'type, stamp, pattern, image, example') throughout the *Commedia* [in 47]. (2) *Libicocco*. Libicocco, the name of one of the devils in the fifth *bolgia* (*Inferno* 21), was a popular word in Dante's time, not a deformation of a contemporary Tuscan family name (viz., *Biccicocco, Cillicozzo*). An etymological connection with a word meaning 'apricot' is proposed.

841. "The Farcical Elements in *Inferno*, Cantos XXI-XXIII." *MLN* 59 (1944): 83-88.

This interlude is explained in terms of the nature of the crime exposed (*baratteria*), which is the focus of the unheroic situation developed in fable form [in 35, 47, 49].

842. "*Decameron* VIII, 9: *carapignare*." With C. S. Singleton. *MLN* 59 (1944): 88-92.

Aldo Francesco Massèra reads *carmignare* in the Berlin ms. Spitzer and Singleton read *carapignavano*, citing other mss. in support. They assume an It. and Flor. **(s)carpignare*, **(s)carpignliare* and point out that Boccaccio's use of a genuine popular or dialectal word (Bruno and Buffalmacco are "tickled to death") proves that the word was still understood.

843. "Zum Aufbau von Petrarca's *Trionfi.*" *NM* 48 (1946): 49–60.

A discussion of classical and Christian prototypes contrasts Petrarch's use of sequential victories in *Trionfi* with Dante's use of the same device in *Inferno* [in 35, 47].

844. "The Epic Style of the Pilgrim Aetheria." *CL* 1 (1949): 225–58.

Previous studies of the *Peregrinatio Aetheriae ad loca sancta* have paid insufficient attention to the "stylistic personality of the author." This analysis considers the *Peregrinatio* from the standpoint of the genre it represents. A study of the uses of *ipse, nam*, anaphora, and other types of repetition shows that certain epic patterns found in later medieval romance poetry are already present in this Vulgar Latin narrative [in 35].

845. "Remarks on the 'Sirventese Lombardo.'" *Ital* 28 (1951): 6–11.

Emendations of the Bertoni (1901) and Francesco Ugolini (1944) editions of the text and textual commentary.

846. "Notes to the Text of 'Ritmo Laurenziano.'" *Ital* 28 (1951): 241–48.

The poem is a rare example of the laudatory *sirventes*. Emendations to and interpretations of lines 16–17, 18, and 35 are offered.

847. "Zu Pontans Latinität." *RF* 63 (1951): 61–71.

A discussion of *hirquitulus* and *Pistiles* in Pontano's first published Latin dialogue, *Antonius* (1491). Both terms are found in excerpts by a Roman glossarist, Pompeius Festus, from the 8th c. Pontano rediscovered these words and incorporated them into his satirical vocabulary [in 35].

848. "Zum 'Cantico delle creature.'" *Trivium* 9 (1951): 241–47.

The individual is not represented as *adjutor Dei* and is set apart from the community of beasts.

849. "L'episodio di travale." *LN* 13 (1952): 1–2.

Fredi Chiappelli, in *Studi di Filologia Italiano* 9 (1951): 141ff., explains the following passage (Francesco Ugolini, *Testi antichi italiani*, Torino: Chiantore, 1942, 100; Ruggero Ruggieri, *Testi antichi romanzi* 2, Modena: Soc. Tipografica Modenese, 1949, 41): "Guaita (a travale) / guaita male, / non mangiai ma' mezzo pane." According to Spitzer, the second *guaita* is an imperative, not a substantive (he concurs here with Debenedetti [*GSLI* 105 (1928): 151]). He cites Provençal examples from the *alba* in support of his interpretation [in 35].

850. "Emendations Proposed to *De amico ad amicam* and *Responcio.*" *MLN* 67 (1952): 150–55.

Proposes emendations to both texts and includes stylistic commentary.

851. "The Text and the Artistic Value of the *Ritmo Cassinese.*" *SMed* 18 (1952): 23–54.

This poem is not fragmentary. Stylistic and linguistic evidence is cited to support the view that it is "the first perfect (and complete) poem of Italian literature" [in 35].

852. "Sul componimento anonimo 'Cosi afino ad amarvi.'" *CN* 14 (1954): 195–200.

Emendations and reinterpretations offered for stanzas 3 and 4. The interpretation stresses especially the poet's state of sensual ecstasy following the lady's encouragement of his advances. There is a "dialogue within a dialogue" in stanza 4, the secondary dialogue being, in effect, a monologue sotto voce, which finishes with the poet's spoken promise to "fare conteze" (*prodezze*). (In a *postilla* R. Ruggieri responds.)

853. "'Istos ympnos ludendo composuit.'" *MLN* 59 (1954): 383–84.

Found in a passage (by N. Wheatley, 1316) treating the composition of hymns, the phrase *ludendo composuit* means 'He composed as a poetic exercise.'

854. "Un passo di una canzone di Giacomino Pugliese." *CN* 15 (1955): 143–45.

A commentary on the fifth stanza in Monaci's revised edition of the *Crestomazia italiana*, especially line 28 (Ernesto Monaci, *Crestomazia italiana: nuova ed. riveduta e aumentate per cura di F. Arese*, Roma: Dante Alighieri, 1955). *Vegianza* (*in presi vegianza*), glossed by Monaci as 'vendetta,' means, rather, 'vista': *prendere vegianza* means, therefore, 'prender vista,' which accords better with the overall sense of the stanza in question. The suffix alternation *-enza*, *-anza*, characteristic of the Sicilian school under Franco-Norman influence, is discussed in connection with Old French parallels *veance*, *voyance*.

855. "Osservazioni sul testo della 'Canzoni di Auliver' (Monaci-Arese, *Crest. ital.*, no. 166)." *CN* 15 (1955): 239–41.

Emendations offered: lines 1, 6, 16, 18, 21, 42, 43, 46, and 52.

856. "Nuove considerazioni sul 'Cantico di frate sole.'" *Conv* 23 (1955): 257–70.

A reaffirmation of the earlier assessment of the "Cantico," in which the importance of biblical and patristic sources in the formation of Saint Francis's thought is scrutinized (response to M. Casella, "Il 'Cantico delle creature,'" *SMed* 16 [1943–50]: 102ff.) [in 35, 47].

857. "The 'Ideal Typology' in Dante's *De vulgari eloquentia*." *Ital* 32 (1955): 75–94.

Dante's methodological innovation in *De vulgari eloquentia* is examined in the light of modern typological theories (cf. A. Rustow, "Der Idealtypus oder die Gestalt als Norm," *Studium Generale* 6 [1953]: 54–59). *De vulgari eloquentia* anticipates Max Weber's methods of morphological classification and represents Dante's efforts to construct the ideal type of Italian [in 47].

858. "The Addresses to the Reader in the *Commedia*." *Ital* 32 (1955): 143–65.

A detailed discussion of Dante's addresses (nineteen in all) shows the poet's concern for establishing the reality of his vision and his closeness to the reader while acting as the reader's spiritual guide [in 35, 47, 49].

859. "L'originalità della narrazione nei *Malavoglia*." *Belfagor* 11 (1956): 37–53.

The originality of the novel lies in the systematic filtering of the narration through a crowd of speakers [in 35, 47].

860. "Postilla all'articolo 'Nuove considerazioni sul "Cantico di frate sole."'" *Conv* 24 (1956): 234–35.

As previously noted, the "Cantico" is divided into two parts—an "Alleluia" and a "Dies Irae"—forming an artistic whole through the litany form itself [in 35, 47].

861. "A proposito del 'Mare amoroso.'" *CN* 16 (1956): 179–99.

The poem is neither a satire nor a parody (Vittorio Cian) nor a "formulario amoroso" (Giulio Bertoni) destined to teach new poets how to write poetry. It is a polemic against a conception of love that is not the poet's own and that he repudiates [in 35].

862. "Il 'Detto del Gatto Lupesco.'" *GSLI* 133 (1956): 1–24.

This text does not form part of the allegorical tradition preceding Dante, nor is it a parody. The protagonist's hybridism is due to the poet's psychological acuity in his dramatization of the professional jongleur's existential conflicts and the precariousness of his life [in 35].

863. "Nuove osservazioni sul testo del 'Ritmo su S. Alessio.'" *GSLI* 133 (1956): 202–07.

A detailed commentary offering new interpretations and textual emendations (lines 5, 9–10, 41, 51, 64–67, 85, 128, 147–50, 175, 206, 219, 240).

864. "*Aivo* nel discordo di Giacomo da Lentino." *LN* 17 (1956): 107–08.

Found in lines 184–92 of the text printed in the *Crestomazia italiana: nuova ed. riveduta e aumentate per cura di F. Arese* (Roma: Dante Alighieri, 1955, 415), *aivo*, a borrowing from Fr., is a transcription of the first-person present of Fr. *aïver* < Lat. *adequare* (It. *adeguare*) meaning 'to balance, to make equal,' which must also mean 'to maintain the equality of two opposites,' similar to OFr. *des(a)iver.*

865. "Altre considerazioni sul 'Cantico di frate sole.'" *Conv* 25 (1957): 84–87.

A reiteration of the main tenets of the earlier discussions stressing the inadmissibility of putative biographical evidence to explain particular aspects of a poetic text (a response to G. Getto, "Francesco d'Assisi e il 'Cantico di frate sole,'" *Publicazioni della Facoltà di Lettere e Filosofia dell'Università di Torino* 8 [1956]: 70) [in 35, 47].

866. "Aggiunti al 'Mare amoroso.'" *CN* 16 (1957): 175–76.

(1) The idea of the *mare amoroso* appears already in *Cligés* by Chrétien de Troyes. (2) Modern skepticism toward absolute perfection is traced through the oscillating pattern of hesitation/assertion in an enumeration of ideal comparisons found in Lope de Vega's *Lo fingido verdadero.* (3) The poetic enumeration of substantives to describe the beloved in the *mare amoroso* resembles that used by Provençal poets. The principal effect is to intensify the significance of the qualities described [in 35].

867. "Osservazione al testo del 'Detto d'amore.'" *GSLI* 134 (1957): 77–85.

An examination of the principal textual and interpretative problems analyzed by S. Morpurgo, A. Musafia, and E. G. Parodi, among others. New readings or corrections are offered.

868. "Una questione di punteggiatura in un sonetto di Giacomo da Lentino (e un piccolo contributo alla storia del sonetto)." *CN* 18 (1958): 61–70.

In this examination of sonnets by the Sicilian inventer of the form, the hypothesis that form and content, often treated in isolation, must be considered together is studied in the context of Lentino's treatment of contrast or paradox. Unity of form and content in these early sonnets is a key to the genesis of the form itself and to the coherence of the sonnet sequence.

869. "La bellezza artistica dell'antichissima elegia giudeo-italiana." *Studi in Onore di Angelo Monteverdi* 2 (1959): 788–806.

An analysis of the elegy's theme and structure, with particular attention to the central episode relating the story of the brother and sister sold into slavery. Other versions are considered in their treatment of *Sion lamentata* ("The Influence of Hebrew and Vernacular Poetry on the Judeo-Italian Elegy," *Twelfth-Century Europe and the Foundations of Modern Society*, ed. M. Clagett, G. Post, and R. Reynolds, Madison: U of Wisconsin P, 1961, 115–30) [in 47].

870. "'For de la bella cayba.'" *LI* 12 (1960): 133–40.
The genesis of the poem is considered in the context of *Frauenlieder* and the popular lyric tradition [in 35].

871. "Ancora, 'For de la bella cayba.'" *LI* 12 (1960): 445.
Two *canzoni* found in G. Vicente's *Tragicomedia da Serra de Estrela* (cited by P. Teyssier, *La langue de Gil Vicente,* Paris: Klincksieck, 1959) use variants of the falcon motif discussed in the preceding article dealing with this poem [in 35].

872. "L'*Aspasia* de Leopardi." *CN* 23 (1963): 114–45.
A coherent view of the text is impossible without considering the relation between the parts and the whole. A review and critique of arguments advanced by others includes an analysis of the development and resolution of the conflict between intellect and sentiment introduced in the first stanza. (Dedicated to H. Hatzfeld.) [in 47]

Provençal and Catalan Literature

873. "Das Sirventes 'Honratz es hom per despendre.'" *ANS* 129 (1912): 388.
Corrects Adolf Kolsen's translation.

874. "Zu Guilhem de Cabestanh's Gedicht 'Anc mais n'om fo semblan.'" *NM* 15 (1913): 179–81.
Clarifications of Artur Långfors's translation (*NM* 15 [1913]: 73ff.).

875. "Zu Långfors' Ausgabe eines Gedichtes von Ozil de Cadars." *NM* 15 (1913): 256.
Corrects meanings offered by Långfors in his edition of this poem.

876. "Corrections au 'Conte d'amour' catalan." *Rom* 40 (1914): 105–06.
Corrects A. Pagës's translation.

877. "E. Niestroy, 'Der Trobador Pistoleta'; F. Naudith, 'Der Trobador Guillem Magret.'" *Rom* 40 (1914): 445–50.
Detailed corrections.

878. "Zu Kurt Lewent's Beiträgen zum Verständnis der Lieder Marcabrus." *ZRP* 39 (1917–19): 221–23.
Line-by-line corrections and additions (*ZRP* 37 [1913]: 313ff., 427ff.).

879. "Zu Kolsen, *Dichtungen der Trobadors III.*" *ZRP* 41 (1921): 355–63.
A discussion of selected lines of Kolsen's translations of the troubadour lyrics collected in this volume.

880. "Zum Text und Kommentar der *Flamenca.*" *NM* 37 (1936): 85–98.
Detailed commentary on the text as it appears in Kurt Lewent's edition (*Sammlung romanischer Übungstexte,* Band 8, Halle: Niemeyer, 1926).

881. "Ancien provençal *sec . . . son agre.*" *MLN* 53 (1938): 186–88.
The phrase "lo colom sec trop voluntier son agre" in the Provençal bestiary (Carl Appel, *Provenzalische Chrestomathie,* Leipzig: Reisland, 1895, 1918, 1920, 204) is probably a scribal alteration of "lo colon set trop voluntier sobre aiga." The scribe

changed *aiga* 'water' to *agre*, because the latter, ultimately a reflex of *ager*, developed semantically from 'field' through 'habitat' and 'instinct' to 'nature.' The line as written now means 'the pigeon follows too freely his nature.'

882. "*Flamenca* v. 7685–88." *A Rom* 23 (1939): 88–91.

The character of Archambaut docs not fit the courtly tradition; he is at first jealous – an unacceptable attitude – and then he is oblivious to his wife's infidelity. Appel's interpretation of the ending as a happy ménage à trois is wrong.

883. "L'amour lointain de Jaufré Rudel et le sens de la poésie des troubadours." University of North Carolina Studies in the Romance Languages and Literatures 5 (Chapel Hill: U of North Carolina P, 1944): 1–74.

In this response to Grace Frank (*MLN* 57 [1942]: 528–34), lexical, semantic, and stylistic material in the *amour lointain* cycle is analyzed to describe the theme of Rudel's poems, *le paradoxe amoureux*, that is, "l'amour qui ne veut posséder, mais jouir de cet état de non-possession." A general study of the troubadour love lyric [in 26, 35, 44].

884. "An Emendation Proposed for the Text of the 'Pistola' of Cerveri de Girona." *Traditio* 7 (1949–51): 464–65.

For *de mars* 'harm' (line 40 in Kurt Lewent's edition, *Traditio* 6 [1948]: 161ff.), we should read *d'emars* = *d'amars* 'bitterness' < *amarum* 'resentment.'

885. "Zu *RF* 61/II." *RF* 62 (1950): 76.

Spitzer disagrees with Gamillscheg's correction of *au mangier* to *au moustier* (*Girart de Rossillon*, line 97) and states that it was customary to read devotional literature to monks at dinner, according to one of Benedict of Nursia's precepts.

886. "*Parelh paria* chez Marcabrun." *Rom* 73 (1952): 78–82.

Based on the concept *parelh*, which the poet exposes through his treatment of the theme in the *pastourella* "L'autrier jost'una sebissa," *parelh paria* is a neologism forged by Marcabrun. It is a derivative form in *-ia* based on *parelh-par-* 'tout à fait égal' [in 35].

887. "Salvatore Santangelo, 'L'amore lontano di Jaufré Rudel' dans *Siculorum Gymnasium*, ns 6 (Catania, 1953)." *Rom* 75 (1954): 396–402.

Santangelo's effort to prove that Rudel's love was Eleanor of Aquitaine is disputed on the basis of what is considered to be a too literal reading of the *amor de lonh* theme. The latter is an eternal theme and a symbol of the paradox inherent in love.

Spanish and Portuguese Literature

888. "La Norvège comme symbole de l'obscurité." *RFE* 9 (1922): 316–17.

Three citations from Portuguese literature (16th–18th centuries) support the contention (Castro, *RFE* 6 [1919]: 184–86) that Norway was a symbol of darkness in that literature.

889. "Bribes de phrases allemandes dans des textes espagnols du XVI siècle." *RFE* 10 (1923): 302–06.

(1) Covarrubias's phrase (s.v. *Lanciscot*) "godt segent licden" 'May God bless it for you' is Dutch *Godt segent ulieden* 'idem.' (2) *Lancaman* 'compatriot' = Ger. *Lanze*

'lance' + Fr. argotic suffix *-man.* (3) *Josefina* (1549) contains several words, including *hasticoz hex tinguert,* from *dass dich Gotts . . . stinkert* 'May God confound you.' (4) Bartolomé de Torres, in *Tinellaria,* writes "nite carne y obbigot," from Swiss *nite carne, yo bi got* 'not meat, yes by God.'

890. "Zur Kunstgestalt einer spanischen Romanze." *NS* 34 (1926): 506–14.
The blending of the present and simple past tenses in *Romanza de Abenâmar* is a baroque device [in 20].

891. "Note sur *La Celestina.*" *RFE* 16 (1929): 59–60.
The nobility of Calisto's lineage is emphasized from the very beginning of *La Celestina,* contrary to what H. García (*RFE* 11 [1924]: 411–12) claims.

892. "Allemand et flamand d'Espagne." *RFE* 16 (1929): 176.
Some apparent nonsense in act 2 of Lope's *El caballero del sacramento* is actually crudely rendered German: "trinkque non denece / y ni te gote fertece" is "Trinken und essen! Nicht Gott vergessen."

893. "Zu Góngora's 'Soledades.'" *VKR* 2 (1929): 244–58.
In Góngora's poetic world, an abundance of forms does not exclude abstraction and distance. An analysis of grammar and syntax in "Dedicatoria al Duque de Béjar," leading up to a more general study of baroque symbolism, supports this conclusion [in 22, 49].

894. "*Betlengabor*—une erreur de Gracián? (Note sur les noms propres chez Gracián)." *RFE* 17 (1930): 173–80.
Gracián's references to *Betlengabor* (Bethlen Gabor, prince of Transylvania) as a former lackey who rose in the world are not to be taken literally. In fact, Betlengabor's fortunes did greatly improve, and he came to be understood as a type rather than as an individual. This explains the plural *Betlengabores* [in 22].

895. "Zur 'Celestina.'" *ZRP* 50 (1930): 237–40.
Calisto's vow to worship Melibea as his God has been interpreted as a Renaissance characteristic in *Celestina.* On the contrary, it is purely medieval: a thing of beauty existing in nature is an indirect representative of God himself, the creator of nature.

896. "Pedro Calderón de la Barca." *Neue Jahrbücher für Wissenschaft und Jugendbildung, Leipzig* 7 (1931): 516–30.
Calderón and Lope de Vega form a typically Spanish unity. Calderón is Lope de Vega's descendant, a classicist bringing order to his forebear. His classicism manifests itself in poetry full of contrast and in an allegorical mode that preserves a rigid rationalism behind a seemingly fantastic façade. Calderón's faith in eternal truth is characteristic of his conservative nature and his Catholicism [in 22].

897. "A. M. Alcover, 'Com he fet mon Aplech de Rondayes Mallorquines,' *ZRP* 51 (1931), 94–111." *ZRP* 51 (1931): 94–95.
An introduction to this article in which Spitzer praises Alcover for his scholarship and devotion to his culture.

898. "Das Gefüge einer cervantinischen Novelle ("El celoso estremeño")." *ZRP* 51 (1931): 194–225.
Cervantes writes in the Christian tradition whereby divine will governs all human action. In contrast, the moral universe delineated in Dostoyevski's short story "A Friend of the Family and the Eternal Husband" is governed primarily by

psychological motivations [in 22]. (Also in *Die romanische Novelle*, ed. W. Eitel, Darmstadt: Wissenschaftliche Buchgesellschaft, 1977, 175–213.)

899. "Zur Nachwirkung von Burchiellos Priameldichtung." *ZRP* 52 (1932): 484–89.

The enumeration technique introduced by Burchiello in his poem "Non son tanti babbion nel Mantovano" was adopted and given sonnet form by Mellin de Saint-Gelais in his satirical "Il n'est point tant de barques à Venise" and finally shaped into lyric poetry by Lope de Vega in his sonnet "No tiene tanta miel Atica hermosa."

900. "Zu Burchiellos Priamel-Gedicht." *ZRP* 53 (1933): 672.

In reference to the previous article (*ZRP* 52 [1932]: 484–89), Spitzer notes that an earlier source for Lope's lyric use of enumeration may be found in Petrarch.

901. "Le pourquoi d'une défaillance de style chez Cervantes." *Investigaciones Lingüísticas, México* 2 (1934): 293–97.

The relative inferiority of the two sonnets attributed to the character Don Fernand (*Don Quijote*, pt. 1, ch. 40) is due to Cervantes's objective: they are the expression of an individual who is a simple, not lofty, Platonist. Through him, Cervantes celebrates the day-to-day world.

902. "Zur Literaturgeschichte. Zur Auffassung der Kunst des Arcipreste de Hita." *ZRP* 54 (1934): 237–70.

The Archpriest of Hita's depiction of personality in the *Libro de buen amor* is the focus of a literary controversy: Werner Krauss argues that the work is too medieval to allow the portrayal of personality; Castro maintains that the archpriest's art is personal and intimate. In fact, the Archpriest of Hita is a conservative writer whose writing is artistically progressive. Although the *Libro de buen amor* is a first-person narrative, the "I" of a medieval tale has nothing in common with the "I" of, say, Rousseau's *Confessions*: the medieval narrator is entirely fictional. Although the characters in the *Libro* may appear realistic, they stem from general types. The most individual aspect of the text is the brio of its author's language [in 33].

903. "Die 'Estrella de Sevilla' und Claramonte." *ZRP* 54 (1934): 533–90.

Sturgis E. Leavitt tried to prove that this play was written by Andrès de Claramonte (*The "Estrella de Sevilla" and Claramonte*, Cambridge: Harvard UP, 1931). Spitzer cites many examples and quotations from the play to refute Leavitt's claim.

904. "Zur Nachwirkung des Gedankens vom philosophischen Gehalt der Fabeleien und des Rinde-Mark-Bildes." *ZRP* 54 (1934): 588–90.

Max H. Neumann (*Revue Hispanique* 78 [1930]: 153ff.) points out the obvious didactic value of *Don Quijote*. There is nothing unusual in this idea, since the work is linked to the medieval tradition of justifying a work of art by its moral content. Furthermore, as asserted by a Dutch journalist, Just van Effen, there are probably two types of readers (a division that the medieval author also recognized): those who enjoy the telling of the story and those who understand the deeper meaning of the work.

905. "En lisant le *Burlador de Sevilla*." *NM* 36 (1935): 282–89.

Commentary on selected passages and elucidations in Castro's second edition of the text.

906. "Notas sobre romances españoles." *RFE* 22 (1935): 153–74.

(1) The word *demorés*, appearing in a Catalanized version of "Gentil dona, gentil dona" (1421), is probably < **de morés* 'of an imaginary Moorish language' < *maurensis*

'moorish.' (2) The same poem may be correctly classified as a rhymed fairy tale of sorts: witness the presence of "serranas," monstrous females representative of nature's sprites and demons. (3) Another fairy-tale romance is the long version of "Infante Arnaldos." Although the truncated version is more romantic, it is not necessarily more artistic. Moreover, the truncation is not proof of "popular" as opposed to "artistic" intervention. (4) Hugo's often criticized "Romance mauresque" is in fact a work of great artistic integrity. That he understood his models is shown by his imitation of their essentially dialogic-dialectic character.

907. "Adiciones al artículo 'Notas sobre romances españoles.' " *RFE* 22 (1935): 290–91.

Short justification of a detail in the preceding article.

908. " 'A mis soledades voy . . . .' " *RFE* 23 (1936): 397–400.

Lope's references to solitude should not be equated with those of the mystics, who made solitude their path to God. Lope's "soledades" are merely momentary intellectual respites from the business of the world.

909. "Kenning und Calderons Begriffsspielerei." *ZRP* 56 (1936): 100–02.

Used in Old Norse poetry, the kenning is an expression characterized by the use of incongruous terms, for example, "storm of swords" for "battle." Paul Trost's assertion that the kenning is an essential part of the baroque tradition has some merit ("Zur Wesensbestimmung der Kenning," *Zeitschrift für deutsches Altertum* 70 [1933]: 235–36). Calderón, for instance, describes a pistol as a metal snake and then proceeds to blend snake metaphors into the story about the pistol. These baroque metaphors underscore a belief in the harmonic unity of the cosmos.

910. "Die Frage der Heuchelei des Cervantes." *ZRP* 56 (1936): 138–78.

A unified and rigorous code of ethics runs through Cervantes's work. Castro's contention (*El pensamiento de Cervantes*, Barcelona: Noguer, 1972) that he is hypocritical is not defensible. Of course, in some of his works Cervantes exaggerates the severity of his beliefs, because the genre (*entremés* not *novela ejemplar*) is not a subtle one. In general, however, Cervantes is serious about the moral pronouncements in his work. A discussion of "El celoso estremeño" illustrates this point.

911. "Un passage de Lope de Vega, l'espagnol *segullo*, et l'étymologie du français *talus*." *MLN* 52 (1937): 79–82.

Regarding Lope's mention of a supposed grass that grows over veins of gold (*Barlaán y Josafat* 1.562): (1) Sp. *segullo* 'soil overlying a vein of gold' < *segutilum* (var. *segullum*) 'idem.' The word seems not to be current in modern Sp. (2) Fr. *talus* 'bank, mound' was attributed in *REW* (first edition) to *talus* 'heel' and in *REW* (third edition) to Celt. *talutium* 'end of slope,' 'sign of a gold vein,' Celt. *tâlos* 'forehead.' An etymology preferable to these is Gk. *talysios* (*talysios artos*) 'bread baked from the first grain of the new harvest,' that is, the fruits that precede all others.

912. "Un passage de Quevedo." *RFE* 24 (1937): 223–25.

In *Las zahurdas de Plutón*, Quevedo enumerates among the ornaments in Satan's chamber "doncellas penadas como tazas" 'young girls who in their punishment take the form of cups,' located in *poyatas* 'shelves.' Some of the secondary associations evoked by these same words enrich the passage: *peñada* also means 'thick-necked' (said of cups); *poyata* suggests *poyete* 'place where old maids sit.'

913. "A propos d'un article de M. H. Meier." *MLN* 53 (1938): 554–56.
Spitzer takes issue with Meier for neglecting to acknowledge his precursors in his approach to the study of Cervantes. Indeed, Meier is following in the footsteps of Spitzer and Hatzfeld, among others, when he insists that details of style be examined in the context of the work as a whole.

914. "Eine Stelle in Calderons Traktat über die Malerei." *NM* 39 (1938): 361–70.
In his consideration of Calderón's treatise on painting, Curtius neglects a basic tenet of baroque theory, namely, the connection between mathematics and painting. For Calderón, arithmetic is a kind of ruler that provides a means to lay out a painting's lines. In his elaboration of the baroque aesthetic of splendor and abundance, distortion and violence, Calderón relies on a kind of numerical mysticism.

915. "Una construcción favorita de Góngora." *RFH* 1 (1939): 230–36.
Góngora's use of the copulative *ser* in passages where *servir* or *causar* might seem more appropriate (e.g., "[fiera] que en los bosques era / mortal horror al que con paso lento / los bueyes al establo reducía") is a patent mark of his conceptism: the copulative boldly equates things that are dissimilar, even opposite, and imposes a difficult synthesis on the reader. This precise usage is not found in Lat.: it is a conceptual innovation, not a syntactic relic [in 49].

916. "El acusativo griego en español." *RFH* 2 (1940): 35–45.
Góngora's use of Latinized (ultimately Greek) constructions such as "desnuda el pecho anda ella" reflects his taste for hierarchizing things: by making *desnuda* agree with *ella* rather than its referent *pecho*, he draws attention to the woman as the most important topic in the phrase.

917. "Thomas Mann y la muerte de Don Quijote." *RFH* 2 (1940): 46–48.
Mann deplores Don Quijote's return to "reason" before his death, a return he attributes to Cervantes's cowardly reluctance to affirm his own universal symbol of man. In reality, Cervantes was acting in accordance with the principle that the purpose of art is not to judge life but to help effect moral edification.

918. "J. P. Wickersham Crawford, 'The Setting of Góngora's *Las soledades*,' *HR* 7 (1939), 347–49." *RFH* 2 (1940): 84–87.
Crawford, trying to find an actual spot in Spain for the setting of Góngora's work, misses the point. Such information adds nothing to the reader's understanding of the poem.

919. "La 'Soledad primera' de Góngora: Notas críticas y explicativas a la nueva edición de Dámaso Alonso." *RFH* 2 (1940): 151–76.
Forty-six detailed commentaries on individual lines of Góngora's "Soledad primera" [in 49].

920. "Para el verso 402 de la 'Soledad Primera.'" *RFH* 2 (1940): 389.
An addition to *RFH* 2 (1940): 151–76 [in 49].

921. "El conceptismo interior de Pedro Salinas." *RHM* 7 (1941): 33–69.
This five-part analysis of *La voz a ti debida* (1933) describes the relationship between the two interlocutors who take part in the interior dialogue within the poetic "I" [in 33, 37]. (Dedicated to P. Salinas.)

922. "El barroco español." *BIIH* 28 (1943–44): 12–30.
Text of a lecture given at Middlebury College translated from the French by Pedro Salinas [in 35, 37, 49].

923. "Los romances españoles: El romance de Abenámar." *Asomante* 1 (1945): 4–29.

The explication de texte method is applied to the romance to show how a single text or passage can be treated as a paradigm of a genre, its epoch, and its national origin [in 35, 39]. (Also in *Explicación de Textos Literarios* 1 [1972–73]: 87–101.)

924. " '¡Dios, qué buen vassallo si oviesse buen señor!' " *RFH* 8 (1946): 132–35.

Parallel examples from *La chanson de Roland* and *Waltherius manu fortis* are cited to counter Alonso's interpretation that the Cid is unconditionally *buen vassallo*. On the contrary, these two hemistyches express the poet's regret over the discordance between the Cid's qualities and his circumstances, a discordance which is eventually resolved in the *Poema*.

925. "Sobre el carácter histórico del *Cantar de mio Cid*." *NRFH* 2 (1948): 105–17.

The *Cid* is a work of art and fiction, not a historical document. It is both representative and idiosyncratic within the European epic tradition [in 35, 39].

926. "Zur 'Cantiga da garvaya.' " *RPF* 3 (1949–50): 186–95.

Supports Carolina Michaëlis's interpretation (*ZRP* 28 [1904]: 385ff.), in which she identifies the "filha de don Pai Moniz" (lines 11–12) as Maria Paez Ribeira, the favorite of King Sancho I. A discussion of other points stresses that historical elements must be examined in context [in 35].

927. "Sobre las ideas de Américo Castro a propósito de *El villano del Danubio* de Antonio de Guevara." *BICC* 6 (1950): 1–14.

A rejection of Castro's "psychoanalytical" interpretation as inapplicable to a work antedating the 18th-c. formulations of "genio original." The poet's conscious strategies are reflected in the rhetoric he adopts.

928. "Dos observaciones sintático-estilísticas a las *Coplas* de Manrique." *NRFH* 4 (1950): 1–24.

A discussion of Manrique's use of the pathetic possessive and the substantivized infinitive in the *Coplas*. The pathetic possessive combines the fact of possession with the natural sentiment of possessing (already) and is a means by which the poet brings his reader into the text. In general, the substantivized infinitive is an intermediate form in which abstract and concrete are combined. Here it is used to signal the poet's liberation.

929. "Sobra la cantica 'Eya velar.' " *NRFH* 4 (1950): 50–56.

Fundamental philological considerations and an examination of word and motif repetition, enumeration, and recapitulation govern this proposal of a new strophic arrangement, which is more satisfactory because it takes into account Berceo's verbal technique [in 35, 39].

930. "Razón de amor." *Rom* 71 (1950): 145–50.

Evidence such as symbolic associations and thematic resonance is adduced to show the unity of the 13th-c. Castillian poem. Underlying the poet's original treatment of the *visione amorosa* and the *débat* is the universal principle *concordia discors* [in 35, 39].

931. "The Mozarabic Lyric and Theodore Frings's Theories." *CL* 4 (1952): 1–22.

Supports Frings's thesis ("Minnesänger und Troubadours," *Deutsche Akademie der Wissenschaften, Vorträge und Schriften*, fasc. 34, Berlin: Akademie Verlag, 1949) that troubadour and Minnesang poems are the products of the popular imagination and are infused with courtly and learned culture. Old Spanish poems originating in the Judeo-Mozarabic poetic school of the 11th c. are similar in content [in 33]. (Also as "Die mozarabische Lyrik und die Theorien von Theodor Frings," *Der Provenzalische Minnesang*, ed. Rudolf Baehr, Darmstadt: Wissenschaftlisch Buchgesellschaft, 1967, 198–230.)

932. "Garcilaso, Third Eclogue, Lines 265–271." *HR* 20 (1952): 243–48.
The theory of pictorial representation underlying the entire passage can be explained through reference to the Greek and Latin history of the It. term *chiaroscuro*. Garcilaso has also appropriated ancient theories of perspective in this poem.

933. "Dámaso Alonso, *Poesía española, ensayo de métodos y límites estilísticos* (Garcilaso, Fray Luis de Léon, San Juan de la Cruz, Góngora, Lope de Vega, Quevedo), Madrid (1950)." *RF* (1952): 213–40.
The implicit assumption that a Spanish work is great because it is authentically Spanish, and that if it is great it is truly Spanish, constitutes "nationale Tautologie." Spitzer contrasts his own method with Alonso's in an interpretation of Luis de León's *Profecía del Tajo* [in 35].

934. "A Passage of Santillana's *Seranilla V*." *HR* 21 (1953): 135–38.
A change in punctuation resolves a syntactical ambiguity. The poem marks an important transitional stage in the development of the traditional figure of the girl cowherd into a Renaissance lady.

935. "'No me mueve, mi Dios . . . .'" *NRFH* 7 (1953): 608–17.
This is not merely an exercise in piety. The tripartite division of the poem parallels the four-part spiritual exercise Saint Ignatius of Loyola imparted to his disciples, that is, memory, imagination, emotion, and will [in 35, 39].

936. "*La cantiga da garvaya* de Paay Soares de Taveiroos." *Rom* 74 (1953): 512–14.
A reiteration of the argument presented in *RPF* 3 (1949–50): 186–95 and a refutation of Rodrigues Lapa's interpretation ("Sobre *La cantiga da garvaya*," *Cuadernos de Estudios Gallegos* 22 [1952]: 169–86) [in 35].

937. "Lope de Vega's 'Al triunfo de Judit' (*Rimas humanas* 78)." *MLN* 69 (1954): 1–11.
The sonnet incorporates medieval, Renaissance, and baroque aesthetic and moral ideas rendered in pictorial terms to create "a spectacle (of God's wrath and triumph) for the moral eye" [in 35].

938. "The Folkloristic Pre-stage of the Spanish 'Conde Arnaldos.'" *HR* 23 (1955): 173–87.
Evidence adduced from other European ballads suggests a French origin of "Conde Arnaldos" [in 35, 39].

939. "A Central Theme and Its Structural Equivalent in Lope's *Fuenteovejuna*." *HR* 23 (1955): 274–92.
The relation between love and musical harmony throughout *Fuenteovejuna* supports the play's "operatic superstructure" [in 35, 49].

940. "Annex to *HR* 23 (1955): 173–87 ("Conde Arnaldos")." *HR* 24 (1956): 64–66.
French and Italian parallels that deal with the lure of the supernatural are cited.

941. "A New Book on the Art of *The Celestina*." *HR* 25 (1957): 1–25.
A damning critique of Stephen Gilman's study of the dialogic character of the

text, its theme, and its representation of love, and particularly of Gilman's approach, method of analysis, and terminology (*The Art of "La Celestina,"* Madison: U of Wisconsin P, 1956).

942. "The Artistic Unity of Gil Vicente's *Auto da Sibila Cassandra*." *HR* 27 (1959): 56–77.

The drama's coherence is based not on implicit symbolic or allegorical relations but on aesthetic criteria. The analysis concentrates on the theme (prophecy), all the characters' roles, and especially Vicente's treatment of Cassandra [in 39].

943. "Die Figur der Fénix in Calderón's *Standhaften Prinzen*." *RJb* 10 (1959): 305–35.

A reaction to W. Kayser ("Zur Struktur des *Standhaften Prinzen*," *Gestaltprobleme der Dichtung*, Bonn: Bouvier, 1957). Fénix is more than a mere embodiment of earthly perfection. A scene-by-scene analysis focuses on the Moorish princess and stresses the garden episode.

944. "Contribution à l'étude d'une oeuvre de Góngora: *Las soledades*." *Les Langues Néo-Latines* 54 (1960): 1–12.

Trans. by G. Floquet from the original, "Zu Góngoras 'Soledades,'" *VKR* 2 (1929): 244–58 [in 22, 49].

945. "Adiciónes a 'Camina del Poema' (*Confianza* de Pedro Salinas)." *NRFH* 14 (1960): 333–40.

Citing R. Lida's article titled "Camino del Poema," which he terms "una elucidación magistral," Spitzer reexamines the relation between *Confianza* and Bécquer's *Rima 4* and pays close attention to the evolution of the title.

946. "On the Significance of *Don Quijote*." *MLN* 78 (1962): 113–29.

An examination of the relation between the critical program established in Cervantes's preface to part 1 and his literary goal, that is, "to destroy a literary genre." How the implications of this program are carried out thematically and structurally is the focus of analysis. (Originally a lecture presented at Smith College, circa 1942, the last five pages of which appear in modified form in *Linguistics and Literary History* 68–73.)

STYLISTICS

947. "Stilistisch-Syntaktisches aus den spanisch-portugiesischen Romanzen." *ZRP* 35 (1911): 192–230, 257–308.

A survey of verb tenses, articles, prepositions, conjunctions, spelling variations, and principles of style in the romances.

948. "Inszenierende Adverbialbestimmungen im neueren Französische." *NS* 28 (1920): 1–30.

The difference in style between modern and 17th- and 18th-c. French prose is due to the use of "stage-setting" adverbial modifiers in modern Fr., such as details of time, place, or manner that are positioned according to their effect on mood (e.g., to contrast or juxtapose objects, human beings and objects, events and surroundings). According to Spitzer, the incorporation of surrounding circumstances derives from naturalism and determinism. He defines three categories: (1) *grundierend*, where an object or event stands out against a background; (2) *drapierend*, where an object or event is ordered or ranked according to a stage-setting plan; (3) *allegorisierend, definierend-resümierend oder den Vorgang in der Gesamtstimmung auflösend*, where allegory, definition, or summary is used to blend the event into the mood of the whole. The modifiers are the result of the author's focusing of vision [in 20].

949. "Zur stilistischen Bedeutung des Imperfekts der Rede." *GRM* 9 (1921): 60–61.

The imperfect tense represents a simplification of narrative technique. By giving the appearance of pseudoobjectivity, the imperfect effects an internal coherence, which frees it from the need for an exact reference to person, place, and time in the narrative.

950. "Sprachmischung als Stilmittel und als Ausdruck der Klangphantasie." *GRM* 11 (1923): 193–216.

German prose has become highly eclectic, no longer distinguishing between oral and written expression or between literary language and dialect. This mixture of styles is characteristic of Alfred Kerrs's prose style. Kerrs's technique is simultaneously representation and imitation, a stylistic anarchy, and results from the author's inability to represent faithfully his impressions [in 20].

951. "Über zeitliche Perspektive in der neueren französischen Lyrik." *NS* 31 (1923): 241–66.

Beginning with a discussion of the use of the present tense in Goethe's *Jägers Abendlied*, an example of *einsame Lyrik*, Spitzer moves on to the use of the present tense and of direct address in pre- and postsymbolist poetry. He notes that the complex temporal perspective present in Baudelaire, Mallarmé, and Verlaine is for the most part absent in earlier lyric poetry. However, the occurrence of Goethe-like *Werde-Lyrik* in French symbolist poetry is not the result of a direct German influence but the product of what Spitzer calls "eine internationale Seelensituation." Stylistic innovations are dependent upon worldview yet reveal what is latent in language [in 20].

952. "Pseudo-objektive Motivierung (Eine stilistisch-literaturpsychologische Studie)." *ZFS* 46 (1923): 359–85.

Spitzer presents a method of interpreting literature that relates a work's linguistic characteristics to the author's soul, to some "inner necessity." By noting linguistic variations, one can establish the inner continuity that connects the text with the writer's psychological disposition. The basis of the method is not biography but an exact reading of the writer's work, the only criterion for interpretation. Spitzer refers to Philippe's novel *Bubu de Montparnasse* (1905) to show how the use of certain idiomatic expressions and *erlebte Rede* creates ambiguities that afford insight into the author's attitudes [in 20, 49].

953. "Zur Entstehung der sog. 'erlebten Rede.'" *GRM* 16 (1928): 327–32.

Spitzer rejects Etienne Lorck's suggestion (*NS* 35 [1927]: 460) that *erlebte Rede*, as an alternative to both direct quotation and indirect speech, allows the writer to be purely receptive. How can the writer alter what another person says? The answer is that *erlebte Rede* is imitation, an intermediate form between speech and report, which, by mimicking the speaker, is both ironic and empathetic. Linguists who deal only with texts, not speech, misunderstand this device.

954. "Diskussion mit Max Kuttner: *visage gendarme; par exemple; que signifie?*" *A Rom* 13 (1929): 195–203.

Max Kuttner's critique (*Deutsche Literaturzeitung*, 1928) of *Stilstudien* is misleading and mistaken. Kuttner charges Spitzer with blithely simplifying difficult issues by emphasizing style, which Kuttner considers a disingenuous formulation of the obvious. Kuttner's failing is that he sees linguistic phenomena not as stylistic phenomena but only as grammatical constructs, abstractions from the concrete reality of language. To take style seriously leads logically to an aesthetic of language, which involves a galaxy of problems more difficult than those entertained by the older generation of philologists.

955. "Zur sprachlichen Interpretation von Wortkunstwerken." *Neue Jahrbücher für Wissenschaft und Jugendbildung, Leipzig* 6 (1930): 632–50.

A poem's language mirrors the poet's state of mind. Unusual language points to a special feeling that the poet wishes to evoke. Very often this is a reflection of the state of the world in which the poet lives. Examples drawn from diverse periods illustrate this point (*Les quinze joyes de mariage*, François Villon's "Ballade des dames du temps jadis," Jodelle's "A luy mesme," Mallarmé's "Le vierge, le vivace et le bel aujourd'hui," and Racine's *Phèdre*) [in 22, 23, 31, 32].

956. "Über individualsprachliche Aufnahme und Ablehnung neuer Wörter." *NMo* 2 (1931): 20–35.

Although an individual speaker's vocabulary may seem at first glance ahistorical, many words that a speaker uses have a very distinct history. In order to work with a system such as Saussure's, it is important to understand how and under what circumstances an individual assimilates or rejects words. Spitzer presents examples from his own experience.

957. "Über individualsprąchliche Aufnahme und Ablehnung neuer Wörter (Schluss)." *NMo* 2 (1931): 84–98.

Spitzer is concerned here with the rejection of words. Since one's language is equivalent to one's soul, there are many barriers to the assimilation of words. The soul protests against words used by those whom one dislikes. Examples drawn from Spitzer's personal experience show how each person's language is unique. Linguists should be aware of this and not be afraid to describe their own linguistic experience when they analyze a language.

958. "Über individualsprachliche Aufnahme und Ablehnung neuer Wörter (Nachtrag)." *NMo* 2 (1931): 570–73.

In an autobiographical monograph, Spitzer's friend Walther Schiller gives an exemplary account of his experience with the word *Frechling* 'insolent person, smart aleck.' His first assumption was that it referred to an animal that was somehow "fresh," by analogy with *Gründling* 'gudgeon,' a fish that is somehow near the ground, and *Hänfling* 'linnet,' a bird that eats *Hanf* 'hemp.' Only later did he associate it with the Viennese dialect practice of using the suffix *-ling* for people of whom one disapproved.

959. "'Et, l'autre salaud qui va nous faire répérer!,' un motif Marcenat." *ZFS* 54 (1931): 48–59.

A response to Kuttner's criticism (*ANS* 155 [1929]: 231) of *Stilstudien*, particularly his rigid perception of linguistic change. Spitzer cites examples to support his fundamental principle: language is continually changing, and there are no immutable laws that govern its use. Therefore, style matters. Spitzer defends himself in general against unimaginative linguists who deny the vitality of linguistic change in favor of the certainty of ossified rules of grammar.

960. "Nochmals zum homerischen *Hysteron proteron*." *ZVS* 60 (1932): 233–36.

Hysteron proteron is a rhetorical figure that reverses the natural order of things, for example, "those who grew up and were born with me," "many has he killed and captured." These are not merely clichés. Homer uses the figure for two reasons: (1) it indicates a subjective, impressionistic, nonlogical sensibility, which evokes the feelings of the characters instead of the opinions of the narrator; (2) it is sometimes used to keep the rhythm of the phrase, more important in ancient Gk. than in modern Gk.

961. "Zeitgebung im französischen Gerichtssaalbericht." *VRo* 1 (1936): 318–33.

A French newspaper report of a legal proceeding reveals a curious mixture of tenses and forms of speech. For example, the apparent confusion of the simple past tense with the pluperfect and of direct narrative with *erlebte Rede* is actually a way of emphasizing the reader's role as participant instead of as witness. By varying tenses the writer can hold the reader in continuous tension of participation and can revitalize the "dead" past. Because of the ambiguous time frame, illusion holds sway over objective time; events appear detached from their temporal framework. (This is not a new technique: mixing tenses also occurs in Old Spanish romances.) Spitzer views the modern newspaper as a linguistic gold mine and advocates a newspaper philology.

962. "Personne étoffée ou personne extériorisée." *FM* 5 (1937): 207–20.

The semantic distinction between "je la suis" and "je suis elle" is not, as suggested by Pichon (*FM* 5 [1937]: 17–32), a difference of "subtle" (*tênue*) and "full" (*étoffée*) reference, but a difference of subjectivity and objectivity. In the former phrase, the speaker merely refers to her inherent selfhood, while in the latter the speaker concretizes or exteriorizes her selfhood by comparing it to a suggested series, "je suis Anne," "je suis Marie."

963. "Les théories de la stylistique." *FM* 20 (1952): 160–68.

A response to C. Bruneau ("La stylistique," *RPh* 6 [1951]: 1-17), who distinguishes between scientific and nonscientific approaches to linguistics and places Spitzer's method in the latter camp. Spitzer defends his approach against Bruneau's criticism that it is impressionistic, and he recapitulates the constituent features described in the introduction to *Linguistics and Literary History.*

MISCELLANY

964. "Schopenhauer und die Sprachwissenschaft." *GRM* 8 (1920): 258–72.

Sophus Hochfeld's panegyric claiming a harmony between Schopenhauer's artistic personality and his language fails to inquire into Schopenhauer's theoretical views concerning the connection between language and style. Schopenhauer believes in an ahistorical conception of language and sees the ruin of language where the linguist recognizes affective expression.

965. "Eine Strömung innerhalb der romanischen Sprachwissenschaft." *ANS* 141 (1921): 111–31.

In the study of language there is a noticeable shift away from linguistics toward literature; in the study of literature there is a shift toward ahistorical methods. In general, this is part of the current dissatisfaction with the performance of the arts and sciences during the war. In particular, linguistics is too esoteric, impractical, and pedantic for the public. Vossler believes that linguistics must prove itself relevant by emphasizing the study of the relation between language and culture. This idea has much to recommend it, but Lerch's attempt to put it to use does not work (*Die Verwendung des romanischen Futurums als Ausdruck eines sittlichen Sollens*, Leipzig: Reisland, 1919). Lerch argues, for instance, that the French use of the future as an imperative reflects their fanatical and tyrannical nature, a view that cannot be supported by the evidence he adduces; his interpretation is based on a virulently anti-French bias.

966. "Abwehr." *A Rom* 7 (1923): 164–66.

Spitzer defends himself against C. Foligno's insinuation (*MLR* 17 [1922]: 197ff.) that his manner of preparing *Die Umschreibungen des Begriffes "Hunger" im Italienischen* as a government censor was immoral and heartless.

967. "Wortkunst und Sprachwissenschaft." *GRM* 13 (1925): 169–86.

Spitzer argues against the impoverishment of philology through the exclusion of the study of style. His method, modeled on Vossler's, is to regard language more as expression than as communication, to scrutinize speech more closely than written language. This reversal of linguistic method results from a historical refinement of the conception of language, traditionally understood as being identical with grammar. To demonstrate the linguistic study of style, Spitzer reviews the development of his own work and its relation to that of others. Since a language is but an averaging of the languages of individuals, the grammatical form of different speech acts, all the creativity and newness of language arises from its individualized use. Syntax, even grammar, is frozen style. Spitzer's mottoes are "Individual style can be described by philological methods" and "The style is the man" [in 20, 31, 32].

968. "Aus der Werkstatt der Etymologien." *JbP* 1 (1925): 129–59.
Etymology is an art that can be mastered only through the use of a wide range of techniques. Those who aspire to be etymologists should (1) realize that etymologies are found by accident rather than through intentional investigation; (2) study words that are intrinsically interesting to them; (3) have native command of the present state of the language studied, so as to know its character and possibilities; (4) place stylistic information about a word on a par with phonetic and semantic information; (5) acquire a broad background covering all humanistic fields; (6) attempt to achieve a fresh perspective on the problem at hand; (7) rely on documentation more than on reconstruction.

969. "Urtümliches bei romanischen Zahlwörten." *ZRP* 45 (1925): 1–27.
Linguistic innovation is not always created by exterior forces. This is exemplified in Romance numerals, which are often erroneously understood to be a continuation of Latin numerals. Four points illustrate the argument: (1) The Romance language vigesimal system. Margarete Rösler assumes that counting by twenty in Fr. is due to Norman influences (*ZRP* 26 [1910]: 187ff.). On the contrary, counting by twenty probably stems from the fact that twenty is the sum of a human being's fingers and toes. (2) Ordinal numbers. Even more difficult than counting is numerical ordering. The original meaning of ordinal numbers is completion of a row, which explains the special linguistic position of "first" in all languages. Citing examples, Spitzer notes generally a continual vacillation in language between individualizing and serializing tendencies. (3) The use of partitive constructions, such as an older Egyptian construction "four of (the category) year" for "four years," is compared with Fr. *en voilà une* and other Romance parallels. (4) The pejorative development of the prefix *bis-* in Romance languages. The duplication of an action in itself leads to a pejorative meaning since an initially unachieved ideal is somehow implied.

970. "Jules Gilliéron." *ZFS* 48 (1926): 506–11.
An appreciation of Gilliéron's teaching style, his scholarly and personal virtues, and his pedagogic achievement.

971. "Zur Meillets Kritik vom *Jahrbuch für Philologie* Band I." *JbP* 2 (1927): 293–98.
Blinded by his typically French desire for clarity and rationalism, Antoine Meillet has produced a simplistic critique (*BSLP* 26 [1925]). For example, he misunderstands Vossler's disagreement with Saussure: in Vossler's view, Spitzer recalls, Saussure does not take into account the constantly shifting nature of language nor is his approach historical enough. Meillet should recognize that Versailles's parks are not the perfect model for all sciences: German linguists have something to offer too.

972. "Der Romanist in der deutschen Hochschule." *NS* 35 (1927): 241–60.
The postwar intellectual atmosphere in Germany has spawned a suspicious judgmental approach to the study of Romance languages. Before the war Romance languages and culture were studied on their own terms, enabling the student to rise above current political tensions. But Germany's historically troubled love of the West has been so traumatized by the recent painful break that the defiant intellectual mood now wants to do without the West. Intellectual life is atrophying, and Germany currently has very little intellectual influence beyond its borders. It is given to the university instructor to revitalize the interest in Romance lan-

guages and cultures; the prerequisite for this task is love of the culture one wants philologically to understand.

973. "Bericht über den ersten internationalen Linguistenkongress im Haag (10–15 April 1928)." *NS* 36 (1928): 439–44.

The Congress reflected contemporary directions in linguistics: the French and Russian synchronic approach introduced by Saussure and the German diachronic approach stressing language's historical aspects.

974. "Atlas linguistique ou grammaire-dictionnaire-textes?" *Revue Internationale des Etudes Basques* 22 (1928): 1–7.

An impassioned defense of the superiority of the dictionary-grammar over the geographical linguistic atlas exemplified by Gilliéron's linguistic atlas of France. Because of the French insistence on clarity and the regulation of language, this type of atlas is intrinsically appropriate for France. A worldwide replication of this method of language study would be a disaster. Language is a living, changing organism; it cannot be captured at a moment in time and frozen.

975. "Zur Methodik der etymologischen Forschung." *ZRP* 48 (1928): 77–113.

Gamillscheg's response (*ZFS* 50 [1927]: 216–98) to Spitzer's negative criticism of *EWF* inspired this article. Spitzer states that, apart from a few examples (which he then discusses in detail), all his previous observations must be upheld. He also responds to Gamillscheg's criticisms regarding his methodology, particularly that his etymologies are based only on sudden flashes of inspiration, that he is incapable of logical thought, and that he uses nonexistent words. Spitzer claims that such flashes are only the impetus of creative thought and are then confirmed by documentation. He applies several of Gamillscheg's criticisms to the latter's own work. In the main, however, he takes issue with Gamillscheg for his conception of language as being *only* rational and for his creation of unnecessary complications. (In particular, Spitzer prefers uncontaminated over contaminated forms.) Generally Spitzer is averse to the trend in linguistics that "depoeticizes" language. Though the object of study, language is a living thing. He also calls for greater tolerance among scholars toward dissenters.

976. "Hugo Schuchardt als Briefschreiber." *Revue Internationale des Etudes Basques* 21 (1930): 591–617.

Selections from forty-five of Schuchardt's letters to many colleagues. Includes a subject index [17].

977. "Zur Vermenschlichung und Versachlichung der Universitätsprüfungen." *NMo* 3 (1932): 80–87.

Students finish their university exams feeling that they are merely performing as machines. The final doctoral examinations should be restructured to consist of an intensive discussion of a single text. Meaningless questions would be avoided, and the student would have a chance to demonstrate the ability to apply the knowledge acquired in the diverse fields of history, linguistics, and literature.

978. "En apprenant le turc." *BSLP* 35 (1934): 82–101.

Spitzer uses his own experience with Turk. to show that, however imperfectly he may know a given language, as a linguist he is able to understand certain aspects of it and to explain them psychologically. A look at the use of the imperative, at syntactic and phonetic reduplication, and at interjections, among other constructs, supports Spitzer's conclusion that Turk. reveals a unique capacity to blend sound and logic to make meaning.

979. "Explication linguistique et littéraire de deux textes français." *FM* 3 (1935): 315-23; 4 (1936): 37-48.

Literary criticism should follow these procedures: (1) study the text alone, without reference to literary history or to the author's biography, and (2) seek to discover the text's essential unity, showing how content and style unite to produce the literary effect. The latter procedure can be carried out by determining the emotive effect of stylistically unusual passages.

980. "Le français en Turquie." *FM* 4 (1936): 225-37.

The Fr. spoken in Turkey ranges from the essentially correct variety spoken by diplomats to the highly decomposed lingua franca of the European quarter in Istanbul. Although the nationalist attitude discourages the use of Fr. by some groups, such as Spanish Jews, a school of languages was established at the university level in 1934 to promote internationalism among university graduates.

981. "Etais-je à Istanbul ou à Constantinople?" *FM* 5 (1937): 325-28.

The suggestion that Fr. should ignore modern changes in place names – for example, the change from Constantinople to Istanbul – should be rejected. Not to do so would be impractical, discourteous, and antihistorical.

982. "Mes souvenirs sur Meyer-Lübke." *FM* 6 (1938): 213-24.

While he was in Vienna, Meyer-Lübke was a commanding figure, a representative of the positivist movement. After he moved to Bonn his fortunes deteriorated, and his once-liberal political views evolved toward reactionism. In character he was prosaic, dull, and rigid, and his works reflect these qualities.

983. "Note sur la prononciation des noms propres." *BSLP* 40 (1939): 31-45.

When used in another language, proper names should be pronounced as they would be in their native context. This is important to the individual both symbolically and psychologically. It is quite common for Americans to Americanize the pronunciation of proper names. This can be interpreted either as an expression of indifference toward the individual or as a sign of acceptance in a country where many immigrants coexist.

984. "Une intonation en anglais américain et son étymologie." *BSLP* 40 (1939): 101-05.

In all languages there are examples of intonation that have become autonomous (i.e., dissociated from their original context and attached to another), such as the diphthongization of "good bye" and "good night" in Amer. The psychological etymology of this phenomenon has to do with the speaker's mixed feelings: regret at leaving and the obligation to depart.

985. "Gerhard Rohlfs, *ANS* 173, 133." *MLN* 54 (1939): 236-37.

In the cited article, a review of a book about France and racism, Rohlfs shows that he is thoroughly anti-Semitic.

986. "History of Ideas versus Reading of Poetry." *SoR* 6 (1941): 584-609.

Spitzer maintains the precellence of the text as a "self-contained work of art" and opposes interpretations that seek to elucidate it according to biographical information concerning the author, source studies that precede an understanding of the work itself, and explications that deal with the ways a given work conforms to a particular genre. The application of the history of ideas to the understanding of a literary text is similarly overrated.

987. "A New Program for the Teaching of Literary History." *AJP* 63 (1942): 308–19.

A critical look at topics raised by Norman Foerster, John McGalliard, René Wellek, et al. in *Literary Scholarship, Its Aims and Methods* (Chapel Hill: U of North Carolina P, 1941). (Dedicated to Paul Friedlander on the occasion of his 60th birthday, 21 March 1942.)

988. "Sobre un nuevo método de tipología lingüística." *Anales del Instituto de Lingüística* (U.N. de Cuyo) 2 (1942): 109–27.

A review of and commentary on the unifying characteristics of the five European linguistic groups adumbrated by E. Lewy. The criticisms concern Lewy's description of the Romance languages. Spitzer is particularly critical of Lewy's rejection of Greek, Roman, and Christian influences on European languages in favor of "an Indo-European mentality," which, according to Spitzer, is too "vague and abstract" to be of typological use.

989. "Why Does Language Change?" *MLQ* 4 (1943): 413–31.

A review of the diverse theories of the causes of language change leads to a rejection of principles of variation alone and to a development of the hypothesis that the conservative instinct itself may inspire and feed phonological and semantic innovation. Spitzer calls for an elaboration of this notion in the face of antimentalist criticism.

990. "*Crai e poscrai o poscrilla e posquacchera* Again: Or, the Crisis in Modern Linguistics." *Ital* 21 (1944): 154–69.

Poscrai became divided into *poskr - ai*, with a sham-radical and a sham-suffix. **Poskr* + *i* and **poskr* + *u* (*o*) are the etyma for the names of the two days after *postcras*. This etymology is the basis for an impassioned discussion of Spitzer's approach to linguistics [in 35].

991. "*Geistesgeschichte* vs. History of Ideas as Applied to Hitlerism." *JHI* 5 (1944): 191–203.

Spitzer accepts Lovejoy's assertion that the ideas of *Ganzheit*, *Streben*, and *Eigentümlichkeit* are present in Hitlerism; however, he refutes the thesis that maintains their historical continuity stemming from German Romanticism. He contests especially what he considers to be an aprioristic approach, adopted by Lovejoy, as a means of analyzing historical events [in 49].

992. "Answer to Mr. Bloomfield (*Lg* 20, 45)." *Lg* 20 (1944): 245–51.

Attacks Leonard Bloomfield's antimentalistic denial of "the human experience that has accumulated in . . . language." The antimentalist is a nihilist who "does not know what the soul is," "has ceased to believe in the meaning of words," and participates in the "process of cultural disintegration."

993. "Deutsche Literaturforschung in Amerika." *MDU* 37 (1945): 475–80.

By encouraging a revision of German axioms and heeding their American public's reaction, German literati presently teaching in American universities may lead the way toward a more cosmopolitan outlook on literature.

994. "The State of Linguistics: Crisis or Reaction?" *MLN* 61 (1946): 497–502.

A response to an article of the same title by Hall (*Ital* 23 [1946]: 30–34) contests Hall's thesis that a mentalistic approach to linguistics means "reaction" whereas a mechanistic approach is "progress."

995. "Addition to *poscrai, poscrilla,* etc. (*Ital* 21, 154)." *Ital* 24 (1947): 253.

Spitzer acknowledges new evidence, brought to his attention by A. F. Engel, to support his earlier remarks on this series of noncewords [in 35].

996. "Elise Richter: In Memoriam." *RPh* 1 (1947–48): 329–41.

A review of Elise Richter's training and development as a Romance philologist under Meyer-Lübke's tutelage includes a description of her method and an evaluation of her success, which, according to Spitzer, lay primarily in her examination of VLat. etyma. Plagued by anti-Semitism throughout her life, Richter never received the title of Professor and died with her sister, Helene, at Theresienstadt.

997. "German Words, German Personality and Protestantism Again." With Arno Schirokauer. *Psychiatry* 12 (1949): 185–87.

A refutation of the notion that word coinage and usage are a reflection of national character.

998. "The Formation of the American Humanist." *PMLA* 66 (1951): 39–48.

Attributes the dearth of adequately prepared and well-respected American-born humanist scholars to the educational background and living conditions of graduate students and to the academic life of the young professor.

999. "Language: The Basis of Science, Philosophy and Poetry." *Studies in Intellectual History*. Ed. George Boas et al. Baltimore: Johns Hopkins UP, 1953. 67–93.

Spitzer explores the dynamics of linguistic expressivity, stressing that language is both a means of communication and a way to achieve orientation in the world. He describes features of development and change that contribute to what he terms the arbitrary, conventional, and ambiguous qualities of any language system, qualities that are exploited in poetry to create an illusion of the suspension of laws of causality. Noting in conclusion that no modern poet has appeared to "make modern science sing," he maintains that age-old myths continue to dominate contemporary language, preventing it from expressing modern mythology.

1000. "La mia stilistica." *La Cultura Moderna* 17 (1954): 17–19.

What others might consider to be a Crocean or Vosslerian influence in Spitzer's work is instead a manifestation of Freudian methods and thought. Both Croce and Vossler were considered taboo by his teacher Meyer-Lübke.

1001. "The Individual Factor in Linguistic Innovations." *CN* 16 (1956): 71–89.

An exploration of the question "Why does a community change its language?" Attributing most changes to certain individuals who have both a reason and an opportunity to effect them, Spitzer describes factors that contribute to such developments. Most innovations fulfill an existing need, a dissatisfaction with the expressivity of the language. Innovation is always relative, however, since it coexists with a certain degree of conservatism – an argument that is illustrated here with contemporary as well as historical examples.

1002. "Riposta a una critica." *Conv* 5 (1957): 597–603.

In this answer to Tullio de Mauro's criticism of his methods, Spitzer upholds the explication de texte method, reproves de Mauro for having focused on earlier rather than later studies, and affirms his belief in the relation between microcosm and macrocosm as a critical index of poetic coherence and harmony.

1003. "Language of Poetry." *Language: An Enquiry into Its Meaning and Function*. Ed. Ruth Nanda Anshen. Science and Culture Series 8. New York: Harper, 1957. 201–31.

In this revision of "Language: The Basis of Science, Philosophy and Poetry" (in *Studies in Intellectual History*), Spitzer examines in greater detail prosodic devices in poetic texts, which expand the expressivity inherent in human language in order to create a verbal universe differing from the familiar one.

1004. "Sviluppo di un metodo." *CN* 20 (1960): 109–28.

Spitzer reviews the major stages of his scholarly development, outlines his central disagreements with principal schools of linguistic and literary thought, and justifies the polemical nature of his writing. Although he maintains the importance of the text's "immanence" and of treating it through a circular process of deduction and induction, he retracts his earlier categorical rejection of source studies, citing his analyses of "Il cantico di frate sole" and Malherbe's "Consolation" as instances in which sources must indeed be taken into account [in 49]. (Complete text of a lecture delivered at the University of Rome, 23 May 1960.)

1005. "Lo sviluppo di un metodo." *Ulisse* 6 (1960): 26–33.

Abbreviated version of the preceding article.

1006. "Les études de style et les différents pays." *Langue et Littérature: Actes du VIII Congrès de la Fédération Internationale des Langues et Littératures Modernes*. Bibliothèque de la Faculté de Philosophie et Lettres de l'Université de Liège, Fasc. 161. Paris: Belles Lettres, 1961. 23–29.

Published version of the lecture Spitzer delivered before the Congrès de la Fédération Internationale des Langues et Littératures Modernes on 3 September 1960, two weeks before his death. He reviews the development of schools of stylistic analysis and their principal adherents and examines the role of stylistics in 20th-c. literary criticism in Germany, Italy, France, the United States, the Soviet Union, and England. Noting that Germany witnessed the first systematic study of style in the first quarter of this century, Spitzer refers throughout to the stages of his own scholarly development.

Index of Persons

References are to entry numbers in the bibliography, except for boldface numerals, which indicate page numbers.

INDEX OF TITLES

References are to entry numbers in the bibliography, except for boldface numerals, which indicate page numbers.

Index of Words and Phrases

References are to entry numbers in the bibliography. An explanation of linguistic symbols appears on page 32.